RUNNING
A PUB

How To and ...
What's it Like?

By Mick Brown

RUNNING A PUB
How To and . . . What's it Like?
By Mick Brown

700+ Tips, Advice, Suggestions, Examples, Warnings, Consequences, Solutions and True Stories.

Education and experience from an Ex-House Manager.

Published by howtoandwhatsitlike.com Publishing 2015
Gloucester, United Kingdom.

ISBN 978-0-9934276-0-2

CONTENTS

ABOUT THE AUTHOR

As soon as I was old enough, I worked behind the bar at the *Kingsdown* pub in Stratton, Swindon. I loved it. When I was 19 I took a lonesome train journey to *Butlin's* at Minehead for the summer. I started as a bar porter and ended up on bar supplies, furnishing each bar with stock. Evenings I waited tables in a huge bar and discovered a new world – **TIPS**. I'd learnt guitar from the age of 14 and on my return from *Butlin's*, turned professional as a musician and went on tour to Germany for two months. I joined another band on my return and left again for months on the road in Germany and later Norway. After much touring in UK theatres as a support act, I turned solo in 1985. I launched 'Drive Recording Studio' in Swindon with my great mate Martin Kilford and George White of BMW and speedway fame - I was really proud of that. After that I lived a double life as a singer/market trader and partner in a shop selling cosmetics and greeting cards with Lynn Ellison.

In 1996 a change was necessary. My girlfriend of the time had been a barmaid and we looked at running a pub. I thought it **TOO EASY**, not a big enough challenge. I can't remember what medication I must have been on – talk about understatement. We applied to several companies and attended an interview day in Weston-Super-Mare for one of these. The company were interested in us, but were worried about my attitude, due to an incident in one of their pubs, involving me and of all the people in all the world – one of the ABM's present that day in Weston . . . What goes around comes around!

We were sent to a pub in Bracknell, to work a week for a tough couple who would put us through our paces. Ken and Pat passed us with flying colours and sent us home two days early. We trained for three months in a pub in Aldershot with Derek and Andrea, leaving my step daughter in full time childcare (a testing time). We were offered a pub in Slough with Andrew Buchanan. With much trepidation and support from Andrew - off we went. I split from my partner and luckily the company kept me on. I then took a unit in Swindon (thank you Mr Dutfield) and later asked to undertake a refurbishment of a new acquisition, again in Swindon – thank you Gerry. That put me close to burn out. After that, I ran two units in Exeter for a great boss (Mark Sutherland) and left the trade to start a family. I have worked around the licensed trade ever since.

I wish I could have bought a book like this when I entered the trade in 1996 - I did try. What would life be like in the licensed trade for my family? How big was the mountain I might have to climb? Was it really doable? Giving up my rented house would leave no safety rope if it all went sour. I was nervous of the commitment – I could find no book. Going ahead, I kept a diary to translate into an aid for future licensees. Being out of the trade for a number of years gave me opportunity to view from a customer perspective. As I wrote away, it became patently obvious where the gaps in service were and what it would take to plug those gaps. The more I visited units in my research (any old excuse), the more furious I became.

AAAAAGGGGGHHHHH!

I've welded my personal experience with ideas on what I call **CUSTOMER LOVE**. I'm not saying what I've written is correct, it's purely my thoughts, but it's not far off the mark - enjoy.

INTRODUCTION

This is my no nonsense, take no prisoners, personal account of running five pubs. What is it **REALLY LIKE** running the show? The answers to problems you may well end up too tired to fathom out, are detailed in forty chapters; including over 700 tips, advice, examples, consequences, suggestions and warnings; saving you money, heartache and years of being in the dark. I will sometimes hint and other times hurl extreme abuse in my attempt to better your odds of success. My views on service are forthright. Mistakes made, lessons learnt and all my on-going research – I pass to you.

Who is it written for? Existing independent operators and house managers, and anyone even **THINKING** of entering the trade. If you've left the trade, you may relate to some of the 50 odd true stories I've included, divulging a host of subjects.

Bonus. Think of your aims and business plan as a game of obstacles. I'll point out all the obstacles you might run in to, how to remove them and later provide what I see as the **MISSING LINK** for almost **ALL** the licensed trade. What you do about that – is up to **YOU**.

Research. I continue to visit all types of licensed premises; the overriding effect it has on me is – **ANGER!**

> ## At least 75% of the staff I run into . . .
> ## Are more a NEGATIVE, than a positive to the business they work for!

No matter how qualified your staff may be; if when they serve they fail to **ADD VALUE** – that is the **NEGATIVE** I refer to.

The measure

Top sports stars will work on every aspect of their body and delivery, to gain one small improvement that might give the edge. In essence, this is exactly what you must strive for in your licensed business. You might be amazed how fewer changes implement a positive effect on takings. Efforts two months down the line when takings show an upward curve, can be like turning a tap on. Most units I visit do more damage to themselves than any competition **EVER** could. Within minutes of entering a building, I can usually identify at least a dozen profit obstacles. I'll provide **YOU** long term solutions, explain **WHY** and the consequences of **NOT**. The measure is . . .

The satisfaction a customer leaves with!

People's expectations are increasingly higher now. Forget service as you know it - you've got to **LOVE** the customer. Being nice, polite, alert, attentive and wanting to be there are the roots and buds of real customer love. **YOU** need to be asking yourself – how do I turn staff education into **PROFIT**.

The answer - TEACH NOT TELL!

The philosophy of *howtoandwhatsitlike* is unlike any 'how to' book. I make no apology in explaining certain issues in depth; merely telling without understanding, is like burying **YOUR** head in sand. Throughout this book I will push, provoke and hope the penny drops you nearer to survival and profit, ultimately guiding you towards a better life for your family.

Terminology. I use **HUMAS** and **HUMAT** throughout. They stand for **HEAD UP MY ASS SYNDROME** and **TERRITORY**. Mostly. I want **ALL** of us to enjoy a better standard of service when visiting **ANY** licensed premises. I **LOVE** this trade and **WANT** it to prosper – enjoy.

1 CUSTOMER ARRIVAL

Why would a new customer choose your place?

On approach, if anything at all puts a customer off, they might simply pass you by. How can **YOU** prevent this happening?

Answer. Better the odds. For customers, outside is where the odds start. Take any blindfolds off and pay attention to the small stuff. Remove profit obstacles and fuel the positives.

Warning. A unit resembling a bag of shit from the outside does **YOU** - no favours. It may well be amazing inside, with great ambience and staff to die for, but losing custom before the door is lazy beyond belief. Why would you let that happen?

First step. Take a prospective customer journey towards you from all possible directions. With a critical eye, identify as many problems as you can that would deter one single person.

Obstacles/opportunities in your shop window

- Are the paths clean?
- Is the outside lighting attractive or not?
- Is there a bucket of nicotine sick at the front door?
- Are there hundreds of fag butts littered all over?
- Are there pretty hanging baskets around the whole unit?
- Are the windows, paintwork and signage clean and tidy?
- Are the flowerbeds attended to?
- If you have a speaker to feed music outside, is the type of music appropriate for the customer base you aim at?
- Is the music at an appropriate volume? Better OFF - than loud distorted drivel blaring at prospective clientele.
- Is the garden furniture in good nick and tidy to the eye?

You'll be paying a lot of money for this shop window - use it wisely.

Mark and learn. List notable problems and potential opportunities both, scoring each from minus ten to plus ten. Anything in the negative mode is a business killer. You must at least **NEUTRALISE** the negatives to minimise loss of trade.

Put yourself in the customer's shoes . . . They're the ones you're trying to impress!

Jet wash. If the paths or block paving need a spring clean; bloody well get on and jet wash, you'll be surprised how much this can smarten the appearance of any unit. Don't hire, think long term; buy a machine man enough for the job in hand, it'll pay for itself within the first two years. Give the garden benches a blast at the same time and re-stain.

Hanging baskets. If you can't afford baskets all around, at least afford to do the entrance areas. This looks attractive straight away (obviously only if this suits your particular unit). Take note - badly maintained baskets look dreadful.

Windows. Don't wait for the window cleaner, do it yourself or delegate. A good team will take on **ANY** job; it's all **PREP** at the end of the day. If you're telling me your staff are too busy to take on this task, you're obviously doing really well, enjoying several holidays a year – is that right?   Purchase a set of squeegees and save anything up to a grand a year. Window cleaning is a luxury if you can afford it, but until then . . .

Assholes and Scumbags. An approaching customer noticing any type of shenanigans outside will disappear - so too will any business plan you may have dreamt up. You need to know what's happening outside, as well as in - most of the time.

A-boards. Anything other than clean and smart, with precise up-to-date messaging is a failure. Target the message, not the detail. Can you read the message from the other side of the road? Is the A-board attractive and will it generate income?

Outside lighting. Are all the existing bulbs working? Is the wiring neat and orderly? LED bulbs and effects can look really attractive, last a whole lot longer and be tons more economical to run. Never underestimate the power of subtle lighting.

Smell. Is there a burnt chip fat, or rotting fag butt aroma, radiating a subliminal message to a hungry customer - not to enter? Is there a scumbag outside smoking a spliff?

AAAAAGGGGGHHHHH!

Entrance. Do the doors open and shut smoothly and quietly? Are all of the panes of glass in the door? Is there a piece of hardboard tacked on, where a bloke put his hand through it last night; worse still - three months ago?

Tip. If you repair this piece of glass before you start trading the following day, most customers will never know you had some sort of fracas in your establishment. Quite honestly, the less customers know about misdemeanours – the better.

Reputation . . . Reputation . . . Reputation

Some units are naturally attractive; others may need a bit of love, attention and imagination. Present what you offer in the best possible light, no matter how demanding of your time.

Maximise your strengths. At the very least - neutralise those negatives. Losing just one customer that could have returned again and again - will always be an expensive pill to swallow.

First impressions do count!

Training story

During my initial training, the licensee made me go out every morning without fail, clearing the car park of all litter, fag butts and foreign bodies. When Joe public pulled into his car park, he wasn't taking anything for granted - including my attitude.

Question. Is your car park cleaned every single day?

Steakhouse story

I took my family to a local steakhouse. Approaching the entrance, I noticed three people in chef's gear - all smoking. Had it not been I didn't want to disappoint my partner, I would have driven away and not come back – **EVER**.

Why? I don't object to people smoking; I just don't want to see it when there's a pretty good chance that person might be cooking my steak. As it turned out; the service was awful and my partners meal came out cold, leaving us eating meals at staggered times - what planet were these **DONKEYS** on? To add insult to injury, the chips had been reheated – bloody hell.

Long story cut short

Every single thing a customer is witness to on approach will make a difference. If the best you can do is eradicate the obstacles - neutral it is, but that won't attract like moths to the flame. You don't necessarily need a gimmick; just presenting in a clean, smart and professional manner can make a difference. Don't blow it before you get the chance to work some magic from the inside. Just to survive, you'll need to cultivate brand new custom on a daily basis. The smoother the approach . . .

The better the odds!

2 ACKNOWLEDGE & QUEUE

Waiting to be served

Imagine you're a customer waiting at the bar. Will you be acknowledged by the server, even though not first in line? Why would a customer arriving a little after you, be served before you? How would this make **YOU** feel? How can you prevent this from happening? Do customers really have to brashly wave a note around like some cowboy in a saloon?

Aim. Raise service way beyond expectation – **ADDING VALUE**.

Failing to acknowledge a waiting customer isn't just failure – it's bloody RUDE!

Example. You are the server. You're already engaged in a transaction, with another customer already acknowledged and waiting. Three ladies enter alongside your existing customers. A simple nod of acknowledgment, and a quick 'I'll be right with you,' is all it might take to secure the note one of them is eagerly waiting to spend. As soon as you've finished serving your initial customer, moving to the second; a further acknowledgment to the three ladies (you know they're still waiting and you'll be right with them) might endorse the fact they are special to you – you care.

The benefit. They will still wait because they'll know you are doing your very best to reach them. Not only that, the server will have started a relationship with the customer before actually serving them – **ADDING VALUE**.

Customers will wait a whole lot longer to be served; in turn boosting chances of lengthening their stay . . .

If acknowledged by a server!

Mental note

Vocal acknowledgment, somehow nudges the **SERVER** to remember who is next. The more you practice this skill, the easier it becomes until entirely natural. I hasten to add - this should be a normal level of service, not a **PRIZED POSSESION**.

A question for you. If bartenders aren't acknowledging waiting customers at the point of service, and by definition taking control of who is next in the queue; clearly fundamental in the art of bolstering satisfaction to the customer journey - **WHY** aren't they?

Correct answer. Because either the person running that business hasn't taught their frontline staff to do so, or they too just don't get it and haven't the foggiest. In which case; how could they possibly have trained and taught their staff?

Prediction. Even if a waiting customer was waving a white flag with '**ACKNOWLEDGE ME**' printed clearly in big letters; 95% of the staff I have witnessed would not register what the hell was going on. And how much would this extra service cost?

Nothing – It's FREE!

You do not have to pay staff **MORE** for any of the extra chores I mention hereafter - you simply have to **TEACH** them to deliver. A premium service will steer you closer toward premium profit.

Do you and your staff deliver this level of customer service?

Why? Customers do not appreciate being taken for granted. Trust earnt - you'll find **THEY** like you a lot. When they leave, they might well acknowledge **YOU**, which you can then return. That collaboration will have laid the foundation for a possible return visit – huge bricks laid to strengthen your profit line.

Bonus

Choosing to train all staff to acknowledge and queue waiting customers will boost your customer love by a 100% overnight. **TWO HUNDRED PER CENT**, if you insist every member of your team say **THANK YOU** every time they take even the smallest cash – I don't see much evidence of that happening either.

If you can imagine me shouting at you . . . I probably am!

Think about your customers. **YOU** will profit in making **THEM** feel special, in however small a fashion that maybe. With as many bullets as you can fire without being OTT, or patronising; enough small positives add up. I don't mean, 'Would you like crisps or nuts with that?' People hate that shit. Being genuinely nice and serving professionally wins every time.

Feel good factor. Being comfortably certain of immediate acknowledgment, can be equally persuasive in the decision to stay for one more round or split. If customers don't have to fight for service, the process will appear far more attractive.

Consequences

Failing to acknowledge and queue, doesn't upset customers that get served, it upsets the **VICTIMS**. Each of these victims could have been a return customer. Mostly, no one minds waiting, as long as they know how long the queue is, and that that queue is being effectively managed – by you or your staff.

Warning. The service you provide is all about delivering premium products via a premium delivery vehicle. That vehicle (you and your staff) should be able to add value to the product; otherwise the customer might as well stay at home, put the telly on, reach in to their fridge and pour it their-self.

Train and teach

Throughout this book, I will repeatedly bang on about how losing just one customer can cost **YOU** thousands of pounds a year. Not being alert to queue customers, is a clumsy mistake by all staff, whether they be a general or foot soldier. Teach **ALL** staff, new or old to visually and vocally acknowledge a waiting customer. Hold hour sessions and create your own service scenarios. Kill two birds with one stone and practice the thank you thing; customers absolutely love being thanked.

Tip. If whilst serving, another customer arrives and another member of staff is free - immediately call on them to serve. Don't wait until a queue develops - service is mostly King. Acknowledgment and queuing isn't an exclusive problem to the liquor trade – it happens in **ALL** walks of retail and service.

Long story cut short

Assuming you've made a good impression on arrival, the very next step **IS** the manner in which you begin service. You are not in competition with supermarkets. The service you provide should bear no comparison to any supermarket I can think of. You will however, be charging a premium price for your products, demanding an impeccable standard of service to justify that extra charge. Acknowledge and queue is a big weapon in that justification. You cannot afford to lose or upset anybody (unless they happen to be an asshole, which I deal with in a later chapter of the same description). Truthfully, you can't please all the people all the time, but acknowledge and queue is a free opportunity to add value for the customer. Don't worry about the competition . . .

Your biggest competition is yourself!

3 SMOKERS

In the U.K. the government banned smoking in licensed premises, but smoking isn't illegal – far from it. It could be argued the licensed trade blossomed on the backs of an awful lot of smokers, but there'll be no U-turn; if for no other reason than staff would have to serve once again in smoke filled, nicotine ridden rooms. I'll leave you to work out the risk assessment on that one - it's just not going to happen. Many blame the smoking ban for a drop in trade. I would argue smoking took the blame to hide the real culprit – the dire customer love on offer, which has eaten away at profits for the longest time. But, if smoking is totally legitimate . . .

Why do we make smoking customers feel like second class citizens?
The trade in general may not have intended that outcome, but that is exactly what has happened.

The smoker's journey

In general, smokers have taken being kicked outside squarely on the chin. With electronic cigarettes now a thriving force, there are big changes afoot. Imagine the mind-set of a smoker from the time they approach, to the moment they leave. What do smokers really think? What are their requirements? How can you improve the feel-good factor a smoker takes with them when they leave? I'd be asking myself . . .

How can I attract busloads of additional smoking customers?

In the supposed good old days of smoking in pubs, it was drummed in to all my staff to clean ash trays, not just at the end of the night, but regularly throughout the whole days trading; at the same time collecting glasses, litter and washing the table with a **NICE CLEAN CLOTH**. After completing this spring clean you would simply start again, often asking customers to raise glasses to wipe their table. I can't remember complaints; in fact – only thanks and the memory of new customers shock and awe at such wonderful treatment.

Harsh truth. So why since the smoking ban, do a huge amount of premises, never seem to empty the odd ashtray provided, the contraption on the wall, plant pots, or any other ingenious container deemed fit to put a fag end in? How undervalued do we actually want to make smokers feel?

Antidote. Send staff to clean the whole area not once a week, but on a regular basis throughout trading hours. Send them with a dustpan and brush to collect butts off the floor, outside the front door, in the garden, on the patio, or in the designated smoker's cage. Send them with a cordless vacuum cleaner. Clear any other litter lurking in the smoking quarter. While they're at it, tidy any furniture and clean any outside tables with that **NICE CLEAN CLOTH** - add **VALUE** to their journey.

Why should smokers be treated any DIFFERENTLY to customers inside?

There is a case to be answered they be given extra special treatment; after asking them in, extracting four quid off them for a pint of lager, and expecting them to trot off outside in the freezing cold. Crikey . . .

Wonder why they'd feel slightly miffed?

Astonishing. There are some absolutely first class smoking zones, providing strong protection from the elements, abetted by outside heating, 48" televisions and sound system to match. Some will have spent thousands indulging their smokers, but still can't be bothered to empty ashtrays. Licensees letting this occur on a regular basis must be near to clinically brain dead. **DO NOT** underestimate the significance of the smoking zone. Ask the cleaning crew to clean outside as well as in from now on; your trading area will have changed since the smoking ban. Transform your smoking zone to a **VALUE ADDED AREA**.

Warning. Adhere to the law of the land and ensure safety of staff and customers alike. Complete risk assessments with reference hoover leads and rain etc. This isn't a book that's going to cover all that, so do your homework. The one thing I will state is - cover your back all the way down the line.

The flip side. Some units will have no area at all set aside for the smoker. You really **DO** have to stand in the cold and the rain with your four pound pint of lager and your 50p fag.

AAAAAGGGGGHHHHH!

Consequences of not providing a smoking zone

I accept there are units that do not have room to house a smoking zone. If this applies - one of three things will happen.

1 Smokers will congregate at the main entrance. They'll merrily puff away, creating a fog that non-smokers will have to pass through (rather off-putting, especially for foodies).

2 They might eat and consume premium products all night long, paying cash to someone else – **SOMEWHERE ELSE**.

3 They might stay at home and order a pizza.

Has that got your attention?

Damage limitation. Do whatever it takes to at least neutralise the effects of not providing a smoking zone.

Action. Cordless vacuum out front regularly. Sweep the pavement. Visibly show punters you care. If this is the least you can do - do it well; smile and be friendly at the same time.

Action. Of course provide metal type objects on the walls outside. Empty often. I witnessed one recently, not only full, but on fire — unbelievable. Supplement these with floor standing butt bins. Like governments - **HIDE** the evidence.

Bonus. Subtle changes will be noticed, especially by non-smokers. Real success would be a non-smoker passing through a smoking zone and not realising. Strong standards of hygiene signal a well-run unit: positive word of mouth - **INVALUABLE**.

Warning. There is nothing worse to deter prospective new customers, or existing customers for that matter, than the smell or sight of damp rotting fag ends in some contraption on the wall, full to the brim, because you can't be bothered to get off your ass and empty the damned thing. Plain lazy.

Pub crawl

Smokers will inevitably choose to spark up when leaving a unit en route to the next port of call - that's what smokers do. To them it will be a natural opportunity — a no brainer. Upon arrival at their subsequent destination, if there's nowhere to put their fag end, what do you think they're going to do with it? On the floor in front of **YOUR** business is where it'll lay.

Cure. Take a walk towards your place from all possible directions. Is there an obvious position to plant a butt holder? Don't just walk the walk; follow through and solve the puzzle. The benefit will be all inclusive.

Functions story

I attended a wedding in 2011, where there was not one ashtray provided for a party of 200 people. I counted roughly sixty odd smokers - I live a sad existence.

Head up my ass territory (HUMAT). What precisely do you imagine smokers at a function do with their fag butts? Do you think they put them in their pockets or handbags and take them home? Course they don't. They chuck them in the hedge, on the grass, on the patio, in empty glasses, on used dinner plates; **SOMEONE** - will still have to clear that mess up.

AAAAAGGGGGHHHHH!

Either you allow smoking outside or you don't. If you do; cater for that group of customers and look like you mean it.

Bonus. Smoking guests at one of your functions don't want a zone, they want their own little **PARADISE**. They might just stay that little bit longer and spend that little extra. They might spread by word of mouth - how well you looked after them.

Ash trays

Question. If you're stacked at the bar and a member of staff down, how can you still provide a service to the smoker?

Answer. How long would it take to brush a dozen or so ashtrays into a metal bucket? Is that too much to ask?

Tip. Another option . . . enough stackable ashtrays in reserve to simply pick up and replace - a quick and easy fix.

What do you do with these ash trays? Cover your back. Make sure staff are trained properly in the disposal of contents.

Warning. Never put an ashtray out still wet. Why would you? A single cigarette these days is an expensive item - **NO** smoker will congratulate you for that!

What is the protocol for washing an ash tray?

I'll bet 90% of staff, including top brass answers that incorrectly. How many would stick them in the glass washer?

AAAAAGGGGGHHHHH!

My suggestion for cleaning an ashtray is . . .

Being outside. Empty the ashtray into a safe and legal **METAL** object with a lid. Use a cheap brush to push the contents in (you won't want to be cleaning your teeth with this fella).

Warning. Don't even think of depositing the contents of **ANY** derived smoking waste in **ANY** type of normal rubbish bin.

Why? Inevitably, it will cause a **FIRE**.

Advice. If you haven't trained a member of staff with **ALL** the relevant documentation - you won't have covered your back. Do **NOT** let staff undertake this simple task unless fully trained.

Wash. Use a large bucket of hot soapy water with a brush. Let the ash tray dry off naturally, for use later. **DO NOT** use the bucket or brush for anything else. Mark the bucket up. Strictly brief the staff on etiquette. Explain **WHY**. Always explain **WHY**. Where you get the hot water from is a problem for you to solve, but in getting rid of smoking from licensed premises, the last thing wanted is to take ashtrays back in at any cost.

Under any circumstances do not. Put ashtrays in the glass washer. It leaves a taste of gone off fag butts in the water and the crystals. Every glass from then on will smell of nicotine. If one of your cherubs does actually fall in to this trap - replace the crystals immediately. Been there, done that – **NASTY**.

I repeat and am shouting now . . .

Don't go near your bar or kitchen with anything associated with ashtrays!

What smoking products do you sell?

If a customer runs out of smokes or cigarette papers after a couple of pints, they'll have to go somewhere else to furnish their habit. **YOU** be the **DEALER**, or they might not come back.

AAAAAGGGGGHHHHH!

Give customers exactly what **THEY** want. Secure the sales, at the same time **ADDING VALUE** to the customer journey.

Grab trade back from garages, supermarkets and that corner shop!

Suggested products

- **Half a dozen of the most popular brands of cigarettes (check the legalities of selling cigarettes behind bars).**
- **A couple of choices of rolled tobacco in different sizes at competitive prices (ask customers which they prefer).**
- **A choice of cigarette papers.**
- **A machine to make roll ups.**
- **A selection of cigars.**
- **Lighters can provide a healthy mark up.**

Got it? Flaunt it! New government legislation probably means you can't flaunt it I'm afraid. Keep abreast of any new bullshit available with a fine attached - hide it if the law demands. Have signage indicating you sell these items (if that's allowed). Word will spread over time **ADDING VALUE**. Overcharging is an obstacle. Don't overcharge – compete.

Pilfering. To sell these items securely, the need for a till system that will account for every single packet of cigarettes is crucial, the profit minimal. Losing just one packet would be disastrous; choosing the right staff all the more critical.

A smoker's bugbear

A smoker has no choice but to go outside and partake. Sometimes that will mean leaving their glass **INSIDE**. Train your crew to be wary and ask questions before removing glasses (even with the smallest amount of product left). Staff might think they're being efficient, but a smoking customer won't look at it like that – they might be **BLOODY FURIOUS**.

Idea. Why don't we provide beer mats with a red **NO-NO**, in a holder, intermittently throughout the unit? A smoker could grab a mat and place it on top of their glass while they're outside. An easy solve - it adds **VALUE** for the **SMOKER**.

Long story cut short

Thousands of smokers have already created their own smoking areas – at home in their back gardens. Spending on decking, shrubs, atmospheric lighting, comfy chairs, proper ashtrays and buying their cans at the supermarket; they might never visit their local club or pub again. **YOU** need to persuade these people back. Next time a smoker visits your place, **THEY** need to **FEEL THE VALUE**. Yes we should be shouting from the rooftops, that passing filthy fag butts on the way in to have a meal is unacceptable, but by the same token; **THESE PEOPLE** could be and probably are - paying quite a lot of **YOUR** bills.

Smoking is still legal in this country. We can't all be Saints. I bet even Saints have the odd ciggy on the sly. My challenge to you is . . .

What can you do to add value to a smokers visit - at the same time improving relations with non-smokers?

4 ATMOSPHERE

I call it atmosphere. You may call it ambience - I don't care if you call it Terry. You may have chosen the trade as your career path and it may well be your true vocation; you may have invested five grand or half a million – the amount matters not. There is something you should know . . .

Warning (imagine deafening sirens sounding right now). Your job is to create the right atmosphere for humans to spend money; key to why some units are busy quite a lot of the time, whilst others are having wooden boards nailed up as we speak. Most units offer a strong product range, so don't apportion blame for poor sales here. Look instead at how you deliver those products and the atmosphere that accompanies delivery.

You will fall at the starting gate if you do not set the scene correctly!

I'm going to take it for granted that your décor is in good shape; no damp running down the walls, or light fittings hanging precariously by the wires. If you can't at least get those things right, best you hand the keys back. Above all, establishing a positive atmosphere is crucial to the **SPELL** you attempt to cast. Let's look at a few negative scenarios . . .

Example. A table of loud mouthed drunks using the 'F' and 'C' words with alarming regularity, whom just happen to be sat next to some of your lovely older regulars (soon not to be). One drunk knocks a glass over - it draws attention. Not to the staff; they're way too busy having a tea towel fight to clock glass all over the tiled flooring. Meanwhile, three customers all wave ten pound notes in the air in the vain hope of service this side of Xmas. Does it happen? What do you think?

Example. One customer in residence, the unit in complete silence, a bartender sat behind the bar reading a newspaper.

Example. On arrival, you pass a girlie smoking in the doorway; she turns out to be your bartender. Does she wash her hands?

Message. It's not just music, TV and lighting that affect vibes.

Music & TV

Some units don't have music on in the background. If this works for you - skip the next few pages. For the majority, cleverly delivered music and TV are powerful weapons.

Music blueprint. Choice of music should be tailored to fit the customer mix for differing trading periods during each day.

Ballpark example.

Morning and lunchtime period. Older shoppers and office clientele consuming food, drink and coffee.

Laid-back afternoon. Shift workers and pool players.

Teatime session. Regular's just finishing work, students and can't be bothered to cook crew.

Evening attack. A younger customer base, party atmosphere and a change in product demand.

> # Think way past the fact that it is music. Start thinking of it as an atmosphere delivery weapon!

Target the atmosphere. The volume at which you deliver this atmosphere is **CRUCIAL** to the whole process. You simply cannot be present 100% of the time, but continuity is paramount. Train key staff to adjust the volume and genre of music to suit changing clientele. Use scenarios to demonstrate the conditions you are trying to create. Explain **WHY**.

Your aim. Set the scene where humans can relax in their surroundings; not send them away, wondering why the landlady lets the bar staff play heavy metal so bloody loud at 11.30 in the morning. All **YOU** wanted was a nice coffee and read your paper (that'll be the last time you go there).

Zones. Different areas might require an alternative canvas to work from - all at the same time. Delivering this type of control will require equipment housing different zones, with different volume and source controls for each and every zone; basically, a tool to direct the weapon.

Example. On a weekday evening, you may have a football game on TV in the main bar. In another bar, a more chilled out scenario with music lightly on in the background. If you want your smoking customers to enjoy that same football game; you may have a television outside in your smoking area, to which you could also pipe the commentary through outside speakers. The loos could have the commentary of the game in one, music in another. This in effect, channels ambience at differing appropriate levels of volume throughout the unit; in other words - targeting your atmosphere.

Warning. Do not however, have more than one type of noise going in the same room. This confuses people. It will drive them away. It drives me . . . **INSANE!**

Why? Most customers won't be able to put their finger on why they want to leave a unit, but this is one of the reasons.

Example. I was present where there were two different sources of music playing on the house system, a telly on quite loud, a slot machine giving it large, all in the same room, all at the same time - **ONE BIG NASTY NOISE**. The bar staff didn't have a clue and couldn't have cared less. I couldn't wait to leave, nor it seemed could everyone else - an empty bar.

Tip. If you have a particularly large bar area, you may require the option of having the volume louder in one part of the bar than the other; in which case you will need to designate two or more zones for the same room.

Tip. Before purchasing any system, plan out in advance all the zones you may require. Add a couple of spare channels to house any new technology on the horizon, or in case of a channel breaking down. Long term, this may by-pass the toll in having to repair or replace expensive equipment.

Tip. Digital sports packages are expensive, always link any big screen or large TV's to the house sound system - it should look and sound bloody marvellous.

Warning. Whatever system you choose to install must be up to the job in hand. Walking into some bar on the high street to watch your favourite team, and being subjected to loud distorted commentary, is akin to cold war torture methods.

CD's. I personally wouldn't consider using CD's in any unit; they have a habit of jumping and sticking. They'll make you look like a cowboy, no matter what investment you've made.

Tip. The worst place you can have loud distorted music is at your front door. If you don't want custom - just lock the doors.

AAAAAGGGGGHHHHH!

Story. One of the pubs I managed had a large separate pool area with two tables plus furniture. It always annoyed me that on returning to the unit from shopping for example, there would be complete silence in this zone - and guess what?

No bloody customers playing my expensive tables!

Lesson. This area had two dedicated volume and source controls, but whenever back from my escapades it would be like the '*MARY CELESTE*'; music out front, but nothing out back. The pool area produced hundreds of pounds every week; food, machine and wets on top of that. Without music, that room became a cold empty shell. You could guarantee after resuming background music; within ten minutes someone would be playing pool. Have you a room like that?

Delivery equipment. Decide upon which type of atmosphere delivery will work for you. Historically this will have been juke box, CD player, or more common now; laptop, tablet or similar, hosting playlists programmed with vibes to suit differing trading sessions. Used in tandem with TV screens, provides a mighty powerful, high-tech, attack force.

Juke box. Employing a juke box will provide an income if well used, but bear in mind you are handing over the choice of music to your customers. If your customer base is older, you must manage carefully the genres of music offered. You don't want your baseball cap brigade playing banging tunes non-stop for four hours, emptying the pub of everyone else, cause by the way - if somebody is feeding your juke box; they will ask **YOU** (quite rightly) to turn it up to **THEIR** acceptable volume. Ask yourself what fits **YOUR** business model?

Flipside. If you want to keep tabs on the choice and volume of music, may I suggest a juke box is probably not the way forward? Forgoing the income that **MAY** result, would put **YOU** in total control of targeting your atmosphere - no bad thing. Whatever atmosphere delivery you choose . . .

It must be on . . .
All of the time - without fail!

Crazy. I had one area manager forbid me to have the jukebox on constantly in the background. Their idea was having the juke box programmed to play a track every fifteen minutes for free, until someone fed it. Paid tracks would then cut in at a louder volume. In between, you would have total silence.

AAAAAGGGGGHHHHH!

Silence in most licensed premises is a business killer. This approach is still used widely, and whether planned or not; to my mind is definitely head up my ass territory (**HUMAT**). If you have a great tool (which by the way you will be paying all sorts of fees to PRS, PPL, TV licencing and god knows whom else for the honour), why would you leave it in the flaming tool box?

Advice. My idea - constantly in the background at low volume until fed. Paid tracks would play at a louder volume, with free background music resuming at the end of credits. Hence no silence and break in atmosphere - **BINGO**.

> ## Remember – You're going to be the one paying rent for the damned thing.
> ## Have it set the way you want it!

In a reasonably large pub, a juke box can add hundreds of pounds to a week's takings. Even a smallish pub or club can add valuable income, but obviously, you must weigh this up with the loss of control in targeting atmosphere. What fits!

Why? You are in the business of delivering alcohol and food to human beings for monetary profit. Along with the way you display your wares and the welcome a customer receives; appropriate music/TV delivered at appropriate volume levels can be a mighty powerful backdrop. Think long and hard as to the right choice for your business plan.

Lighting

Having all your lights on one or two single switches provides **NO** control over any mood you may attempt to create.

This is utterly bloody useless!

They'll either be on or off. Ability to control the amount of light in each zone via numerous dimmer control's, lets **YOU** paint the picture. Combine that, with targeting music at appropriate volumes and it can become a bit like retail science.

Example. At dusk you may want to slightly dim the lighting, portraying an altogether more intimate backdrop; also useful at the end of the night for bringing the lights back up indicating the evening over, we'd like you to go home now ta. A bit like instant coffee, this is instant atmosphere. It sets the scene and adds **VALUE** for the customer

Lighting effects. Reasonably priced laser and LED effect units can add flair and ambience to a busy night time session. Fixed units, means little wear and tear with no bulbs to replace. Ensure they are sound to light (meaning they react to the beat of the music), this will save buying a controller. Look at uplighters too; these shoot coloured rays up walls.

Advice. Have each item on a separate switch, enabling a choice of effects at any one time. As a bonus, most lasers and especially LED's, are economical to run.

Female friendly

I guess most women, would not enter if a unit looked unwelcoming from outside. If at the door they're welcomed with heavy rock at ear splitting volume, several men leering as the door creeks open – they might turn away. An extreme example yes, but it's all atmosphere. How would you score?

Summary

Shoot all negatives influencing the customer journey - **DEAD**. A smooth approach to the building and the first steps inside; acknowledgement at the bar, a welcome attentive service from both male and female staff; all of this playing out to a backdrop of perfect background music and clever, controlled lighting; it's the equivalent of casting a spell. Top that off with premium products, great smelling meals delivered by smart looking staff, a thank you for payment, and it all starts to come together; a subtle use of weapons the average person might not particularly notice. Subtract pieces of that puzzle and customers might well perceive a marked difference, but not necessarily put their finger on what was missing. This may well cut their stay short, or discourage a return outing.

Suggestion. Visit a busy unit that doesn't use music. Pin your ears back, have a good listen - it won't be silent. What can you see or smell? It's all clever stuff. What could they do better? How could you do it better? How could you do it differently?

Long story cut short

Traditionally, it may well have been the warmth and personality of particular licensees getting a lot of things right. Whilst still a huge advantage - successful modern units won't rely solely on that; they'll provide enough positives to make that the topping on the cake. I once again refer back to the fact that some pubs seem naturally busy. If you look under the surface at what is going on, you will discover the key elements helping that recipe work. This can work for you too. Subtle use of music or not, TV and lighting, will lay a good foundation. Feeling safe and secure to let ones hair down leads me perfectly on to my next subject . . .

5 BANNING ASSHOLES

Asshole introduction

You've invested your life savings in this new venture, made the outside of your pub look inviting, spent thousands on a new sound system with TV's linked in, and trained your staff up to acknowledge everyone. Improved customer service is paying dividends and your new cook is working out really nicely. Takings are increasing and you've a hundred odd people watching the midweek football on your satellite TV - brilliant.

Problem. Unfortunately, you have this public asshole within, whom each time his team miss a shot, shouts at the top of his voice, the plural of a four letter word beginning with **C**.

Warning. In the scenario mentioned earlier about a group of louts on a table using the 'F' and 'C' words very loudly, I can tell you this happens on a regular basis. It is one of the key reasons customers might leave a unit earlier than planned.

Flipside. There are units where this is completely normal; if that's you and takings are through the roof I congratulate you, but certainly don't envy your task. I also accept that swearing can be second nature these days. Used in context is usually not a problem. Loud mouthed and encroaching is a different beast.

Consequences. The majority of licensed houses are damaged if this behaviour goes unchecked; it undermines **YOUR** authority, makes staff feel vulnerable and customers **LEAVE**. Bad for reputation and a top notch suicidal business plan.

What to do? I can't tell you exactly what to do; we're all different with no exam to pass on the subject. I can give you examples, consequences and subsequent advice to help you make your own mind up - enjoy.

A typical asshole story

One pub I frequent has this guy, a known local character. As soon as he enters, you see people visibly shirking and turning their backs. When he spies someone he recognises, he sort of sets about them. They in turn act as if they're pleased to see him. Really, they want the earth to swallow them up, or more preferably – **HIM**. The last time I encountered this chap, he was sat down with a really nice older couple (regulars). Whilst talking, he was spitting all over the table (as is his manner when he's had a few). They had to put their hands over their glasses without upsetting him (to evade the spitting). Understandably, leaving a third of a pint each, they made their excuses and promptly left - they really did. This chap is also very rude. He swears at the top of his voice, seemingly every other word. After the couple had left, he managed to nauseate another group of customers, before eventually departing himself - in search of more pray I expect.

How much damage can one person do?

Consequence. If two lovely customers decide that staying at home is a safer option from now on, it'll be a quick trip to the supermarket and another nail in the coffin – **YOURS**.

Work the figures. The couple come in for three hours on a Sunday afternoon and consume about four pints each. That's roughly £25 a session, assuming they only attend once a week. At a conservative estimate, that's £1300 a year lost from just two customers. Has that got your attention?

Double bubble. They are wonderful customers, the sort that light up a room just by being there. They add atmosphere in truckloads - without lighting and music. Would you, or do you put up with a similar character that drives **YOUR** custom away?

Decisions for profit

I would argue; the loss of even one customer via a loud mouthed bully like this is enough to warrant a lifetime ban. Every brick of trade you build, **THEY** will be knocking down. Every investment you make, guys like **HIM** - will tear apart.

Advice. Of course you can't just ban anyone because they swear or make a mistake, but you must differentiate between people whom really are a bloody nuisance and customers who are just slightly out of line. **YOU** need to make that call.

> # Humans need and like to know the top and bottom lines they can mess around in-between.

Advice. **YOU** must demonstrate what those lines are. When the mayhem calms down, the customers will just get on and enjoy themselves between the parameters **YOU** have set, leaving **YOU** in control and not the assholes.

> # In the five pubs I managed, I banned just over twelve hundred people in total. Trade increased in every single unit!

The customer journey. Experienced licensees tend to acquire an uncanny knack of being able to spot a scumbag or asshole at a thousand yards. Whilst at the same time delivering exactly what customers want, you also have to say **NO** and stand your ground – **AN AWFUL LOT**. Remember why you're there. Folks come out to relax, have a laugh and let their hair down. Every penny you take will depend on the atmosphere you have no doubt worked really hard to create. Ambience in whatever form - does not include assholes.

A table of idiots

You can turn what seems to be a troublesome lot, whom just might need to know the rules, into almost well behaved regulars. The outcome will be apparent almost straight away.

Showtime. Pull whoever seems to be the **LEAD ASSHOLE** to one side. Have a quiet chat to them about table manners and the behaviour acceptable in your establishment. They might well decide to leave anyway at that point - job done.

Flipside. Raise your voice from behind the bar and tell 'em straight, especially if noticeably losing customers the effect.

Result. They'll either wind their necks in and show respect, or become abusive; in which case you must ask them **ALL** to leave and ban in one foul stroke. This demonstrates to **ALL** customers, **YOU** will **NOT** put up with this behaviour under any circumstance; at the same time sending a message that **THEY** are safe and sound in your professionally run hostelry.

Bonus. The idiots will tell their mates that your pub is not worth drinking in, as the landlord is a **MOODY GET**. Exactly the message you want to reach the idiots mates - job done.

Big warning. The cold reality . . . The bunch of assholes might turn nasty: chuck a glass, a chair, a bottle, a plate, or any damned thing at you, your bar, your windows or your staff. They might kick the door on the way out, smash a window in your door, even worse try and have a bash at you. If you sense this is going to happen - try and stay behind the bar with the flap down (locked if possible).

What to do? Pre-warn staff the possibility this might happen. Have someone either in sight, or slightly out of sight, ready with the phone to ring the cavalry – **DON'T DILLY DALLY!**

Have you trained your staff to do this?

Tip. Sometimes it will pay to announce you have already rang the police. Other times, it may be applicable to signal a member of staff to make **THAT** call from behind the scenes, leaving the perpetrator no clue you have a plan 'B' in motion. You will have to go with the flow; it's called living on the edge.

Warning. Don't shout about your CCTV capability unless forced to. CCTV is your defensive weapon – keep it as such.

Sorry. If you're new to the game, it's probably the last thing you thought running a pub was all about. Learning to deal with all this crap is all about practice. The more incidents you deal with, the better you will become at handling any given situation and outcome. How sad is that?

Drunken assholes

Its Sunday teatime and the joint's humming. You've a live singer jollying things along. Suddenly one of your younger regulars starts falling all over the place, nearly knocking into the singer. He spent sixty quid in your place the previous evening and nothing to eat today. Now he's on his arse on your carpet. I've seen this happen a hundred times and mostly dealt with in the same predictable fashion.

What happens? This regular will fall over half a dozen times. The first occasion will be jointly laughed at by everyone, including bar staff and licensee. Half a dozen times later, they'll fall over a table of newly bought drinks, upsetting a group or family, at which point all hell breaks loose – **NASTY**.

Result. That successful, profitable session will be at an end. Those customers won't be coming back any time soon. Trade will suffer on forthcoming entertainment days and everyone will think **YOU'RE** a prick for not dealing with it earlier.

Seriously. I have witnessed mass brawls after such scenarios. Black eyes, glassing incidents, police called, bad feeling carrying on for months. The victim's screaming at the landlord about who's going to pay for those five drinks - **OUCH!** Having to pay dry cleaning for the lady who's had red wine spilt on her frock with flowers to say sorry - been there, done that.

AAAAAGGGGGHHHHH!

Warning. Do not expect to take people's money day in, day out, without being totally aware of what is going on within and around your unit. You cannot plead you were so busy you didn't notice **JACK** falling over, or **JILL** falling asleep slumped over the table. If you work in a business that has no alcohol involved; invariably when you get busy, you can just focus on being busy. When you add drink to the mix, liken it to throwing a hand grenade into a room, the surprise element of not knowing whether or when it's actually going to go off - **TRICKY**.

Showtime. Remove any drunk from the premises with immediate effect. No messing, no going back on it; no being persuaded by their mates, family, girlfriend, boyfriend and god knows who else swears blind they'll vouch for them, stand with them, hold them up and keep them out of trouble.

Why? These people will have no idea what it takes to look after someone in this state. They will more than likely be two parts to the wind themselves; in actual fact . . .

What the hell has it got to do with them?

Bottom line. You're in charge. You make the rules. Take control and dissolve any problem before it becomes one. Never back down. If you cannot do this – get another job.

Drunks are bad for business – full stop!

Cover your back

Let's be honest, you'll probably be only too happy to serve an individual as much alcohol as they desire, until such time as they do start falling all over the shop. Morally and legally however: you might have a **DUTY OF CARE** to this customer whether you like it or not. If some harm comes to them, you'll be on thin ground if it can be proved you've been negligent. In any case, you might not want to lose this **REGULAR**, who on average spends a hundred quid a week. That's five grand a year from one customer – has that got your attention?

AAAAAGGGGGHHHHH!

Suggestion. Ring the bloke falling over a taxi. Get his two mates to go with him. Pay the driver yourself (obtain a receipt). Get the money back from Jack the following day. This will improve your standing in the community; someone whom can look after their herd in a caring, but equally - no nonsense way.

Don't however. Let the piss be extracted by this individual. If it happens again and again, I'd be pulling **JACK** to one side. If this carries on he can drink elsewhere. Explain that whilst you like him very much, he's becoming a real pain in the ass; the legal consequences for **YOU** no joking matter.

Advice. Next time Jack does it, ban him. The joke will be wearing thin; not only with you, but other customers too. I reiterate - drunks on display are really bad for business.

> Do not hide your head in the sand, hoping a magic carpet will miraculously whisk a drunk back to their abode and tuck them up in bed - it doesn't work like that!

Landlords taxi story

I was in a mate's pub. One of his regulars **WAS** falling all over the place. One minute he was fine; the next, completely out of control. Willy not only removed him bodily from the building, but walked straight over to his own van, belted him in like a little boy and ran him home. I'm certainly not suggesting you become a personal taxi service, you certainly won't have the time or inclination, but you must always solve the problem.

One bad egg can devastate takings!

Watch your trade vanish out the exits, as he or she practice their own brand of witchcraft in **YOUR** front room. I banned hundreds of these numpties. When confronted, they'll be only too pleased to show their true colours. I can't tell you who these people are, but customers have personally thanked me for banning a particular person. You will almost feel the palpable relief in atmosphere as trade returns, as if by magic.

Stress. It wasn't till my third pub, that I really started to make decisions faster. Before that, I'd spend many a sleepless night, worrying about actions taken that day, or the knowledge I had to deal with an individual the following day – **JUST HORRIBLE**.

Advice. If you've decided an individual has to be banned and it's not been wise or prudent to have done so previously - wait until you know that that person is due. Wait at the door if you can. On their approach, inform them they are no longer invited to enter your premises. Tell them straight. Tell them the truth.

Why? It will catch them off guard, hopefully without any mates to back them up. It is altogether a different playing field to push past, or assault you in that setting; a psychological barrier they hopefully won't want to climb over.

Spit story

Sometimes you have to ban someone immediately. A guy stood at the bar and cleared his throat a couple of times. Unbelievably, he proceeded to gob it up on the bar floor, right in front of myself and a member of staff. Worse, he casually picked up his drink and carried on as if nothing had happened.

AAAAAGGGGGHHHHH!

Occasionally, you just can't believe what you have witnessed. The member of staff and me looked round at each other, as if in slow motion. I think it fair to say – I am not a small person. When I'm angry, people tend to realise within a fairly short space of time, along with anyone else in the surrounding area. It all seemed a trifle surreal. It didn't last long. Nor did he as I grabbed his pint, threw it in the sink, walked round and frogmarched him out the nearest exit. **DIRTY BASTARD.**

Warning. Be careful, the law is an ass. You can't just put your hands on people as far as I'm aware. **SHAME REALLY.**

Cover your back. Find out what you can and can't do in this unfair world we live in – do some homework. This is **NOT** a book for current intricacies of licencing, or law and order. Whatever sex, whatever build; you must deal with all this nonsense as best as you can. Look after your customers, staff, yourself and family, at the same time as protecting trade.

Tip. Some women have a fantastic way about them when dealing with situations. Find the way that works for you.

The police. Preferably before you sign on the dotted line, consult the local bobby (if one exists) and licensing officer. Use the opportunity to explain what your plans are. If you need to call the police, can you do that with confidence? Ask for their support and guidance. Is there a local pub watch you can join?

Prediction

Continual government cutbacks have resulted in dwindling
police numbers on our streets. Less police means priority
policing on a grand scale. Naïve excuses for politicians play a
dangerous game with our security. That will carry on until
totally anarchy breaks out – and it might.

How does this affect you? An unqualified dignitary's sidekick
armed with a calculator, might advise there is no way police
can afford to keep visiting the same licensed premises time
and time again: and that as they say – will be that. To some
extent that already happens and could get a lot worse, but . . .

Sometimes not to act . . . is not an option!

If a scenario has got way out of hand and you've lost complete
control – ring the police without hesitation. All this bollocks
about not ringing the police too many times is all well and
good, but it won't help whilst you're recovering in hospital, or
in some wooden box on your way in to the **BIG FIRE**.

Big warning. This does not mean you can call the boys in blue
every 5 minutes. I'm pretty sure that would go down like a bad
case of the clap. Think of it as a weapon of very last resort.

Long story cut short

Erase any obstacle that prevents a sale on your premises. Die-
hard regulars will benefit - but they are not your prime target.
There lies a whole world of new customers out yonder. Just to
survive, you'll need to attract new custom on a regular basis,
who through your door will provide opportunity to wow with
all the ammunition you can muster. The ultimate goal, that
fantastic prize - the return customer. Let me be clear . . .

Assholes will destroy any chance of that!

6 TOILETS & THAT SMELL

Male urine

The most underrated and never talked about threat to any licensed venture . . . Is the smell of MEN'S URINE!

Like it or not: when the male species of this planet go for a wee in your loo, most will be aimed directly into the urinal. The rest ends up over their shoes, trousers, hands, top, up their arms, everywhere. They don't mean to do it, but boys will be boys. Until we can wave a magic wand and solve human hygiene problems - it is what it is. However, if they're having a bad spray day, that spray will circulate all over the shop. On the tiles, walls, floor and the bloke standing two places away.

AAAAAGGGGGHHHHH!

Warning. The memorable facet about urine is - it smells. It smells bloody awful. Worse still; not cleaned away, it smells ten times as bad the following day. **THAT** smell will bleed into any connecting corridor and leak all through the trading area.

Be honest. Are your toilets a positive selling point to your premises, or an obstacle to profit? I would suggest that if you can smell a loo either before, or on opening the main door to those loos – it is without doubt an obstacle to profit.

Please explain to me why we would expect our customers to enter an area, which can only be described as smelling like an ELEPHANTS SHITHOUSE?

Prediction

Human expectation of hygiene will only go one way. I envisage super clean loos will become pivotal to any future business plan. In visiting hundreds of units, the general standard of men's in particular, is rank beyond belief. This provides tremendous opportunity for **YOU**. The trade has seen big changes in recent years and a global economic disaster of tidal wave proportions, but there are success stories. These units tend to get an awful lot of things right. Loos are one of them.

Advice. You may have inherited the foulest smelling loos in the land. Maybe the place has been shut for a while? Maybe they just haven't been cleaned properly for a number of days, weeks or longer. In that case; you may never (without total refurbishment of said loos) get them smelling sweet. You must however, do enough to neutralise **THAT** smell. Unless in pooing mode, men simply aren't programmed to sit down and merely wee. Without a urinal, more often they wouldn't even bother to raise the seat. Hence, that cubicle would have to be cleaned fifty times a day to remove urine now coating the seat and adjacent surfaces. Urinals are a necessity – it is a problem.

How long do you plan to, or give your cleaners?

Two hours to clean the whole unit? Breaking that down, probably only leaves twenty minutes in and out to clean both men's and ladies. Can I suggest this is highly inappropriate (cloud cuckoo land actually). Whilst you don't want to go bankrupt, employing an army of cleaners to rival the Queen; attaining and maintaining high standards of cleanliness in loos is far harder to achieve, than you might imagine. What do your cleaners do? Do you know? If you don't know – why don't you?

Suggestion. Ambush your cleaners after finishing. Guide them back to the toilets. Ask them to take you through their journey step by step. Reassure them all is ok, you just want to understand the job they do. How long does it take at present? Ask them to be honest. What do they think?

Why? You may be surprised at what you can learn on a little trip like that. What does it highlight? Do you need to allocate more time? Can other staff take on extra jobs elsewhere to make that work? Toilets are a slice of the picture you paint, an essential service you provide as a backdrop to profit.

Ignoring smelly loos is the equivalent of burning fifty pound notes at regular intervals . . . EVERY SINGLE DAY!

Suggestion. Clean the loos yourself. See how long it takes. Have you got the correct cloths, cleaning agents, sponges, buckets, mops, soap, toilet rolls, rubber gloves, warning sign etc? Just cleaning the WC, tiled floor, throwing a few smelly cubes in the urinals and replacing empty toilet roll holders, doesn't even touch the side of bringing a loo up to standard.

Housekeeping

1st on the list. Durable, easy to clean floors are an asset in toilets, but need time to dry. Always commence the daily clean in the loos. After returning each loo area to the standard you set, finish by washing the floor. Back yourself towards the exit, leaving the floor to dry thoroughly before commencing the rest of the unit. That leaves plenty of time before your adoring public enter the auditorium. It also might prevent being sued by anyone **SLIPPING** on a wet floor.

Tiling around urinals. Clean with spanking hot soapy water
EVERY SINGLE DAY - remove the stench of yesterday's urine. If
you only add one thing to duties – add that. Supply gloves and
a mask. Think about that spray effect – **NASTY**. You can employ
as many companies as you like, supplying as many gadgets as
you can reasonably afford, but in my opinion . . . .

No amount of air freshener sprayed into any foul smelling dirty toilet will make the slightest bit of difference.
It will still smell like a BABOONS ASS!

Hot and cold running water. Do both function with ease on
each basin you provide? If not, why not? Are they squeaky
clean? This is a fundamental service you **MUST** provide. Think
about the customer journey. Remove obstacles - **ADD VALUE**.

Mops and buckets. Use a different mop and bucket for the
men's and ladies. Label them on both handles and buckets in
permanent marker. On no account use them for any other
reason. Change the men's mop head at least – **TWICE A WEEK**.

Throw it away!

Ensure the water used in these buckets is scalding hot and
doused with an appropriate detergent. Find a detergent that
leaves a nice lingering smell, rather than a choker. Empty
buckets outside in a drain if safe. **NEVER** mix these buckets up
and **NEVER EVER** take anywhere near your bar or kitchen.

Advice. **TEACH** all your staff the etiquette of mops and
buckets. Merely telling employees to do things **DOES NOT**
work. Explain precisely why; in this case, in as brutal fashion as
you can invent. This will go a long way to removing any chance
of cross-contamination between loos and food areas.

Why would the bar area smell of piss?

Please don't tell me the mop and bucket used in the men's toilet, is used on the bar floor at the end of the night.

AAAAAGGGGGHHHHH!

Does this happen? I really **DO** witness this, on a regular basis. How do you know? The whole trading area will honk with the stench of men's urine. What other result could you expect? Consequence. Funnily enough, customers don't like it either.

Warning. If the ladies stink of men's urine, you'll know the reason why. This wouldn't be classed as lazy – it would be . . .

Licensed house suicide!

Female friendly

Ladies loos. The room must be trying to smell as good as possible, with unblemished, well lit mirrors and good décor. Supply soap and moisturiser in dispensers, which as a bonus will leave a nice smell in the room every time used. Avoid soap bars - women hate sharing soap. Women like to be pampered and treated respectfully, not subjected to: **NO** toilet roll, **NO** lock on the door, **NO** sanitary towel bin, tired décor and **THAT** smell lingering. Each small detail should **ADD** to the value.

Women are more likely to be far fussier about standards of hygiene and décor than the average bloke!

Tip. Physically take a journey from the bar to your ladies loo. How can you add value for lady customers in that journey? Ask female friends - what would they appreciate, or hate to experience? Think out of the box – **FIND THE VALUE.**

Nice loo story

Ian, a friend of mine, invested heavily in both his toilets. He runs a country pub with first class food. His loos are absolutely **TOP NOTCH**. Lights, taps and urinals all fitted with sensors; top of the range tiling to rival any five star hotel. Hand dryer and towels both provided - consistently so damned clean; an investment which compliments the high standard of food and premium products he offers. The finish - sublime.

What does this tell a customer? In Ian's case; nothing is left to chance. With no words it just says everything.

Long story cut short

Each to their budget of course, but setting a standard of décor and cleaning vigilance is only half the story; maintaining that standard the hard part. It'll only take one piece of bad service in another part of your delivery, to alert a human's antennae to other misdemeanours. Smelly, dirty loos are an easy target.

Challenge. The next time you're in a licensed house loo, run your hand up the tiled wall. Is it slimy? Are all the pipes and surfaces clean and smart? Are there puddles on the floor? Is it urine? Can you smell **THAT** smell? Would you still order food?

Download. I have provided a free download of a suggested list of tasks to clean a men's loo at *howtoandwhatsitlike.com.*

Next. In the following four chapters, I'll deal specifically with blocked urinals, cubicles and locks, toilet seats and lastly; toilet doors, rolls and fans. Some of you will think I'm completely crazy by now and that's ok, but if you want to succeed in this game – you have to complete the jigsaw. Some of you will get it. I'm going off to sit in a darkened room for a bit.

7 BLOCKED URINALS

Urine sediment

Question. How many times do you enter the men's toilets to discover one of the urinals is overflowing, leaving pools of water and manly emissions all over the floor?

Answer. It happens **ALL** the time.

Aim. Your objective is to literally wipe this problem out.

Why? One hell of a health and safety **RISK** in causing a fall, might subject you to - one helluva compensation claim to follow. Worse still; a health and safety **HAZARD**, the fact you have bodily fluid contamination. Oh and by the way, all those chaps will be merrily spreading urine along adjoining corridors; proceeding to tread all over your new lounge carpet, tiling and floorboards. Now the **WHOLE** unit might smell of men's piss.

AAAAAGGGGGHHHHH!

Astonishing. If there was a similar leak or blockage behind the bar, you would deal as a matter of urgency. Why is a leak in a loo any less urgent? You tell me?

What is the cause? Mostly from a build-up of sediment in the u-bend that links the urinal to the main waste pipe. This sediment is the remains of urine, held together by pubic hair, chewing gum, phlegm and god knows what else. A soapy, greasy, sticky, stinking blockage - nothing can permeate.

Consequence. It exacerbates **THAT** smell about a hundred times over, leaving a nasty taste in your nose and mouth. The aroma can stain your clothes, a bit like cigarette smoke used to. This time – no one will escape the honk.

THAT smell is a profit stripping killer!

What do you do? Unless you can do it yourself, you have to ring a plumber. However, the mere mention of this tradesman should send a shiver down your financial spine.

Advice. You wouldn't dream of taking on a pub without at least basic knowledge of working the cellar. The same applies to toilets. You can hide mistakes within a cellar behind a locked door – you can't do that in a public toilet, it's there for **ALL** your customers to **SEE** and **SMELL**. It will chip away at **YOUR** reputation. Find a local plumber prepared to carry out an inspection of your toilets. Pay them. An experienced tradesman should take no more than ten minutes to suss out any problems which might arise on a regular basis. Get them to explain this as if you're an idiot – a simple picture please.

Tip. If you have visible u-bends beneath urinals, take an existing u-bend down to a plumber's merchant. Purchase a spare for each urinal. A plumber might see this as a threat to their livelihood, but pay them to train **YOU** to fit one of these in an emergency. Emphasise the need to cover your back from a health and safety perspective. In the event of a blockage during a busy evening session, the ability to change a u-bend in less than ten minutes will go a long way in damage limitation.

Warning. Prepare to feel extremely sick, during and after changing a u-bend – certainly not for the faint hearted.

Bonus. If you don't feel confident in changing a u-bend, or just don't want to go there - still purchase spares. Invariably, a blockage will always happen at the least convenient moment. At least when you have to call a plumber out at three o'clock on a Friday afternoon, it'll better the odds no question. All they'll have to do is turn up, spend twenty minutes tops, complete and wait for you to cough up a load of notes.

Warning. Time is money to a plumber – **YOUR MONEY**. Not organised with spares in house; will mean the plumber turning up, diagnosing, disappearing across town to collect parts and returning forty five minutes later to complete - all the time the clock still running. Into the second hour and life starts to get expensive. Last time I looked, a brand new u-bend was no more than a tenner tops. Get the spares. **DO IT NOW.**

Tip. Prevention being the best cure, regularly change however many u-bends you have every six months, or more frequently. To a plumber this is a ten minute job per urinal. One hours work will see all your u-bends changed for new. If you've supplied the spares at cost, one hours labour is **GOOD NEWS**.

Tip. Regular monthly maintenance is an alternative. Ask at the plumber's merchant for an appropriate cleaning agent.

Extreme warning. This will be corrosive. Health and safety, risk assessments and special training – **COVER YOUR BACK!**

Tip. Whenever **ANY** tradesman chips up at your place, always offer tea and coffee. Like customers, treating tradesman with respect will generate relationships - nearly always beneficial.

Unit manager. You may not have access to a local contractor, which can become a problem on a Saturday afternoon when a customer reports your latest flood. The likelihood and probability of someone travelling fifty miles down a motorway to change a u-bend at that time - debatable. The fact you have Joe the plumber sat in your bar won't count for tuppence. **YOU'LL** be completely in the shit (pardon the pun).

Astonishing. It has always shocked me that big companies, who probably take the lion's share of their weekly income, between five 'o'clock on a Friday and Sunday at closing time, shut down their head office and maintenance teams for the exact same period. Do you work for a company like this?

No spare u-bend and too late to get a plumber?

I used to have a bucket in a locked cupboard; an extra-long screwdriver, old fashioned wire coat hanger, disinfectant and long red rubber gloves ready and waiting. No spare will mean unscrewing the existing u-bend at both ends, scraping out the blockage with the screwdriver or coat hanger, flushing clean with water and re-attaching. While you're at it, hook more sediment out of the adjoining pipes with the coat hanger, just in case the blockage is there instead – that's if you haven't been sick by then, with **THAT** smell infecting the whole area.

AAAAAGGGGGHHHHH!

Bad news. If it's still blocked after all that – you really will have to wait the arrival of a plumber. Worse still, even after washing your hands half a dozen times and showering - you'll still be haunted by an extreme dose of – **THAT SMELL**.

In the interim. If you've a stopcock that covers the urinals only, turn it off until the plumber arrives – why doesn't each urinal have an individual stopcock? Use several of these yellow warning signs and mop the fluids up. Cover the offending urinal up. Do whatever it takes to prevent humans using it until fixed. You simply have to get the floor dry. Spring clean that night, and again and again until **THAT** smell dissipates.

Long story cut short

Urinals are a waking bloody nightmare. Personally, I would change all u-bends on a regular basis and yearly change the whole piping. It's got to be cheaper than calling a plumber out thirty times a year. Whatever you do – cover your back, but . . .

Lose the puddles of piss at all costs!

8 WC CUBICLE DOOR LOCKS

Number two scenario

You're out with friends having a nice time. Meals have been ordered and the atmosphere is perfect. Suddenly your body starts talking - time for a **NUMBER TWO** (that's a poo to me and you). You've been enjoying yourself so much, you're not thinking that hard. Pushing open the access door, you take a quick visual and nasal scan to check for a level of cleanliness before deciding - look out pan here I come. Into a cubicle and shutting the door is followed by the sound effect of an alarm ringing - there exists no working lock on the door.

AAAAAGGGGGHHHHH!

Please do not come up with any excuse as to why one or more of your toilet cubicles has no working lock on it.
Believe me . . . No excuse currently exists!

Prediction

If a survey was taken right now, I predict only 50% of all cubicle doors would have a smooth working, lockable door mechanism. I further predict; at least 10% of all cubicles would have no lock whatsoever. Call me Victor, but it would not surprise me if that figure was a conservative estimate.

Why is this so important? This would count as a major intrusion to the customer journey – a jolt back to reality. That customer was in bar heaven until **YOU** woke them up. On top of that, someone else just entered the only other cubicle. You **KNOW** that lock works having just heard it slide across.

Observation. I cannot for the life of me understand why cubicles aren't fitted with more substantial and hard wearing locks. As soon as these locks start to malfunction, they become a complete pain in the arse in more ways than one.

Warning. I have seen admirable refurbishments of door locks, augmented by huge plates of natural plywood, held together by huge bolts that will now last longer than the door itself. Not only does this look Rog the bodge, it provides rough surfaces that are almost impossible to clean thoroughly. Impossible!

The lock on the inside of all toilet cubicles must be cleaned (and be cleanable) every single day without fail!

Why? When both sexes have finished in a cubicle, they will have wiped their bottoms and touched their bodies god knows where, before being left with no choice but to unlock the door with dirty hands - have I put you off your dinner yet?

By the way. Back to that tour you got your cleaners to take you on; did they mention how often they clean these? I'm not a betting man, but would think it fair to predict these locks may **NEVER** have been cleaned since the day they were fitted.

AAAAAGGGGGHHHHH!

Long story cut short

You'll still be paying tax for every square foot of any cubicle at your disposal – useable or not. The higher the fence you build for the customer to jump, the more likely they'll find an excuse to chip off home and watch that TV. Locks on cubicle doors must exist and be 100% smooth working – **NO EXCEPTIONS**.

9 TOILET SEATS

The ballcock incident story

My family and I visited a popular and famous seaside resort. Come lunchtime we chose to eat in a seafront pub/restaurant/hybrid evening venue. After ordering cod and chips twice and something for one of our cherubs, my partner visited the ladies loos with our daughter. On her return, I inquired how that had been for her. She replied it had certainly been interesting. Without wanting to cause alarm to our children, but having just ordered food in this joint, I thought I'd just check the men's out. Approaching the door to the men's, I could smell the familiar stench of urine sediment – **THAT** smell. On opening the door I was greeted with dirt, dust and pure shit (the real stuff) all over a wall. Both cubicles had stainless steel all in one plinths. One had a worn black seat that was in two separate pieces, neither actually fixed to anything, just placed in the right position on top of the throne. The other toilet had no seat at all. Both aluminium plinths and cubicles were filthy.

AAAAAGGGGGHHHHH!

Escaping, I gave the same reciprocal remark back to my partner, praying they'd leave our cod and chips in the fryer long enough to kill - any bacteria picked up along the way. There were actually two men's toilets on the premises. The second was blocked off, with **OUT OF ORDER** scribbled on a piece of A4 paper, taped to a chair in front of said loo. A chap whom I can only assume was a plumber, emerged from the loo carrying this ballcock thingy. He started to chat with the main man behind the bar, to the order of, 'I need to replace this'.

Problem being. The plumber chap was waving this ballcock thingy, directly over the cutlery tray on the bar between them. It was dripping blobs of liquid from that loo - onto the cutlery. Neither of these **EXPERTS** noticed. Nothing was said or done.

AAAAAGGGGGGHHHHH!

I remarked to my partner that I was glad we had already collected our cutlery. We will not be returning **ANY** time soon. No training, no standards, no clue whatsoever. **BLOODY HELL!**

Without fail. Make sure all the cubicles in all your loos enjoy fully functioning toilet seats - why on earth wouldn't you?

Be prepared. Visit your local DIY store and get a couple of spares to keep in your store cupboard – you'll need them.

Long story cut short

Let's get this straight – a visit to the loo should enhance the customer journey, not shit on it from any height whatsoever. I regularly witness male cubicles, with ill fitting, dirty, broken and non-existent toilet seats. If you cannot bother to provide this fundamental service, you are in the wrong business. If you can't afford to spend a few quid on a spare toilet seat – then shame on you. Toilet seats are a noticeable component in a smooth running visit to the loo. I don't care whether you think this is relevant; nothing untoward in the picture you paint should be noticeable to a customer. Remove obstacles, return a positive and then perhaps I can stop - **SHOUTING**.

Ignoring something as simple as a broken, missing or dirty toilet seat is the equivalent of . . .

Walking around with your own head up your own arse!

10 TOILET (doors/fans/loo rolls) + TOILET SUMMARY

The most infected item in licensed premises?

A big percentage of men **DO NOT** wash their hands before leaving a toilet area. What would be the point anyway?

Meaning? A bloke visits the loo. He has a wee. He does not wash his hands. He has to pass through a door to exit the men's loo. He has to use the inside door handle to exit. So will the gentleman who carries a personal cleaning gel on his person and has spent five minutes scrubbing his pinkies. It won't matter a jot, he'll still have to use that same handle.

The exit door handle in any toilet, has got to be the single dirtiest item in licensed premises . . . ANYWHERE . . . ANYTIME!

Double bubble. A customer using a cubicle will not only spread germs to the cubicle door, but failure to wash their hands will further contaminate the exit handle in the process. 100% of every visitor to that loo will have to touch that door handle to escape, regardless of what ailment they may have, or what the hell else they have been touching in your loo.

AAAAAGGGGGHHHHH!

Furthermore. I'm afraid the bad news doesn't stop there. If there are adjoining doors to any corridor: in order to re-join the main bar area - 100% of **ALL** customers using that corridor will have to touch **ALL** those door handles too – **NASTY**.

Alarm bells ringing. I would hazard another guess. This particular handle might **NEVER** have been cleaned in the whole time your premises have been in existence. Harking back to that trip I suggested you take cleaners on; did they indicate this was cleaned every day? I bet they didn't. You could use toilet paper to grab the handle, but what if both cubicles are in use, or bereft of toilet paper?

Suggestion. Layout permitting; get rid of entrance/exit doors wherever possible. As germ carriers go they loom large, coupled with the fact your toilets aren't honking anymore (are they?) - it's a solution. An example is in some motorway service stations. Perhaps staff will have less time off sick, customers too - all of which might increase your **PROFIT** line.

Ladies loo. I'm really not ignoring you. Truthfully, I didn't visit many. I'd have probably been arrested, but same advice really.

Tip. Can't lose the door? Provide a paper towel dispenser at the exit with a bin below. Do it anyway, it's a nice touch.

Fundamental. **TEACH**, not tell the cleaning crew the importance of adding door handles to their ever growing cleaning routine - they'll have to use the bloody things too.

Ventilation

Are all the fans in your toilets working correctly? Are they man enough for the job in hand? A fan cannot make a filthy loo smell nice, but can remove **POST POO** aroma in a clean and neutral space. A loo well cleaned every day will still smell nice later in the day - with adequate ventilation.

Flipside. Bad ventilation will destroy any amount of cleaning you undertake. If a fan isn't working correctly, or makes that horrible whining sound, it's a distraction – replace it.

Toilet rolls

My pet hate. A cubicle without toilet roll, or some plastic contraption, that with every pull, the paper tears off - me wanting to smash it to smithereens.

Advice. If you check a cubicle and find a toilet roll near the end of its life – change it. If you've a busy session ahead and two members of staff ring in sick; the last thing you want to worry about mid-session - is re-filling the freaking dispenser.

Tip. Make sure the dispenser IS free flowing and doesn't require a degree to work out how best to liberate the paper. If faulty - change it. If you're purchasing paper from a particular supplier, dispensers might be free of charge – CARRY SPARES.

Tip. Keep a good stock of refills/rolls via your stock and order book (please tell me you have one) so as NEVER to run out.

Suggestion. If you are guilty of having a customer ask you for a toilet roll at the bar, you need to either review how you are running your premises, or get another job – UNFORGIVABLE.

Loo check story

If you introduce loo checks - be careful what you wish for. I was in a loo where a member of staff walked in, went straight to this A4 chart on the wall, signed it and disappeared out the door. I was standing in front a blocked urinal full of yellow piss, a lake sized puddle of piss, toilet paper all over the floor, an empty soap dispenser and a bare wire on the hand dryer.

AAAAAGGGGGHHHHH!

Warning. You are the people who employ these profit draining, success assassins. YOU MUST TAKE RESPONSIBILITY. Train all staff within an ounce of their life and explain why.

Baby changing/ disabled facility

Upon finding a unit that is family friendly, parents with young children will return again and again. If a parent using the facility for the first time finds it in bad order - they might not. It may have been clean at opening time, but babies make a mess. Check and clean as a matter of course. Make sure safety straps are available, spotless and in good working order. Cover your back. Many baby changing rooms double up as a disabled facility. These spaces should please the customer. Think about that. They will usually be on the ground floor and should not be used for convenience by the general public.

Toilet summary

The negatives in the last five chapters don't amount to much when taken singularly. String two or three in line and you create an altogether crueller beast. A visit to the loo should be no more than a passing glance in the customer journey; a slight interruption at most, before re-joining the ambience of a visit. It **SHOULD'NT** be littered with obstacles, distract and chip away at the **MAGIC** you as a host, might have succeeded till that point in creating. To that end, thorough, honest cleaners are worth their weight in gold. Good luck in finding them.

Warning. Making changes in cleaning protocol is easy. Enforcing those changes takes stamina and an iron will. You have to be all over this like a rash, day in – day out.

P.S. If you're wondering what the hell you can do to make your place more female friendly – a good start will be offering a quality experience in the ladies. Ladies just love a clean loo.

Add nothing but VALUE to the customer journey – remove the obstacles!

11 INHERITING STAFF

Takeover scenario

It's your first pub. You've paid a hundred grand to take this place on in fees and whatever deal you may have signed. The pub takes nine grand a week on average. At that level, you can just about come out even, as long as no great disasters happen on a regular basis forthwith. You inherited six members of staff from the previous owner and the cleaning crew; a husband and wife team who are there for two hours a morning, six days a week. Being so busy, you've just had to let the cleaners get on with it, though the place looks fine on the surface. They however, seem to spend more time drinking tea and having a fag outside, than they do cleaning. A mate of theirs covers on a Sunday morning to give the loos a consolatory once over. You still can't seem to work out what **THAT** smell is though.

AAAAAGGGGGHHHHH!

Of those six staff, there is not a cook amongst them. Only one is of any worth, another is leaving. You're absolutely positive two of them have their fingers in the till and one can't seem to go half an hour without popping out for a fag. (Where do they get the money?) The last one you only met yesterday when she popped in to say hello, having been on the sick for the last two weeks (which didn't prevent her from putting away the best part of five pints of lager while she said hello). The most galling thing being; this lady, whom **YOU** are now paying and have only just met; shouts back at you, whilst nearly falling over when leaving, 'I'll let you know when I'm better'.

Who's the MUG?

The trap. Trouble is; just when you've taken on a boozer, it can be financially fragile. After a deluge of rain the other night, you now find that water is leaking through the roof, in not one, but three separate places; the urinals are blocked for the fourth time this week and the ice machine stopped working yesterday. Suddenly, the 5K you intended for working capital is looking decidedly sick. You have to pay for this week's stock in cash when they deliver and that'll be **YOU** on dodgy ground, joining all the other pubs, clubs and bars in the same shitty position - hoping in hell they have a busy weekend.

AAAAAGGGGGHHHHH!

Warning. Apart from the previous licensee having taken on individuals totally inappropriate in providing service to humans (possibly down to the idiot only ever providing two hours training on their 1st day); one of the biggest threats and financial obstacles, inherited or not, will always be . . .

Employing the WRONG staff!

A really big deal. Whether an incoming manager appointed by a large company, or an independent; you will be making a tremendous personal and financial commitment. It might well be the career you've always dreamed and planned of . . .

Staff transferring to your employment won't give two craps about any of that!

Look at it from their shoes; the only **NEW** member of staff as far as they are concerned - **WILL BE YOU!**

Immediate consequence. It's very easy to find your back against the wall, before you even know it.

Consider too. With long term servers, what consequences would arise should **YOU** ever want to sell that business on?

Pre-emptive homework

The ideal situation taking over an existing business, would be to start from scratch. Hire a new team, with the existing team given a chance to re-interview for their jobs. I think you'll find the protection of employment laws, state that any transfer of business will simply transfer those workers with it - by rights. In other words – you can't just ride roughshod over the hillbillies. Nothing is simple in this world I'm afraid. This isn't a book that delves into laws and regulations; besides, what I might state now, could change tomorrow and I personally wouldn't trust any government to look after my socks. I can only advise you to check out the latest rules and regulations on employment law, before making any big decisions. What **CAN** you do?

If taking over an existing business, feel free to be clinically cynical. Ask yourself - exactly why are the owners moving on? Even if a valid explanation is poking you in the face, I would still look very closely for . . .

Tell-tale signs!

Look at the profit and loss (P&L) figures for the past three years. If these are not available - why aren't they? Pay special attention to the stock results. I know we haven't covered stock or P&L as yet, but these are pivotal to any decision you make. Without skipping to chapters covering these issues, you should be achieving at least near a 100% stock yield for wets (drink).

Example. If you're missing 10 bottles of one particular lager from your fridges at the end of a day, you should have the cash and till readouts to account for those 10 bottles. If you can only account for 8, it'll reduce the stock yield to 80%. In cash terms, if one bottle costs you £1.50 and you sell it for £3.50 – losing two bottles will have cost you ten pounds total – **OUCH**.

How do you work that out? Not only has it cost you three pounds to buy the lost stock - you've also lost the seven quid you could have sold it for. A tenner lost – **OUCH AGAIN**.

How would you lose stock like that? Unless you believe in fairies, only a human being can remove bottles from fridges. You, one of your family, one of your staff, or one of your customers will have stolen two bottles of lager from the fridge. Maybe a member of staff has rang in the bottles, but pocketed the cash. The outcome is the same. Maybe two bottles smashed on the bar floor – you could check the wastage book.

And what the hell has this got to do with staff transferring to your employment?

Work the figures. Identifying a stock problem within the books, might also give indication as to whether, existing staff are **STEALING** from their **CURRENT** employer. Find out what products the current employees drink. By the same token; find out what products the current employer drinks, they might be responsible for stock loss - nothing would surprise me. Pursue all avenues of evidence. Ask the relevant questions; otherwise you're in head up my ass territory (**HUMAT**).

Electronic point of sale (EPOS). If the unit already has an EPOS till system, you should be able to pinpoint products that continually show a lower yield – that means **STOLEN** mostly.

How? Every time a sale is made, the till logs that information and **REDUCES** your stock by one count; i.e. one pint of cider sold, will reduce how much the system will think you still have in the barrel - clever stuff eh. The really important bit? It will tell you exactly what you **SHOULD** have left, otherwise . . .

The drinks are on YOU landlord!

How does this help? Being able to paint as closer picture to the truth, will probably be some distance from what you are being told by the vendor, attempting to escape what they might see as – **A ROPE AROUND THEIR NECK**. When shown round as a prospective new owner or manager, you might be fed all kinds of horseshit – **REMOVE THE DARK GLASSES**.

Why? A real-time picture might well make you **THINK TWICE** before proceeding with any business or career move. It might at the very least, stop you making the offer you were thinking of and carve out an altogether better deal - for **YOU**.

Visit incognito. If you really want to get a handle on what's happening in a unit, and before you sign on any dotted line; visiting before making yourself known makes common sense. Not just at busy times, but late afternoon when things are generally quieter. Finding out what traits staff follow and tell-tale signs first hand, can reveal an awful lot.

Upon takeover. Hold a staff meeting. If you've done your homework, visited incognito, read previous stock results, profit and loss reports and attendance records of all existing staff; you will already have formulated a business plan of attack.

When? ASAP. You only get one chance to create a first impression - use it. Spell out in no uncertain terms, your determination to raise the level of customer service to new heights. Take the opportunity to lay down the law as to mobile phones, fag breaks, no more leaning on the bar likes it's some kind of pillow etc. etc. Above all - it's your chance to re-motivate these people and give them **HOPE**.

What will happen? Generally, employees who care will love the fact they're going to be managed and trained properly. You may well find anyone on the lazy side, will look for another job before you find them out.

Help in making your mind up

Proof. I make no apology reiterating the need to see concrete figures. If a vendor cannot provide daily records, why would you believe a word they say? How can you explain one bartender taking £400, another only taking £50 on the same shift - with fifty no sales showing up? How could you possibly even know if you hadn't seen the figures? What effect did this have on the stock for that period? Who was the bartender?

Would you really pay a premium for BULLSHIT?

Advice. If I was thinking of taking on a unit, I would want to see full and detailed records. I would spend at least one whole day deciphering. If I didn't have the experience to carry that out, I would employ a clever stock taker/auditor from outside the area to clue me in. It might save me a lot of money.

Long story cut short

This business is brutally harsh on newcomers. It might chew you up and spit you out, leaving bills to pay, divorce courts to visit. It can however, be exactly the right move. Right move or not, you will **NOT** have the luxury of carrying anyone; especially if they've got fingers in the till **BEFORE** you arrive. Not to make stringent investigations on staff you may inherit would be lazy. If I was investing a 100K, I'd personally want to interview **ALL** employees I might inherit without exception. If it was legal, I'd expose them and the owners to a three hour interrogation, hooked up to a lie detector that passed a 1000 volts of electricity every time they actually lied. Get the gist? Covering my back. The electricity thing was a **JOKE!**

12 RECRUITING NEW STAFF

I initially wrote dozens of pages on this subject; I've shrunk it to bite size chunks easier on the pallet. I advise you to read every damned word. If one sentence prevents a huge mistake or sets you in the right direction – it's worth the read.

Hiring the right person will be the single most important ingredient in your success, mediocrity or downfall!

Your aim

Find the best possible candidate to fit and enhance your team. To simplify the process, I provide a list of questions you might ask when interviewing, a suggested summary sheet to help evaluate how the interview went and a bullet point checklist targeting recruitment for the licensed trade. You can download these for free from the *howtoandwhatsitlike.com* website by clicking on the free download button for this book. Being busy, you'll need all the help you can get. Feel free to edit these and devise your own template to suit.

Consequences. To best appreciate employing quality staff, you must first understand the severity on your profit line of drastic errors. Not following correct protocol for interviews and references is like playing Russian roulette. After choosing the wrong candidate, you may never be aware anything is wrong. The damage may continue for years unchecked – as might your takings. You can forget targets, bonuses, holidays, generous pension schemes and other suchlike pipedreams. Recruiting mistakes are **EXPENSIVE** - and yes I am **SHOUTING**.

Prediction

If you were to ask any experienced licensee what had been the biggest pain throughout their career, they'll more than likely tell you; finding reliable, honest, hardworking staff – is the hardest thing to achieve. As if that wasn't difficult, you have to build a whole bloody team of these people, whilst attempting to pay a pittance - it's a problem. On top of that: in recent times we have bred youngsters that can play computer games with a high degree of skill, text at great speed on their mobile phones, but seemingly possess no social skills whatsoever. Their ability to concentrate on repetitive jobs and attention to detail is truly miserable. I predict a wall to climb.

Relief (of my bonus) story

I took a two week holiday. The company supplied me with a relief manager and I checked in to a rest home for disturbed licensees. The guy seemed ok. I stocked out and left my little world in his hands, just hoping he wouldn't destroy all the little gains I'd worked really hard to achieve. While I was away he took on this barman. He started him on a weekday morning and had a busy lunchtime session. About three o'clock, he ran upstairs for a quick wee and came straight back down. On his return to the bar, he noticed both till draws were open. All the notes and pound coins were missing. There was no sign of the new barman and no customers in the pub either.

AAAAAGGGGGHHHHH!

This guy had about £650 quid away and that was my stock and bonus for that quarter staying firmly in the 'Promised Land'. Guess what? No CV, no references, no proper interview, and no money left in my tills - thanks pal.

Bear in mind. Money and stock missing will decimate your business (see **STOCK CONTROL** and **STAFF AT IT** chapters).

Consider though. A problem that may become familiar will be one of need and desperation. That may be strange to suggest, but the number of times I felt I had to compromise myself and the business I have been running (for the sake of my own sanity) and hire a second best option - were frequent.

1st pub story

My first unit was in a town centre in greater London, turning over 5 – 9K a week. My partner was chained to the kitchen. Our Area Business Manager I nicknamed God, would probably have sacked us if we weren't providing food seven days a week for the majority of each day. I had one full time barman, another four part-time bar staff, and a cleaner. Suddenly a couple of the staff put their notice in and the full timer went on the sick. Thanks a lot.

Consequently. Two weeks later and I've been stuck on the bar for up to 13 hours a day, every day. That's on top of cellar duties, ordering, counting tills, receiving deliveries and a hundred and one other bloody chores that make the wheels turn. At this point all humour will vanish, personal life relegated to a wish list. Any ideas of how to build the business up are left gathering dust, when it's all you can do to put one foot in front of the other. It seemed like one, long, never ending marathon. Oh, and don't even think of being ill. I was a bit stuck, because I couldn't replace the full-timer. He was coming back, but I was still getting hit for his wages, even if it wasn't the full whack on the sick. It gets to a point though.

Sod it! Sign in the window - staff wanted.

Problem. One after another, people stroll in and enquire about the part-time bar staff job advertised in the window.

What's the problem? You'll be on your own serving a customer, another waiting - a possible staff member wafting in the background. Suddenly, there'll be a glimmer of light in what up to now seemed a very grey day. You might only be able to throw a pen and paper toward them and request a number with a promise to ring later. It's not ideal.

Example. One particular girly came in. I quickly fired a few questions at her. What's your name? Have you got any experience? What hours are you looking for? Can you work tonight? By that evening, Helen was working for me and turned out to be one of the hardest working, loyal staff I ever had. For the most part it was desperation and in that case - pure luck. I also made awful decisions that nearly cost me my job on more than one occasion. **I KID YOU NOT**.

Key qualities and avoiding recruitment mistakes

You can avoid the majority of blunders by simply interviewing properly. Ask well aimed questions and follow up references and attendance records in previous employment. Even if you're desperate for staff, there are lots of boxes to tick when weighing up the suitability of the person standing in front of you. Even if this person can juggle five glasses at once, whilst pouring a perfect cocktail and hold a conversation at the same time - the two key ingredients I'd be looking for are . . .

Will this person be receptive to training to deliver a higher standard of service and do they look like they want to be here?

Question. How many staff currently serve in units with little advance, let alone on-going training of any kind?

Answer. Quite a lot I would hazard to guess. I would expect managed houses to have a better record of forcing employees to pass NVQ's on all types of backcovering subjects, but from where I'm sitting, I see little evidence of investment in the customer love side of the equation. I hope I'm wrong.

Why? Anyone can serve anyone with no smile, no courtesy, no thank you and no investment of any type of customer love. Imagine someone with a little hammer, continually chipping away at your building, each day managing to remove a brick. Eventually a wall will give way where there used to be bricks. In layman's terms; don't unleash anyone on your customers until sure they're not going to damage your business. The right recruit, should be able to add **VALUE** to the customer journey.

From evidence I witness on a regular basis you may as well hire a cardboard cut-out!

Planet Zog. You may well be reading this thinking, 'this bloke is living on another planet if he thinks all these dream bar staff are going to knock my door, begging me to hire them.' I would have sympathy with that, but these people **ARE** out there.

Applicants. If a dozen people apply for a job and none tick enough boxes – don't make a rash decision and employ **ANY** of them. Better to resist hiring someone whom is just plain second best. If so desperate it cannot wait, re-interview select candidates and choose a close first. A mistake need not be the end of the world - that's what a trial period is for.

The hard part. If a choice does turn out to be unsuitable, it's never nice having to say to someone it's not working out, but in that period within the letter of the law – **SAY IT YOU MUST.**

The hard truth. You will be running a business, not a charity. The main hindrance might be; the time you'll have wasted in training them for two weeks and letting them bond with existing staff; which might prove damaging if they've been a bad influence. Plus, the sheer expense of all that. In the process you might have missed a better candidate, whom might have applied in the period since you took down all your staff wanted signs. Two steps forward, six steps back.

Backcovering. You don't need to be an expert in employment law, but you do need to know the basics. Find out current legislation that specifically affects the licensed trade.

Tip. If an independent, find a solicitor with experience relevant for you. Half an hour is all it will take for a run down of the basics. Heck, you might even get that for free first time.

Tip. Pay solicitors bills with **IMMEDIATE** effect. You never know when you may be grateful for **IMMEDIATE** advice. Better to be broke and well informed, than broke and thick as a brick.

Area business managers (ABM's). Ask their advice. Backcovering is a professional sport to these characters.

Trade body/Union. Could you benefit subscribing? Do they offer support and guidance in employment matters?

I re-iterate. **DO YOUR HOMEWORK**. Make sure whatever decision you may have to make – is **CURRENTLY LEGAL**.

Advertising/C.V's/being organised.

First decide on where you advertise a vacancy. Let's say you are looking for a part-time bartender. Personally, I wouldn't dream of listing a vacancy in a jobcentre. You are looking for solutions, not problems. I'm afraid an ad in the jobcentre will bring more problems than it is worth.

Why? You'll require someone who actually wants that job, not three hundred people completing targets in order to qualify benefits. Whoever set this system up really does suffer from **HUMAS**. I repeat: this is only my personal view. If an efficient jobcentre exists I'd be surprised. Good luck with that.

Instead. Design an advert on your laptop. Keep it simple i.e.

Part time bar staff required.
Apply within or phone 123456

Tip. Do not write by hand. Whilst I don't think you need to go overboard, signage should look professional, not amateur. Produce several different job vacancy titles and laminate for future use. Immediate and efficient, store them where they'll stay pristine. Scruffy signs are an avoidable obstacle.

Tip. Always include the unit phone number. Passing parent's might not always want to come in, but might take that number in order to encourage their cherub to start earning money as soon as humanly possible – and leave. It worked for me.

Tip. Before you advertise, place a clipboard with pen and contacts book attached behind the bar. Take a name and **ALL** numbers. Ask them to drop a C.V. in or post. Have paper slips clipped on that board with your name and unit address to hand out. Before they leave, impress on them - as soon as a C.V. is dropped in you will arrange an interview. C.V. received; start a file on that candidate within a box file. If your first choice doesn't work out, you'll need to review the situation. Having previous applicant details in one place and not in the bin, will be a luxury you actually planned. You may already have several good prospects sitting in that box file.

No CV? No interview full stop!

Recognition. Don't underestimate what a nervy ordeal it is for someone walking in off the street to ask about a vacancy, it shows metal. Remember, it's not all about you. At this point in the proceedings; they'll still be weighing up whether **THEY** actually want, have to, or fancy coming to work for you. Their brains might be working overtime looking for obstacles that might prevent **THEM** from giving **YOU** a chance.

Contacts book. Keep it confidential. Applicant's personal information shouldn't be left around for all and sundry to read. This would be entirely inappropriate.

Answer staring you in the face?

If there's someone you come across in your travels – why not ask if they're interested? I know of two young people that regularly serve me in a local capacity. They both exude personality and consistent customer love. It's worth a shot.

Arranging interviews

Schedule your diary for interviews and arrange cover on the bar. Personally ring applicants and create a written trail of whom you have rang and when. E-mail if you wish, but talking on the phone can tell an awful lot. If the keenness they displayed in-house seems to have gone on holiday, that's probably what they'll be like working for you – on holiday.

AAAAAGGGGGHHHHH!

If that happens, ask there and then, 'you don't seem as keen?' If they start Umming and Ahhing; stop them right there and end the conversation . . . **THEY** will be wasting **YOUR** time.

I say again. You'll need people who really **WANT** to be there.

Where do you interview? I have two trains of thought. All the advice I have absorbed on interviewing, has been to find a private room. Yes this will provide a space without interruption, enabling you to focus completely on the matter in hand, but is this the correct approach for you to find the correct bartender? The second train of thought: interview your prospective employee at one end of the unit, with everything singing and dancing in the background. Most experienced landlords and managers will be used to multitasking. It shouldn't be too difficult to keep **YOUR** concentration, but it might be interesting to see how **THEY** react to stuff going on in the background. Can they keep their focus and not be distracted by general unit noise. After all, it will be the usual habitat **THEY** will have to perform within.

Advice. Choose whatever suits you, but interview everyone in the same manner. This will help you compare the difference between candidates more accurately.

Application forms. A CV **IS** their application form. Unless you work for a large company demanding such formality, why complicate the issue? If demanded by a higher force - produce an application form on offer of employment at the earliest.

Tip. Favour candidates that can actually listen. They might listen to customers and more importantly – listen to learn.

Setting. The last thing you want, is your existing staff all on a coffee break, outside having a fag, leaning on the bar half asleep, answering their mobile phone behind the bar to their drug dealer . . . When a candidate arrives for an interview.

Why? A quality individual will more likely to want to work in a professionally run unit. What you present is exactly the image they'll meet on that first date - first impressions do count.

One last decision. Do you want to make your candidate at ease from the word go, or should it be more challenging? You can be challenging and friendly all at the same time, adding a couple of spiky questions to test the ground, but don't lose sight of what you actually wanted in the first place.

What questions should I ask? Some of you will be more nervous than the interviewee. There'll be no room for doubt or insecurity on your part. The only way to evaluate performance is to ask the candidates the same questions. Have a set of questions readily to hand and ad-lib through their C.V.

Free downloads. In the next few pages: I have provided a suggested bullet point summary for taking on new staff, a suggested introduction, a list of questions to fire at your prospective employee, and a suggested interview summary sheet to score your candidates. All of these are accessible to edit from the website. Feel free to doctor these to suit.

Advice. Have a partner, colleague, or someone you respect business wise join you. A silent observer could take notes on your behalf during. Let's call this person a buddy. Unless you're the brain of Britain, having someone take notes could be really rather useful. You may prefer and be fully capable of managing this whole process on your own. Time will be a factor.

Tip. If you're doing more than three interviews in one day, or appointments are spaced over separate days, having good notes to draw from might be a godsend.

Warning. Don't be surprised to feel completely shattered at the end of a day's interviewing. I doubt very much if the average licensee will be the proud owner of a gold medal in interviewing technique. You may well be operating far outside your usual comfort zone and struggle with the intensity. Either way, it will prove exhausting working with such focus.

<u>Bullet point summary for taking on new staff</u>

- Determine exactly what you require from a new staff member and how they might fit in to your team.
- How exactly will this add profit?
- Decide the minimum level of competency you will need to achieve from a new team member.
- Purchase a contacts book, pens and clip board and have slips printed with your full address on.
- Put staff wanted signs up, in and outside the unit.
- Collect C.V.s from prospective applicants and start a file on each candidate from word go.
- Remember - NO C.V. – NO INTERVIEW.
- Set a date for the action to commence.
- Let all parties know by phone and agree a time they can make it. Keep a written record of conversations.
- Subject all candidates to the same setting and questions in order to more accurately measure performance.
- You shouldn't have to do this, but make sure all existing staff be professional in the background.
- If possible, arrange a buddy to sit in and take notes throughout. Have several pens available that actually work. You're in the business of hospitality: offer candidates a tea, coffee or water. Make them welcome.
- Do the interview.
- When a candidate leaves – write assessment of what has just taken place. What overall impression were you left?
- Mark your 'out of 10' assessment sheets.
- File away for decision later and future perusal.
- Stretch your legs, wee etc.
- Next please.

Intro & questions suggestions

- **Shake the persons hand and introduce yourself** leaving room then to ask their name i.e. **'and you are?'**
- Offer refreshments and explain your role within the unit.
- Tell them – **'I'd like to get to know all about you'**
- Tell them - **'I'm going to be firing a few questions at you.**
- Start – **'How was your journey? How did you get here?'**
- This says are they local? Can they get here fast if need be? Read through their C.V. and ask pertinent questions as they arise. This will give you some info on them slowly, slowly. It will also help them feel at ease; leaving you to lap up all the gory details and delve into what the hell they've been doing all their life. Get to know them.
- **Fill them in on the 'full' job description** Go through every single chore in detail and discuss as you go. See how they react, facial expressions etc.
- **What would you say your strengths are?**
- **And your weaknesses?**
- **Can you tell me why you have applied for this job?**
- **You will be expected to work over the Xmas period – is that a problem?** The answer should of course be **'No'**.
- **If you are successful in your application, how long you might be thinking of staying with us? Is this a short term fix or can we expect a longer term commitment?**
- **Have you got any questions that you'd love to ask me?**
- **One last thing – should we offer job and you accept - is there any problem with us following up your references?**
- **Thank them and let them know you really appreciate them making the time. You will let them know ASAP.**

Advice. In reading the C.V. slowly through as the mainstay of the interview, it will provide opportunity to adlib as you go. You can question any bits that ring alarm bells and hopefully erase any doubts. On the flip side, you may well decide you'd rather be publicly boiled in a pot of dog shit, than choose to employ this donkey sitting in front of you.

Big tip. Always ask for permission in following up references. If ever a question was designed to trip someone up - this is it.

Reaction. If the candidate shows any doubt or nervousness about you ringing Tom, Dick or Harry, to confirm what they've stated on their C.V. - you can bet your bottom dollar there's more to that than meets the eye.

Tip. Practice the interview scenario with your partner, a friend, or colleague. Don't overdo it though. You just need to be reasonably familiar with a set of questions and the order of delivery. Rehearsal is fundamental in releasing space in your brain - to measure and process an applicant's performance.

Interview summary

As soon as the candidate leaves, you'll need to make some quick notes as to how the process has panned out. Note two or three main things that have stuck out (no more than that). Fill in the marks **OUT OF TEN** questions on the summary sheet illustrated on the next page. Alternatively, download and customise this list relevant to requirements from the website.

Evaluate. You need to **MEASURE** the profit of adding a particular individual to your team. In scoring marks out of ten: should there be no obvious choice at the end of the interview process, it might be far less painful narrowing down the field. Don't throw them away - the first choice might not work out.

Interview summary score sheet
Name

State three things that stood out during this interview!
1/

2/

3/

(Mark the following questions between minus 10 to plus 10)

A/ Are they a good communicator?
(This includes good eye contact/likeable personality/
Nice smile/confident/polite/ability to listen)

B/ How did they present themselves?
(I.e. Smartness/hygiene/late/early?)

C/ Were they keen and enthusiastic to fill the post?
(I.e. how much do they want to be here?)

D/ In your opinion, could you train this person?
(Are they capable of listening? If already experienced will you
be able to break any bad habits, or are they headstrong?)

E/ Can you visualise them behind your bar?
(Yes or no?)

Beware, beware

Even if convinced the person you have just seen has been sent from heaven, you may have another dozen to see. You may not pay too much attention to the next candidate if you're dancing on the ceiling. The next might well have been the **HOLY GRAIL** if you hadn't taken your eye off the ball.

Past experience. When reading someone's C.V. and noticing they have past experience in hospitality, it will be important to question them at length about that employment. How long were they there? Who did they work for? What training did they undertake? In what form did that training take place?

I made a bold statement in my introduction that 75% of all staff I run in to are more a negative to those units than a plus. Consequently, that means at least 75% of all candidates for any bartending job you interview claiming they are experienced – might well be shite.

Experience is not always an advantage!

Why did they leave? Are there references for that employment? Will they accept a new way of working?

Warning. These individuals, at no fault of their own, may have picked up bad habits from other suchlike staff. Guvnors, whose only idea of training, will be sitting at the end of the bar getting fat on the stock. Bad news is - you could be sat in front of someone, supposedly trained by one of these dipsticks. This shouldn't put you off, just in full ownership of all the facts.

Example. I witnessed a licensee shouting at a young female bartender not to pick up a broken glass, only for this know it all to make his way from behind the jump, crouch down and commence picking up the big pieces. Yes he did cut himself and yes he did carry on serving. What a prick!

Close the deal

Having made your choice, speak personally by phone that second; don't get beaten to the post by another employer. Arrange a start date and honour leave of notice to an existing employer. Make sure you let all the unsuccessful candidates know the score without exception; nothing worse than having someone drop in occasionally to find out if they got the job or not. Plain embarrassing, when the person you've taken on is stood beside you at the time. Been there, done that.

Tip. If it was a close run thing, a couple of other applicants having been strong contenders; make sure you speak to your first choice and confirm before dishing out any bad news. That choice may have taken another position already, which'll leave you in the embarrassing position. Don't burn bridges.

References. Contact all references without exception. Make the new choice aware that you will carry that out forthwith, in the same phone call as offering the job. Again, don't dish the bad news until those check out. If things do go sour, you may still have another option available within said cookie jar.

Long story cut short

If you've a track record of employing many hundreds of staff with only positive results; don't hesitate, write a book on recruitment - we need your secrets. If however, you're new to the trade, or a mere mortal like the rest of us; the better the preparation - the better the outcome by miles. If trained correctly, a **SUITABLE** candidate can increase goodwill and professionalism by hundreds of per cent. Put a price on that.

Recruiting is a piece of cake. Making the correct choice - far more difficult!

13 STAFF TRAINING

Why is training crucial to success?

According to size and expense, each unit will have its own monetary threshold to reach - each and every week. Failure to achieve this threshold figure without counter balance, might mean sinking in to the robbing Peter to pay Paul predicament. For a manager - it will mean constant pressure to do better, with danger of dismissal. For an independent - stress and worry beyond belief. **SOD THAT!**

What are the magic beans?

True success depends entirely on the satisfaction taken home by the customer - return visits the dividend. If the route to improve the customer journey is employing individuals that appear like they want to be there; subsequently, it will depend on the amount and quality of training **YOU** provide.

Return customers ARE the magic beans!

Burning piles of fifty pound notes story

I recently visited a brand new unit, where the investment must have been half a million plus. If I was being polite, I'd class the service as negative to say the least. I was truly shocked. I revisited a week later just to check my sanity. The server didn't move from where she was leaning on the till and was plain rude. No thank you, no smile - minus bloody ten. Astonishing!

AAAAAGGGGGHHHHH!

Warning. Having a great idea and setting a business up doesn't mean it will work. It cannot be left purely to chance.

No better opportunity than now!

Whether you're an independent entering the trade, or a manager for a big company; raising the level of customer love delivered by staff would knock any competition senseless. From my experience since leaving the trade; apart from the odd individual I've come across - there is no competition.

How? You'll need a team of some kind behind you. You'll need to train that team. Put bluntly — the better the training, the better the profit. Not training is definitely **HUMAT!**

Why? It is impossible to serve everybody yourself. In the kitchen running around like a headless chicken, serving drinks, clearing tables and preventing customers helping themselves while you're changing a barrel in the cellar. It simply isn't possible. You need staff in order to delegate the thousand and one jobs requiring attention, day in, day out. If delegation is the key to success, training your staff is the key to delegation. Achieving all this just isn't that easy to accomplish I'm afraid.

Why? Taking for granted the premium products and the environment you have created are tip top; that only leaves the delivery part of the equation — **HUMANS**. Finding staff will be hard enough, but as previously mentioned; the amount of money you'll want to pay them to smile all day long and work like Trojans will be problematic. But - there may be light ahead.

How? Waves of youngsters have been cast adrift by successive governments, who quite frankly - I wouldn't trust to tie my shoelaces. Older generations left on the scrap heap have much to offer. Even if they don't want a career in the trade, a second part-time job can be a statutory requirement for years of one's working life - paying bills an uphill struggle. I can't see that changing any time soon. To be well trained for that second job could be advantageous for **THEM** - hugely profitable for **YOU**.

Who will train the staff?

Whoever is in charge of running a unit has to become just the best trainer **OVERNIGHT**. Big companies may have the means to employ a team of tutors, but most of that training will be aimed at the unit managers. They in turn will drill their own army. An independent must do the same, but without the back-up of experts on Freephone all hours of the day. For an independent to gain a level playing field, you must simply learn as fast as possible to be the best coach. Unable to afford trainers on a regular basis, will mean soaking up as many a course as the pocket allows; a strategy to raise the quality of customer love - paramount. Strong man management and encouragement may see you through the first hurdle, but moving forward; not knowing what the hell you're doing will be divisive. Learn, learn and learn some more. It will simply not be enough to have your name over the door, hold the big set of keys and swagger around being the guvnor. That will **FAIL**.

Someone has got to train the staff!

From what I can see, there isn't much training going on in any walk of life; and if there is − it's lukewarm. Training is costly; mostly in time and effort, but training equals long term profit. If you were to ask most licensees how many hours in total they've spent training staff in the past week, they'd probably look at you as if you had three heads − all spouting shit. They'd probably accuse you of living in cloud cuckoo land if **YOU** think **THEY'VE** got time to spend training people - perish the bloody thought. However, I expect they're supremely talented in holding a conversation on their mobile whilst serving someone. In this digital age, they'd probably call that - multi-tasking.

AAAAAGGGGGHHHHH!

Training comparison

When a coffee shop takes on a new trainee barista, you can bet that that new trainee won't be anything like proficient in the use of these all singing, all dancing with bells on coffee machines. Some of these companies whisk their new employees off to a training school for two weeks, before unleashing them in a particular unit to do their on the job training. Two weeks? The average bartender will be lucky to get two hours, let alone two weeks intense training. If this doesn't ring alarm bells for you, perhaps I can stick some dynamite in an appropriate orifice, cause' it sure rings alarm bells for me. These coffee shops are on a high street near you. They'll be paying a premium rent, in a premium position, flogging their own brand of hot flavoured milk, in their own particular themed surroundings. They don't look like going bust to me. Oh and by the way, they're stealing the money that used to be spent in pubs - from right under your nose. **OUCH**.

Ambition

Your team should be like an army of trained assassins, killing customers with love and attention to small detail. You need to hire staff receptive to your ideas about delivering high standards of service; then proceed to train them in all aspects of that delivery. In other words - they need to be **UP FOR IT** before you start investing, time and energy in a never ending training regime. In employing a bartender for your team, there will be three forms of training to undertake. Let's look at these next with a summary before moving on.

INDUCTION, THE MISSING LINK and ON-GOING TRAINING

14 INDUCTION of BARTENDERS for INDEPENDENTS

Common sense

Building a house without laying strong structural foundations would be risking financial suicide. Put politely, this course of action would probably see the builder being labelled as a cowboy of massive proportions. I'd call it – bloody scary. Start a bartender tonight without **ANY** whiff of formal training, and as long as nothing goes wrong, you'll probably get away with it.

This is head up my ass territory! (HUMAT)

Consequences. Yes you can start Sandra on the bar tonight, but if Sandra . . . slips up behind the bar on a puddle of lager beneath an overflowing drip tray; in the process, snags her toe on a metal post holding the bar up (in the flip flops she arrived wearing); her upper torso falls on to a crate of fruit juices, left in the middle of the floor by the fridge, and cuts her arm on splinters (from a glass dropped an hour ago not properly cleaned up) – it may prove to be an expensive first session.

AAAAAGGGGGHHHHH!

Managed houses will usually be geared up to provide a targeted induction for **ALL** staff. For an independent just about to sign contracts, the last thing they might be thinking about, is pre-training their new team on a whole bunch of regulations.

Why? An easily accessible to all induction – doesn't appear to exist. However; you'd still be stark raving bonkers to plonk anyone behind **YOUR** bar, not having received at least basic instruction in health, safety and evacuation in case of fire.

What usually happens in larger organisations?

Essential health, safety, fire and hygiene tuition is taught as an on-going exercise: in other words - an hour here and there filling in NVQ books or similar current vehicle. The employee might have to finish relevant chapter/s of an induction before even being allowed to work. This is called covering ones back.

For Independents

The art of covering your back isn't always straightforward, but it should be. A simple, reasonably formal induction; mixed with questions, examples, interaction, and small amount of humour; completed by the employee manually writing answers down, would be a great way to introduce employees to their new environment. There's something about physically writing stuff down that makes it all the more memorable.

Have you done this training yourself?

It shouldn't. Be another layer of red tape, difficult to procure or understand for employer and employee alike. It should be easy to access, easy to teach and easily understood.

Suggestion. Why on earth don't the major trade bodies and big business get together, lock their experts in a room and bash out a simple, A4, 4 page induction for new bartenders universally to adhere to? Downloaded for free, it could provide a perfect platform from where all further training ensues, a level playing field for one and all. Still – back to reality.

> **I warn you again . . . Before an employee steps foot behind your bar, you have to cover YOUR back – THEIRS TOO!**

Backcovering. In the following pages, I'll list topics relevant. Before I do so - I must cover **MY OWN** back with . . .

WARNING. This is a **SUGGESTED** list of issues I personally feel fundamental to the safety of staff employed; at the same time aiding and assisting the employer. It is **NOT** a legal document. **YOU** must check current legality relevant to my suggestions. I am merely supplying ideas as a basis for a suitable induction.

Fire safety

Here is a scenario in regard to a new bartender (Tim) in his first week. It demonstrates why you must at least touch base on given subjects, before releasing an employee behind the bar. Even if started on a training vehicle, he will not have covered much in the first week. He might only have filled his name in.

Scenario. It's Tim's second day and you leave him on his own whilst popping upstairs to have a wee. Tim has had no formal training. He has been taught how to pour the lager that's a bit lively, how to work the till, and where you keep the ice. He has no idea that the pub phone is hidden in a cupboard. An electrical problem causes the juke box to catch fire on the wall. There are five customers in at the time. There are flames.

What does Tim do?

Showtime. Brave Tim spots a fire extinguisher, grabs it and heads over to the fire all guns blazing (pardon the pun).

Stop! (Sound of screeching brakes)

Brave Tim hasn't had in-depth tuition on which fire extinguisher to use on which fire. He's about to throw what effectively is - a bucket of water on an electrical based fire.

AAAAAGGGGGHHHHH!

Warning. Unless a trained fire fighter, you cannot just show staff where fire extinguishers are positioned and expect staff to know which to use on what type of fire. This in itself needs hours of training and application by someone qualified to pass on this specialist information. Yes it might be part and parcel of an on-going training vehicle, but unless an employee has undertaken that training and holds a certificate to say so – they probably shouldn't make use of an extinguisher full stop.

Why? If Tim has been the epitome of the 'last boy scout', he might have got those five customers out before tackling with an extinguisher full of water. He might now be unconscious on the floor (on his own) after taking a few thousand volt shock. What was just a fire, might now be a hundred times worse.

Question. If lucky, he might still survive; though fairly singed all over with a bad headache – who will take the blame?

YOU WILL!

Prediction. Truth be known six months on; having passed whatever training has taken place making it legal and safe to use extinguishers safely, I would bet at least 90% of staff when quizzed on what extinguisher to use on what fire - wouldn't answer correctly. This type of training needs constant refresher tuition. You have to be able to answer correctly in seconds. There'll be no time to look it up on-line.

Exercise. At regular intervals; ask all staff individually to face the back of the bar, shut their eyes and tell you exactly where all fire escapes, extinguishers, fire alarm and pub phone are. If you've ten staff and they score a 100% - I'll eat my hat. If most don't know, including long term employees, I'd suggest pulling you're bloody finger out. All employees should know this stuff from day one, never mind what extinguishers do what.

Fire alarm. If you have a fire alarm - where is it? How does it work? Is it linked directly to the fire brigade? What does it sound like? Why is it important to alert senior staff with immediate effect? Might there be family in upstairs accommodation? How do I alert them? Do you have to press a number for an outside line to ring the fire brigade? What exactly should I do first? Do **YOU** know the answers?

Get the training – cover your back!

Fire exits. Point out every fire exit. Explain fire exit signage and where that exit leads. Provide options of escape should a route be blocked. Instruct whereabouts of evacuation point (where all staff congregate in order to check all are present and correct). How does one go about ordering all customers to evacuate? Should I check all loos and rooms if safe to do so?

In reality. There is no way Tim or any rookie is going to remember everything after a paltry two hour induction, with 15 minutes on fire safety. But, emphasising raising the alarm, location of phone, fire exits and evacuation would be a start. Whilst on the subject of fire, two questions for you.

Question. With regard to natural entrance/exits, what can you do to stop new customers unaware of a towering inferno inside - from entering?

Question. A table of four has just started their meal. Upon being made aware a fire has broken out somewhere in the building, they refuse to leave – what can you do?

Suggestion. One of my best mates (Griff) is a firefighter. In the run up to the opening of a refurbishment I managed, he held a training session for all my new staff. Although informal, it paved the way for those staff to relate to further formal training with ease. Brilliant actually – why not try that?

Health & safety at work

Think about every aspect of the following questions. In on-going training vehicles you might deal with these in detail, but should you cover some of these in your induction process? Think mostly about consequences for both staff – and yourself.

- **Why should you wear appropriate, protective and comfortable footwear behind the bar?**
- **Why should you keep the bar area free of obstacles and remove spillages at the earliest possibility.**
- **What is the correct manner in which to lift crates or cases?**
- **Why should you not even think of going near any barrel, until fully trained and signed off in manual handling?**
- **Make staff aware of any substances hazardous to health in your workplace. Why? What could happen?**
- **What should happen in the event of a glass smashing? Dealt with in the wrong fashion, what might result?**
- **What should happen next after any incident or accident?**
- **Why is it important not to touch equipment you haven't been trained to use? What could go wrong?**
- **Who is the first aider? Where is the first aid kit? Is the first aid kit fully stocked? When did you last look at it?**
- **What other health & safety issues might be applicable in your particular set-up?**

Proof of age

Why is it very bloody important not to serve anybody under age? Totally avoidable, what are the exact consequences? Whose head will be on the chopping block should **THEY** and **YOU** both receive a whopping fine? When explaining, if anybody's laughing – feel free to work on removing the smile.

Personal hygiene

What do you mean I can't pick my nose behind the bar? Why is this so important? What is the effect on business of bad personal habits? This cannot be left to common sense. Walk into any bar you care to mention and watch for five minutes. I pretty much guarantee it will open your eyes to bad personal behaviour. If included from the start, good personal hygiene will prove to be a key player in the future of hospitality.

Bonus

Induction isn't just rules and regulations, it's also opportunity to welcome and begin the process of bedding in to a friendly and helpful - well drilled team. Humans need to feel safe and secure in your employ; rather comforting to feel under the wing of somebody who cares, providing a platform from which the other thousand jobs can be hammered home.

A no brainer. Source and partake current training courses in health and safety, fire and hygiene for **YOURSELF**. Any induction will inevitably link to health, safety and fire education. How the hell can you inform staff without the knowledge? This all may bore the hell out of you, but ignore at your peril. Merely displaying your A2 health and safety at work poster (a legal requirement?) won't mean all your staff are fully trained – or you for that matter.

Warning. Induction is not a replacement for a more formal training vehicle. It should however provide a safer platform from which to travel. Do not belittle on-going formal training. It underpins the extra measures you must take in raising the satisfaction a customer takes home. I will cover these in the next chapter. They are all layers of the cake.

Listen again - an induction MUST take place before setting foot behind the bar!

Teach not tell. If you instruct, or tell somebody without explaining why - will they understand? Forced to tell someone time and time again will mean one of two things. Either; **YOU** are telling and not teaching, or – they're as thick as a plank. Both are bad news. The real message – teach not tell.

Cost. New employees simply won't be able to compute too much information, that's what an on-going training vehicle delivers. It is entirely wise however, to cover your back – and theirs. Every single minute you employ staff is an expense **YOU** must benefit from. Of course it would be monetary suicide to send all new staff on expensive training, when they might only last a week in your employ. However, not to cover your back, or care about the well-being of employees, is the equivalent of wearing a cowboy hat, sheriffs badge, holster and toy guns on a regular basis - stupid (unless attending a fancy dress party).

Long story cut short

If you view health, safety, fire and hygiene as a complete pile of crap akin to watching paint dry, I'm afraid **YOU** need to change attitude, get with the plan and stop being the dog on a lead. Running any type of licensed premises will be a lot easier if you're on board and paddling fast. Don't leave it to chance. Provide a targeted, fast track, basic rules of the jungle to adhere to – on day one. You may have no choice but to sign up to a training provider for induction. Ask advice from trade bodies on current options and consequences of not.

Embrace the crap and become its master!

15 THE MISSING LINK

Premium service equation (for bartenders)

Enrolment in an NVQ type of training vehicle, learning how to pour the many and varied products and most subjects covered in the long chapter on working the bar; will all come under the banner of on-going training. On-going training is essential, but for me is merely a backdrop to the real game changer. The road to profit is **ALL** about the customer journey. That journey must be attentive, obstacle free, professional and attractive. A bit like a coffee without the beans - you'll need to add extra ingredients that **CONSISTENTLY** provide – **EXTRA VALUE**. Simple though it may seem, set aside just twenty minutes to hammer home the following service equation.

Acknowledge and Queue

Immediately ADDING VALUE to the customer journey.

Greet, apologise and serve

ADD VALUE by rewarding customers with a warm welcome. Deliver in a non-patronising and attentive manner. Start with an apology if been kept waiting anytime whatsoever.

Deliver great looking products

FULL VALUE delivered without fail every single time.

Thank the bloody customer for the money! At EVERY SINGLE opportunity.

Acknowledge and queue. Customers do not want to be getting in to arguments about whose next. If **VOCALLY** acknowledged, **THEY** will note that even though staff may be busy, service is being dealt in a professional manner. They will feel relaxed in the knowledge the bartender is in complete control and has treated them with respect. **IT ADDS VALUE.**

Greet, apologise and serve. Even in the busiest bar scenario, you should still smile and greet whilst apologising for any wait. It adds **SO MUCH VALUE** - it takes seconds. A warm welcome is a huge opportunity to build some bricks, yet often missed.

Deliver great looking products. Whilst the other three points of the equation add extra value, pouring should be part of the entertainment. The customer might well be licking their lips in anticipation - the server will be fulfilling the dream. Customers paying a premium price, will expect a product to be poured and presented in the best possible light, adding **FULL VALUE** for the charge – **EVERY** single time. It may reveal weakness in serving ability (not fixed in twenty minutes), but at least you'll know. An honest conversation with each server might remove more obstacles. Have **YOU** trained every single member of your team, the ideal pour of every single drink?

Thank the bloody customer for the money? It's not just in pubs and bars you don't get thanked when you hand over the cash. This is a disease widespread in general retail. No matter how busy, you must always finish a transaction by thanking the customer, removing another obstacle and **ADDING VALUE.**

What have you got to lose?

If you read every word of this book and enforce nothing other than the four points mentioned; you will remove four possible obstacles and vastly improve customer love – in one stroke.

The general standard of service I witness on a regular basis is quite frankly – SHITE!

To what standard do your team deliver?

At what cost? An exemplary standard of service, increasing return custom, is actually free to you the employer. Yes - **FREE!**
How come it's free? You simply have to train your front line staff to deliver on the equation every time they serve. You might need a cattle prod with forty thousand volts running through it (I am joking mostly), but shouldn't have to pay more wages to achieve this. **YOUR** job is to keep barking until your team get it. After a while; they **WILL** queue customers without being prompted, **WILL** greet appropriately, **ENSURE** products are presented exactly as they should and **ALWAYS** seal the deal with many thanks. This is all free - because that is what they should be delivering anyway (I'm shouting again).

Extreme warning. The average price for a premium product is now in the three to four quid range, soon to be a fiver. Price doesn't always put punters off - bad service will. Staff failing to deliver a premium service - are the negative I bang on about.

They will lose you money - all day long!

Why? A customer not paid due attention when it's their turn to be served; may have one drink, might not stay for another. They certainly won't become a regular return customer. More and more I notice staff behind bars, treating the customer as if they're doing them some kind of favour just being there.

AAAAAGGGGGHHHHH!

Long story cut short

The manner in which; you greet, serve, dispense, deliver your premium products and seal the deal - is crucial to creating profitable conditions. You can have the best equipped, most attractive looking unit in town; if your frontline service is naff, you'll find it hard to cultivate new custom to return. You might be scratching your head wondering where it all went wrong, or simply missing extra profit – that was there **ALL THE TIME**.

Flipside. Compare a tired unit; carpets that look like they were laid in the seventies, but ambience cracking and service friendly and attentive – business might be booming. Both units will have premium products – what's the difference? Probably the standard of welcome and overall service score.

Upshot. If the standard of service is only as good as your weakest link, let me be the public asshole. I can see hundreds of weak links in my travels. **YOU** can easily raise the bar on your team performance, by raising productivity. You really can.

Warning. You may have to educate your crew in the art of being genuinely nice and smiling - I'm really not joking. Watch any children's TV presenters; they smile naturally as if their life depended on it. Watch your staff - how do they perform?

A5 Premium Service Flyer. I've produced an A5 staff hand out available from the website *howtoandwhatsitlike.com* at small expense. Educate and re-educate all your staff from that moment on. It will take stamina on your part, lots of stamina.

Aim. Going out is a fundamental human self-reward scheme. Your job is to breed regular customers. Dedicate just twenty minutes to drill this four part equation. Your aim is profit.

Sometimes the simplest solutions can be staring straight at you!

16 ON-GOING TRAINING of BARTENDERS

Benefits

After induction, on-going is exactly what it says on the tin; starting the moment you commence employment and carrying right on. An NVQ type training vehicle alone will not cater for the real learning curve of actually serving people in situ. It will however, underpin all on-going training and benefit from a legal standpoint. A true record in hard copy of each staff member learning rules, regulations, legal serving measures, and a whole host of information employees would probably class as boring – is a mighty valuable document.

For the employee. The laborious nature of filling in what seems to be endless pages of answers, is actually a very workable tool; like being back at school – no bad thing.

Example. A bartender needs to be conversant with wine glass sizes, and indeed the permitted size of glass. You cannot just serve wine in any sized glass you wish. Manually writing in a training vehicle sinks the info deeper, also providing a point of reference for the pupil. It will not however; teach the pupil the intricacies of your wine menu, the advantages of upselling, or for Christ sake don't fill past that line cause I start shouting really loudly. These too class as on-going training.

For the employer. Staff filling out and signing each page of an NVQ type training vehicle is - **BACKCOVERING HEAVEN.**

Example. If little Johnny your star barman picks up three crates from a floor position and doesn't bend his legs in the correct manner - **YOU** might end up in the small claims court.

But. If you've previously told him not to lift more than two crates at a time and witnessed him not bend his legs; better still, caught it on CCTV having previously put Johnny through his NVQ on manual handling, signed off with an appointed NVQ trainer countersigning - his days of being the star bar man could be numbered. It's one thing to pay him statutory sick pay, but totally out of order to try and fleece you of four grand. Training makes the employee responsible too.

One to one training

The longer you invest in chaperoning new students, the better. In those early learning hours; far more important to slowly instil the **QUALITY** of service you require, than brain overload. You being called away to change a barrel after half an hour, distracted by customers and then having a coffee - just won't work. During this process, you will need to give these pupils your **FULL** attention. This will eat into your time, sap your energy and test your concentration. Anything less than **FULL** attention and you will **FAIL**. Half measures will not pay the bills and definitely not see you on the road to a good pension.

Long story cut short

The more time you devote to training, the easier delegation will become. **DELEGATION** provides **YOU** time to spend on other parts of the business – or yourself. If you end up running around like a headless chicken (seemingly the only one who knows what they're doing), what bloody good is that?

Start from scratch. Take a step back, think about it, take a deep breath, retrain everybody and lay the bloody law down.

Continual training WILL pay dividends!

17 TRAINING SUMMARY

Join the dots

Induction. This is not a serving period; it's a learn the house rules (backcovering all round) and welcome to the team session. Everything from sorting uniform, bank details for payment, to where the fire exits are. Why washing hands should become second nature and why getting caught supplying drink to underage humans an expensively bad idea.

The missing link. You'll have gathered by now how alarmed I am at the general standard of customer service in licensed premises. Just to survive you will need to build trade. The premium service equation is a simple insurance vehicle to limit human damage and promote a new standard of customer love. You cannot leave it to chance. After induction; immediately introduce new bartenders to the service equation. Inspire your team to be the best, to stand out in the crowd, to **ADD VALUE**.

On-going training. Continual reinforcement of the service equation in conjunction with an NVQ type training vehicle (bolstering knowledge of health, safety, fire and hygiene requirements to an altogether deeper understanding), will benefit both employer and employee alike. Mastering how to pour every drink known to mankind and the hundreds of affiliated jobs supporting service, is forever on-going I'm afraid.

The day you stop training . . .
Is the day you stand still!

The customer journey

Customers leaving a unit happy, won't stagger down the road screaming what wonderful service they've just experienced, its way more subtle than that. Premium products served in appropriate surroundings, with superb customer love will be the answer. They won't know that. All they'll know is - they had a good time and they'll be back. If you were to ask every customer how they scored their stay, how they would mark you? If minus ten means they'll never set foot in your place again and plus ten being they want to move their bed in - you need to be scoring in the early plusses to be building trade.

Long story cut short

Example. I recently visited three units; two of them brand new builds. Not one of these units acknowledged me, welcomed me, or thanked me for the cash. One girl replacing glasses in an overhead hanger, sneezed all over the bar and the drinks being poured either side. Not one of the three staff blinked – they just carried on. One of the girls rubbed her nose eight times in about ten seconds. Two customers noticed; one visibly winced and started shaking their head - it wasn't me.

AAAAAGGGGGHHHHH!

Why would you even consider sending untrained staff on to the front line of your business? You'd be better off putting your money on a horse. If it lost, at least it'd all be over in a matter of minutes, instead of years of self-harm. I simply do not believe all these new staff mentioned above are shite. They have to be taught. The only one who can do that is . . .

YOU – I'm quite willing to beg!

18 FIFTY JOBS & ISSUES
Relevant to WORKING THE BAR

Reality check

I've heard it said **ANYONE** can work behind a bar. Well if the pub I was in the other night is anything to go by - I'd rephrase.

Any donkey CAN serve behind a bar!

A full-time bartender might well refer to themselves as a **PROFESSIONAL**. For the most part I'd use that term loosely. I've come across very hard working and organised individuals in the past few years, but these are few in-between. A small percentage in the middle will turn up and do a job, but the rest merely make up the numbers – and I'm being polite.

Untrained, inattentive, unhygienic, thankless bar staff will lose you money . . . Every single hour you open!

If I sound bitter and twisted, let me put you straight – I am. The sooner the battle to regain custom from coffee shops, betting shops and digital TV packages at home can begin – the better.

Chicken pinkies story

If you ever get a hint of chicken flavour as you're drinking your favourite tipple, it probably came from the bartender's hands feeding on chicken crisps, shortly before they wrapped their pinkies around your glass to serve you. This happened to me. No, he didn't wash his hands. That part of his brain wasn't functioning; he did however choose not to pay for the crisps. It appears some cogs were turning - just not the correct ones.

Attention deficit story

In the same bar as chicken pinkie: on the same night, there were two girls on duty. I was sat on a stool, an empty glass in front of me waiting to be served in a round of three. One of the girls walked up, removed my empty glass, but failed to even look at me. On several occasions, both girls placed empty glasses in the washer situated right in front of me, then turned to serve someone obviously far more important. I was holding eight pound coins openly in the palm of my hand, clear to see. One of these girls actually served four groups of customers before me. My bloody hand was aching.

Question. Do we actually have to stand at a bar with nothing less than a twenty pound note, waving frantically in order somebody might at some point - realise you are waiting?

This quality of service is not only shite, it's actually far worse - It's negatively SHITE!

Prediction

Implementing the premium service plan outlined in chapter 15, combined with perpetual on-going training and getting shot of assholes that infect your trade - might well increase the odds of success dramatically. Relevant to the last two stories, the owners of the bar in question could see takings rise within a fairly short period.

Exaggerating? I don't think so.

Aim. The big profit awaiting harvest in all licensed premises requires a sea change in approach and human delivery. My number one target for each reader of this book, is to improve service in place, or planned – even by a small margin.

All for sale

Everything a customer can see behind the bar area should be for sale, service or display – **FULL STOP**.

Why? Space behind a bar will be limited. If it's not for sale, service or display - get it the hell out of there. Every inch of your bar is also your second shop window; the first being the outside of your premises. Don't **WASTE** a single customer gaze.

Example. Managed houses are disciplined on this issue. On first impression you can usually tell the difference between a managed house unit and a couple in their first tenancy.

How? The managed house will have nice displays, clean mirrors, hardly anything not for sale or service in view. The new tenant will have all sorts of crap behind the jump. Shelves of CD's, stereos of all types and sizes, quiz books, first aid kit, ornaments, cups, framed photos of their dead dog; all sorts of shite taking up oh so valuable working space. Not to forget the obligatory mobile phone and charger to boot. Boot? That's exactly what I'd do with it. Remember, you'll be paying business tax for **EVERY** square foot you inhabit.

> **Personal mobile phones should not be seen or heard within the service area!**

I used to swap and change the bar around until I found the most efficient and attractive manner I could devise. Yes the bar is merely a tool to deliver premium products, but alongside your staff – one gigantic marketing opportunity. A smart professional looking bar is a fantastic weapon, but one that takes a lot of thought and sweat to make the most of.

> **Get rid of the crap and utilise every single space - you'll need that space!**

Punctuality and preparation

All staff should be on time and actually ready to serve before the allotted time; not rushing through the door five minutes late, coat zipped up, still talking on a mobile. Furthermore: if there's no ice, scant supply of fruit and no change in the tills; you're going to look a complete prat – **YOU** being the person running that unit. Any interruption to service will be a reflection on **YOU** and how you manage. If customers are already queuing at the bar, obviously a bartender will just have to get stuck in at the coal face, but arriving ten minutes ahead will usher prep time. Any bartender should already have a till **CASH CHECKED** and **FLOATED UP** by whoever is in charge that session, but ice and fruit should be down to them. I'll leave you to argue about odd minutes served over and above, a fair manager will always find ways of paying that back. Remember: independent or not - businesses need managing at all levels.

Fruit and condiments for the session ahead

When building drinks, the customer should be offered the fruit of their choice: lemons, oranges, limes and cherries at the very least; depending whether you serve cocktails, will determine needs. Sauce, salt, stirrers, straws, cocktail sticks, napkins, corkscrew - whatever is required. An organised set up might have fruit pre-cut, wrapped, dated, stored in a kitchen fridge.

Warning. Beware cross-contamination and general hygiene.

The customer journey. If a customer requires salt for a tequila - you shouldn't have to search for salt. If a mummy wants a straw for little Ella's bottle of pop, all the straws being locked away in the store cupboard – what bloody use is that? Remove the obstacles and prep accordingly for a smooth ride.

Ice in drinks

This is not a book to teach how to pour individual drinks; that is best demonstrated real time, but if customers see good looking, well presented, attractive concoctions coming over the bar – they might fancy one of those too. A variety of drinks require ice. Of course the first question should always inquire whether the customer requires ice and fruit. The reason you'll need a bloody good ice machine is . . . You'll need an awful lot.

Don't be tight on the ice!

Added value. You aren't actually giving a customer any more product than you would in a smaller glass. All you are doing is serving with crap loads of ice. Marketing gurus might label this value for money. I'd call it **SLEIGHT OF HAND**. Call it what the hell you like, but serving the product in the most attractive wrapping paper you can imagine - visually **ADDS WORTH**.

Example. Tell me which of these you prefer. A vodka and mixer in a short stumpy glass with just one lump of ice, or the same drink in a half pint, hi-ball or similar, packed full of ice? That's a no brainer for me. Pack it full of ice and decant the requested spirit over the ice. After determining the mixer and the amount of mixer; dispense the product again over the ice until nearly full. A two second decoration and Bob's your uncle – a weapon of profit and a customer satisfied.

Example. If served the most fabulous cocktail over crushed ice, melting in your mouth, all delicious – a customer might indulge their self to one of those expensive treats every time.

Warning. Be consistent. The first time a customer returns for their weekly fix and the bartender doesn't crush the ice - the product will fail the audition. That will be that; the spell will be broken and **YOU** might lose a regular bonus ball.

Shovels. A nice thick shovel, man enough for the job and big enough to scoop enough ice in one foul swoop, will increase speed of service. Remember to clean the shovel.

Ice barrel. No taller than about 18cm. Watching staff dig the last two cubes out of a deep bucket is painful. Not all staff will be six foot tall. Think about the staff journey too.

Warning. Never ever scoop ice via a glass - the glass will break. You will have to throw all the ice away within that container. You also might end up in casualty with a cut that needs stitching. You might have bled all over the bar. Oh, and the customer that waited seven minutes while you were jumping around like *Skippy* on a bad day - will have left.

Extreme warning. Never let customers pick ice out of the bucket with their hands or **ANYBLOODYTHING**. Ice buckets on the front of the bar for customers to help themselves - what's that all about? How are you going to police the hygiene on that one? How many customers do not wash their hands when visiting the loo? Do you think it acceptable to expose customers to the possibility, that someone who has just been holding their willy, is now helping themselves to some ice via some pair of tongs? Worse - scooping it out with their fingers.

AAAAAGGGGGHHHHH!

Remove all ice buckets from the front of the bar – RIGHT NOW!

If you can't be bothered to put the ice in a glass, why not direct customers to the nearest supermarket for a real no-frills service. Yes I am shouting and I hope the proverbial penny is dropping. Service is the **ADDED VALUE** for money you provide; the very thing separating you from a supermarket.

Cold fresh water

Water will be an important component to you, but largely ignored. How do you access fresh clean drinking water? Do you fill cumbersome jugs, stacked on the bar taking up valuable room? No water jug might demand filling a squash or a whisky straight from a tap. Do you bend down to a low universal chore sink you pour all the waste down and rinse dirty cloths? Is it the same place you always wash the outside ash trays in?

AAAAAGGGGGHHHHH!

Essence. Working the bar is all about smooth service. No task should be difficult. Difficult indicates obstacles, or no training.

Example. Filling up a pint of orange squash from some dirty under the counter sink - with stale water (the bartender failing to let the tap run for 20 seconds to get rid of the foul taste). Think it doesn't happen? – It happens all the time.

A solution. On the bar next to the beer pumps, install a cold water spout fitted with a water filter.

Good news - No more bending down and water fresh as a daisy.

If you get nothing else from this book than a filtered water feed on your bar, I'll be happy. Have it fitted professionally. If your bar is large, throw the boat out and have two. As a condition, demand the plumbers merchant, or plumber, show you how to change the filter cartridge, it will save a call out every six months for a new filter that shouldn't cost the earth. Hey presto – ditch the jugs on the bar taking up valuable space. I have one at home and quite honestly – I really couldn't be without it. If you want the industrial version it does become more expensive. Fresh water is fundamental - just an idea.

Personal hygiene

Every single time a member of staff enters the bar area, they should wash their hands without fail. I'm taking a wild stab here, but it's almost as if we've completely ignored the fact that any drink is classed as food. Did the whole of the licensed trade get up one morning and undergo some sort of mass telepathic message?

From now on we'll just forget that serving food in one form or other, accounts for somewhere north of 90% of turnover. If none of us wash our hands, the customers bound to think that's completely normal!

AAAAAGGGGGHHHHH!

The average customer will not register the absence of good hygiene, because from what I can see - it simply doesn't exist. Unless their hands get particularly sticky, I would be surprised if the average bartender washed their hands many times at all during a session. This is a storm waiting to happen.

What customers will notice . . .
IS someone who does wash their hands,
IS conscientious and DOES give a damn!

Instead of worrying about competition, look at yourself. Is your hand washing sink easily accessible? How often is it cleaned? Do you have one? The dividend will come from a level of diligence unheard of, transforming **YOUR** reputation and **YOUR** sales. You do not have to pay staff more wages to adhere to high levels of personal hygiene, but you do have to teach them.

Hair story

I was in a bar with some mates in a big UK city. The girl behind the bar had this fantastic head of long jet black hair - it was striking. Problem being, she played with that hair almost every other minute. Not once did she think of washing her hands. Pour a drink and let it settle - play with her hair. Fingers back round the top of the glass – **TWIDDLE, TWIDDLE, TWIDDLE**. After topping the drink and serving, she'd look round to see who was waiting. She had no clue which of three groups of customers was first, having **FAILED** to queue them as they arrived. This wonderful professional, served the only group who were looking at menus and came in first – **LAST**. They had one drink and left (without ordering food). She was still playing with her hair when we left – **TWIDDLE BLOODY TWIDDLE**.

AAAAAGGGGGHHHHH!

So that's contaminated hands serving food and no queuing of customers as they enter the killing zone. Well done girl, you are last in the class, shut the door on your way out. Oh and turn the lights off at the same time cause we've just gone bust.

Warning. I cannot stress how much of an effect bad hygiene has on takings. The effect however is cumulative.

Negatively Cumulative!

A customer made aware something's **NOT QUITE RIGHT**, might break the selling spell you have cast. Asked what it was that put them off - they may not be able to tell you.

Observation. Customers these days have much more choice and can be oh so fickle. The slightest hiccup may leave the bed un-maid. They can just as easily visit the coffee shop next door, even though these are just as dear to purchase food and drink and suffer from similar service blunders.

Challenge. Visit any bar you care to choose. Watch the staff. How many times do they touch their body, not washing hands afterwards? Would you be happy to let them serve you next in line? Would you say something or just leave?

Common sense. If your bartender touches their nose, ear or anything associated with their body, it would only be good manners to expect them to wash their hands thoroughly.

Warning. This is a repeat prescription I'm afraid. It can be tiresome and frustrating reminding staff time and again to wash hands. You'd think a 4 year old could learn quicker, but the penny does drop eventually. TEACH the consequences.

The sink thing

If you are planning a refurbishment, why not incorporate washing hands as a unique selling point - how refreshing that might be. A dedicated hand washing sink with surgeon style taps, fixed at a suitable height, nullifying bending down all the time to use the bloody thing. If you want customers to visibly notice hygiene standards, why not embrace personal hygiene as a weapon. We are living in the dark ages if we continue installing low down, pain in the arse, universal chore sinks.

Clean as you go

How many times do you lean on a bar and stick to it? Every time that occurs – you will have FAILED. That's YOU by the way. It's a bartender's job to keep the bar and all the tables clean and tidy, including food and litter abandoned underneath those tables. Removing spent glasses and plates is fundamental. Have a CLEAN CLOTH available at all times and offer to clean a customer's table as a matter of course.

Tip. Ask the customer to lift their glass while you wipe away. The public are unfamiliar with such acts of customer love. All these little pieces of the service jigsaw - **ADD VALUE**.

I call this - breeding regulars.

Litter. Never walk past a piece of litter. The cleaner you keep the unit, the cleaner **THEY** might keep it, the easier your job becomes. Sometimes you get back some of what you put in.

Vacated tables. As soon as a table is vacated it must be cleared and cleaned ASAP. Wipe all around the rim thoroughly.

Why? When new customers enter, the first thing they will take is a quick recce of all that surrounds them. Remember that most customers will have been looking forward to this visit for some time. If all you can offer them on that first impression is a room full of tables littered with dirty plates and empty glasses - **YOU** will have officially **FAILED** the visual exam.

Consequences. Every time you fail to clear a table once vacated, it will be reducing your seating capacity. Put simply; your ability to take money will be hit each time you fail to clear. Failing to clear on a regular basis could be cumulatively choking your business to death. Successful units develop a sense of urgency. They can adapt and step up a gear, a different pace, whilst still appearing calm. Its clever stuff, but this can only happened if working as a team and well drilled.

Example. An eating house with thirty, four seat tables, gives you a capacity of 120. If half those tables are vacated and littered with debris, your capacity is cut in half. Arriving customers might walk away and eat elsewhere. I'm not suggesting as if by magic you'll fill all the tables automatically, but filling seven or eight of these tables for another sitting, might increase turnover that day by hundreds of pounds.

It's hard enough to get customers through the door - to lose them once they're in is an unmitigated disaster!

Clean cloths. I make no apology in mentioning the use of a nice clean cloth throughout this book. The array of cloths I witness is staggering. Mostly, these poor excuses for a cleaning cloth appear in the form of a dirty rag - what's that all about? Again you are chipping away at all those building blocks - not that I see much evidence of staff cleaning tables anyway.

What should I use? My own preference was the white stockinette; strong, rugged, rinse-easy and washable. Have lots. Even in a smallish bar you would go through at least a dozen cloths a day. Once either visually dirty or at the end of each day; new for old and into the laundry bag.

Warning. You cannot **CLEAN** with a dirty cloth.

Tip. Dirty cloths need putting through a washing machine on prewash/deep clean every single day without fail. Leaving in some kind of bag on the premises for two or three nights, before eventually remembering to put them on a wash - is **LAZY** (they'll honk the place out and deteriorate very quickly). If a cloth starts looking grubby – throw the bloody thing away.

Imperative. A washing machine and dryer is a must. If it's living quarters upstairs; place the machines there, a sort of bonus for the live in staff. If that's you, it won't feel like a bonus. By the time you've added all the dishcloths and tea towels from the kitchen, the machine seems to be on all day. When you want to get three hours kip before the night session, the washer droning away in the back ground, shortly before launching into spin mode - you might wonder.

Cleaning detergents for tables? If I **HAVE** witnessed table washing, it's mostly accompanied by a plastic bottle of one detergent or another. Unless there is some scientific reason I am unaware of for this expensive habit, I really do not see an advantage. A hot cloth will do this job for nothing.

Cleaning pong story

I visited a unit with my friend late at night. The unit had changed hands a while back and was now much busier. After purchasing drinks, I noticed a young man cleaning tables with you guessed it – detergent. I had noticed a slight whiff when I came in, but now this whiff was altogether stronger and stifling. So I'd just spent nearly eight quid on two drinks and had to put up with this bloody honk. It smelt a bit like posh BO.

AAAAAGGGGGHHHHH!

Lesson. If you must use detergent, make sure it smells nice. Sometimes neutral is good enough. If you want to make tables smell nice, I thought that was helped by something called . . .

Furniture polish!

Baby chairs

Would a mummy or daddy be impressed if the high chair provided was sticky and manky, the harness coated in crap?

The customer journey. They didn't walk in in a bad mood, but all it will take from that moment onwards; is a meal not to be quite right, or take too long to arrive, which might fire an impression. They might decide not to even bother ordering in the first place. How many other people might they tell?

AAAAAGGGGGHHHHH!

I have a young family. Many units don't carry enough high chairs; often grubby, and yes the straps particularly disgusting. I have other choice wording. Not confined to licensed premises, coffee shops suffer from the same dilemma, yet another opportunity to get the edge. I re-iterate; don't worry about competition - look at the standard of service **YOU** offer.

Warning. If the safety harness attached to the chair is not in good working order - withdraw this seat from service. The last thing you want is a claim being made against you after little Jimmy falls out of the flaming thing.

Tip. Upon purchasing a high chair, find a seat offering the option of purchasing the safety harness separately. If you have several chairs, you could carry a couple of spares as a rule - its small potatoes. Before you purchase - are they washable?

Advice. Each time a chair is used it'll need the once over, just like cleaning a table. Whoever's walking the floor or serving the food – make a point of asking the customer **NOT** to return the high chair to the high chair station, but to leave it in place as, 'We like to give it a good clean'. Actually cleaning chairs in front of customers spreads the word. It visually **ADDS VALUE.**

Reputation doesn't happen by accident!

Tip. At least once a week, you will need to **DEEP CLEAN** all the baby seats. You will have undertaken some kind of written risk assessment of baby chairs, to keep in your health and safety files won't you? Can I suggest that in your weekly deep clean, you check and record the condition of the straps? Sign and date this weekly check. Just like all the records you take, of all machinery and checks – never throw away, keep them safe. Cover your back. Cover your back. Cover your . . .

All I wanted to do was serve a few drinks!

Glasses and plastic mats

At least weekly, **ALL** the glasses in your establishment should be spring cleaned. Cleaning each glass after use is **NOT** enough. Wipe the rims of **EVERY** single glass to remove scum or lipstick. If you can't get a glass clean for some reason, just throw the flaming thing away (safely). Don't think twice, just chuck.

Point of order. Before commencing this process, deep clean the actual glass washing machine. Don't just clean the glasses, put the plastic mats through the glass washer and clean the shelf itself with a spanking hot clean cloth (safely).

Warning. If the plastic mats your glasses sit on, stick to the shelf underneath - you are **NOT** taking care of business. It won't be water holding them down, it will be contamination. You'll have been serving food in glasses sat on contaminated shelves - **DISGUSTING**. Have you checked your shelves lately?

Chosen glass. Varying premium products may demand a unique choice of glassware. This glassware is designed to add value to that product. Whatever glass you use, always glance at eye level for cleanliness before pouring that expensive stock.

Broken glass etiquette

When some anonymous hero of a customer bends down and picks up pieces of jagged glass – they **WILL** cut themselves. They'll duly bleed all over your nice carpet or newly polished flooring. They'll then proceed to bleed all along the corridor to the loo, where they'll smear blood all over the tiled floor and your lovely clean white basins. The last thing customers want to visualise is blood stains all over the chinaware. This could be a local, a member of your staff, or indeed it could be you. Either way it'll turn out to be a pain in **YOUR** ass.

NEVER ever start picking up broken glass with bare hands!

Observation. On the last dozen or so occasions of witnessing glasses dropped in pubs; staff and customers alike have all bent down and began lifting small and large pieces of broken glass. At least half of those occasions, the licensee in question watched as all this played out in front of them - I do wonder.

Damage limitation. At the very moment a glass drops, the only loss will have been a glass and a small amount of time for a member of staff to clear up.

Aim. Your job is to limit the damage to just that.

What should you do? Upon alert of a broken glass/sharps incident occurring, the nearest member of staff needs to drop whatever they are doing, apologise if in the middle of serving and take charge. Just like in a supermarket, they must stand over the broken glass until handed thick gloves and a dust pan and brush to remove the glass. Even if it necessitates shouting at customers to make aware – **TAKE CHARGE THEY MUST**.

May I point out? The member of staff taking charge may be the only sober person in the room.

Warning. Broken glass needs to be emptied in to a metal waste glass bin. This should be empty at the start of every session. You don't want that knocked over whilst dealing with the present situation, making a two minute job - tons worse.

I would return to the area with a battery powered hoover to scoop up any splinters of glass awaiting customers to stab (this means keeping said hoover on charge constantly). If the glass was full of drink in the first place, you might have to soak up the spent liquid with heaps of kitchen towel. Thick gloves should be worn all throughout with a coat of common sense.

Warning. I often see a mop and bucket used to soak up the excess of a full pint. This is fine and dandy, but after mopping an area with glass splinters, it would be advisable to just chuck that mop head away afterwards – why wouldn't you?

Are all your staff trained to deal with broken glass incidents?

Backcovering. You cannot just trust staff will deal with scenarios like this with copious helpings of logical thinking and practical judgement - leave nothing to chance. Train all staff the etiquette you decide to follow in adherence of current health and safety rules and regulations. How is it covered in your training vehicle? Draw up risk assessments. Use these assessments as a training tool. Like fire drills, run broken glass drills - involve your team. Make them very aware of the consequences of not being in control.

Bonus. Customers love witnessing good management.

Doing nothing is not an option!

Mopping the bar

The bar must have its own mop and bucket. Mark them up. I favoured the galvanised metal job, they last forever. Change the mop head as often as necessary - you reap what you sow.

Warning. I repeat - you cannot **CLEAN** with a dirty mop.

Never forget to mop at the death of a trading day. Even in the cleanest of buildings, the bug and insect build-up overnight is challenging. Do not let **ANYBODY** step on that floor till dry. It's the one time a day you'll secure to wash the floor with no one leaving their stain. Personally, I would go absolutely **MENTAL** should anyone even approach my drying floor.

Cleaning outside

We covered the importance of keeping the smoking area clean and **ATTRACTIVE** for smokers, but smokers aren't the only ones to enjoy the outside area. On a nice hot summers day, any customer might enjoy being outside, or sat on a patio sipping their ice cool product, whilst their children play.

Example. In this wonderful world of supposed super service we live in, I watch staff **ALL** the time; saunter outside to deliver a meal, proceeding to head back indoors as if they've been blindfolded. Passed tables stacked with plates and glasses left three hours ago - you wouldn't imagine writing the script. Lesson. When you work the bar, all of these areas are **YOUR** responsibility. You must beaver away **ALL** of the time. There will always be a job to do. Never **WASTE** a single journey.

Loo checks

After a couple of rounds, a customer might visit the loo on a regular basis. That visit, must in no way distract the customer from the good time they might be enjoying out there in the bar. Whoever's in charge on any given session, should be visiting the loo frequently during trading hours. Does every cubicle have toilet paper? Is the supply close to the end of its life? If so - change it anyway. Are there any new leaks in the men's? How is the supply of paper towels? Are the dryers working? Are the taps clean and working efficiently? Does the soap need replacing? Are all the locks working smoothly? Is there any mess to clean up? Is there any sign of drug activity? In essence. Loos need **CONSTANT** upkeep. After the cleaners set your loos up, it's over to you. Removing obstacles as they arise will maintain the smoothest customer journey.

Bottling up

Replenishing stock should always take place at night, as soon as the last drink has been served and the tills withdrawn.

Why? If left till the morning, a bottle will simply not have time to acquire the **DEEP COLD QUALITY** expected by the customer. Charging a premium price for premium packaged products is all well and good, but serving warmish bottles will go down like a bag of shit. This is completely avoidable.

Not bottling up at night is plain lazy!

Tip. Sometimes at the end of a session, customers slow down the rate at which they consume. Both traditional and on-going; by all means get someone making a list for bottling up, but . . .

Warning. It may be false economy to load the fridges up until you're absolutely finished serving. Mixing warm bottles with cold could result in serving a customer a warm product by mistake. It won't be the customers fault – it will be **YOURS** (another totally avoidable argument). Having worked really hard to win a customer spending £50, why take the chance of spoiling it? Having to replace (and loose) a bottle at the death is bad enough; worse still - you'll have to smile while you're doing it. If the bottles cost £1.50 with a selling price of £3.50, how much will you win and lose in that scenario?

First in/first out

First in means the oldest stocked product in a fridge must leave first (first out). If you've got lines of six bottles deep in your fridges and have sold three from the front - you need to pull the last three forward and put three new ones in behind them. All bottled products will have a best before date printed somewhere. Being lazy might cost **YOU** money and reputation.

Tip. If you have a line of five or six of one particular product that doesn't seem to sell; a further half crate left in the cellar, due to go out of date in two months – sell them off on a promotion. Keep a sharp eye on best before dates. Better to get some money in than have to chuck down the sink. Get rid.

Advice. If you haven't sold one single bottle of a product for months: once you've sold it off, do not stock again. Be decisive. Yes someone will come in and ask for one in a year's time, but non-selling items take up valuable space in your fridges. It costs **YOU** money to keep things cold.

Tip. Try and keep all products in fridges, in dozens or half dozen groups. Keeping an eagle eye on your stock and the ability to easily count that stock, will be a big part of your working life. Stock in easy to count denominations, might add years to your life expectancy – I'm really not joking.

Advice. Make sure all your fridges are working efficiently. I reiterate the fact you are selling a premium product at a premium price **YOU** will expect. This all amounts to a crock of crap if the product isn't served at the optimum temperature.

Warning. Do not trust fridge temperature indicators. Use a thermometer and record daily results to recognise problems.

Bottling up during session

If a unit has a habit of selling out of certain bottled products during a session, through lack of space in front line fridges, it will obviously necessitate a restock in the middle of the action.

Warning. You **CANNOT**, repeat **CANNOT**; fill back up with bottle store temperature product. This sends a shiver down my spine (pardon the pun). Reputation is burnt to a cinder the moment you start selling warm product – why take the risk?

Instead. Identify the products selling out within the capacity of your bar and hold extra chilled storage behind the scenes.

Example. If you're in a small unit with only enough storage for a dozen of your most popular bottled lager front of house, these selling out by teatime - I would suggest at least one little fridge back of house, holding another four dozen of this product, so to never run out of cold supply.

Flipside. In a huge unit with a dozen fridges and capacity to hold at least twenty four dozen of one particular product: if you sell out by eleven 'o'clock on any given evening, it goes without saying, you'll need a big mother of cold storage behind the scenes to handle that dream problem. Another problem might be - how long it takes to count the money.

Bottom line. It takes forward thinking to be organised in this detail. A big unit might well have extra staff to cope, but it would still need driving. In a smaller unit, it might just mean grabbing any two minute window to replenish.

Word of mouth harm. I've had friends tell me they don't frequent this or that bar any more after a certain time of the evening - for fear of being served warm product.

Bottle skip

Throwing bottles in a skip, even from a short distance is utterly thick. It's usually a habit of the younger, more exuberant bartender from my experience. Any bottle thrown in this manner can end up in fifty pieces. Do they think this is clever or cool? Was this part of their job description? Have they been trained by a more qualified prick to do this? Let me tell you . . .

**It's neither clever nor cool . . .
It's thoroughly irresponsible!**

Dunce story. I witnessed one of my bartenders launch a bottle toward a skip from about three yards. It smashed to pieces – one of which struck a customer on the neck. Luckily the customer thought it was quite funny – I didn't.

Ultimately. **YOU** will be responsible. I got away with it, but my barman got severe earache at the end of that shift. He didn't do it again I hasten to add. Furthermore; inevitably, if I hadn't seen it happen, some poor sod would still have to empty that skip and dodge the bullets - thanks a lot.

Showtime. If you witness this amateur night behaviour, ask the individual to personally explain to you why it was a bad idea to throw that bottle. When they've finished, put them right on everything they've just got wrong. Ask them to explain how they are going to safely empty that skip of all the broken splinters in a safe manner? Get them to do just that.

Induction. When showing a new bartender round the bar, explain why **PLACING** bottles in a skip makes common sense.

Waste book on bar

Let's just assume you can provide some kind of stock result. This may be a modern till and back office system, able to tell if you are down by a single bottle or measure of any given product. It may also come from a pile of invoices and till receipts in a bag, handed to your local freelance stock taker.

AAAAAGGGGGHHHHH!

Stock is a valuable and important currency that you will have had to **PAY** for. The important figure you'll need to know is . . .

How much money am I losing on average in stock every day?

Why? It's a bit like having a petrol leak in your car, but not knowing you've got a petrol leak in your car. You normally put £50 a week in the thing, but without taking much notice, for the last three weeks that's risen to £90 per week. Thing is, you've been so busy what with one thing and another, the penny simply hasn't dropped. This doesn't make you a bad person - it just means you are not in control.

How does it work? Assuming you **CAN** obtain a figure of how much stock you are losing on average each day (please tell me you can); a quick look in your waste book might compare any deviation. Finding out a loss of £9 a day, with your waste book indicating £8 a day on average - you're not far off the beaten track (assuming the stuff written in that book is genuine; not an excuse for a free staff drink thank you guvnor). This might validate and explain certain losses, but it may well send you running to the quacks (to check your blood pressure) should there be no explanation – always a nasty surprise.

Implementation. Train all staff to document any wet losses on an on-going basis. A vodka mixer poured instead of a whisky mixer (the bartender simply pouring the wrong product). A 250ml glass of dry white wine a customer refused to drink (due to the last consumer's lipstick being still being present on the rim of the glass) and was really rude to the server (so would I have been). **ANY** loss of stock – write it down.

Please stop story

I witnessed several staff in a bar having trouble pouring lager producing a massive head. They'd keep pouring until the head was eventually small enough to be acceptable to the customer. I watched one drip tray after another be poured down the sink with no record or measure taken.

The landlord figure appeared and asked if everything was alright? The reply positive - he disappeared upstairs, obviously deciding to let the lunatics run the asylum. These were deep old drip trays. He'll have had to purchase this product before his loving staff literally poured it down the bloody drain.

AAAAAGGGGGHHHHH!

Point. This wasn't a managed house, he was a tenant. Lager frothing like that could indicate one of a number of issues, but if you don't know it's happening - how can you deal with it? It is fundamental to communicate **ALL** stock loss, if for no other reason than job security of all who work your kingdom.

No sales and voids

Lots of managers **NEVER** let their staff use the void or no sale button, and this may be company policy. This is policed by not allowing the key fob that works the till, to be programmed for this purpose. The main problem with this approach: **EVERY** single time a mistake is made on a till, or a customer requests change for machines, a superior will have to be called over **EVERY** single time to correct, or give access to that till.

Consequences. The real time cost of this policy is twofold. It will destroy any speed and quality of service you have delivered up to that point. It also might reveal the fact you don't trust any of your staff as far as you could throw them and think they're all a bunch of thieves.

In reality. If you want speed of service, you cannot take this route. Think about it – you can't trust them to void or no sale, yet at any given moment there may be hundreds of pounds inside that very till. If you can't trust them, what the hell are they doing working for you in the first place?

Accountability. Every time a void or no sale is made, get the person responsible to print a receipt off and state the reason.

Warning. Yes there's a fine line between giving responsibility to a member of staff and them ripping you off, but did you follow up those references? Were you totally happy with the references? Did you interview properly and ask pertinent questions relevant to **YOUR** future?

Solution. Thieves will steal no matter what you think, do or say. They won't care if it's raining, or you part your hair to the left for a change. They'll just rip you the hell off every single time an opportunity arises. Stopping no sales and voids on your till is a form of control, but can also interrupt a smooth customer journey. Being in full control is the answer.

Yes it's your job to catch the thieves, but you can't do that without the right tools.

However. Being informed you're losing thirty quid a day in stock and an average of twenty pounds in cash from the tills, would make me want to nail the bloody tills shut and employ an interrogator specialising in torture (only joking – mostly).

Never leave the service area unmanned

If there's no-one to greet and serve a customer on arrival, it will be an opportunity missed. Just as important will be the security of tills, stock and anything remotely **NICKABLE**.

Does it happen? Yes, I'm afraid it does. On one occasion I had to get the beer delivery in with the pub open, all my staff having rang in sick. Don't ask me how I managed it, I just did. At the end of it I felt like a nervous wreck - I didn't do it again. Being naïve, I felt I'd get the sack if my boss pulled up and found the pub shut, even though working, not shirking. **MAD.**

What should I have done? Having no choice but to receive the delivery, and no chance in hell of letting any delivery personnel in my cellar unsupervised; I should have prioritised and shut the pub for ten minutes, asking the one customer to wait outside - bribing with a freebie afterwards. If you've got thirty customers in and you don't know any of them – it'll be a problem. Remember – trust is **NOT** an option.

What might you do in that scenario?

Busy pub, but losing custom story

I was in a busy lounge bar with live entertainment performing. Between two bars, five bartenders were on duty, including the landlord. All the staff filtered into the public bar, leaving the lounge unattended. A couple entered the lounge. They waited 3-4 minutes, looked at each other in staggered bemusement a number of times - before walking straight back out.

AAAAAGGGGGHHHHH!

Lesson. There had been two or three staff serving non-stop all afternoon in that lounge. When a staff member finally reappeared, there were four people now waiting. She was quickly re-joined by the other two. You can never leave a bar un-manned, especially when busy. Why would you? If there had been at least one crew member manning the trench, they could have served two of the waiting customers, whilst queuing the other two and engaging apologetic dialogue with the couple that left never to return.

Warning. Even the busiest bars that seemingly don't have a problem paying bills, can unwittingly lose a fortune smaller bars would die for. As in this case - they won't even be aware. Busy units need to work extra hard – just to keep their crown.

Fine detail. The fact that the managers of that boozer don't realise how much more money they could be turning over, doesn't surprise me in the least. Once you start taking that sort of cash, it can sometimes get a bit blurry. You tend to focus on the big picture ok, but lose sight of all the fine detail that helped you achieve success in the first place. Being successful can be a dangerous time. Building trade and turnover is a fantastic challenge to certain individuals. Sustaining that level of success is an entirely different beast. That's when managers need to manage. In reality, it's still the same battle; staying in the premier league will mean attracting new custom daily.

Getting to know you

After successfully acknowledging and queuing, an opportunity will arise to cement the server/customer relationship

Greeting and choice. If you're the bartender, within the space of about two sentences, **YOU** need to make the customer feel at ease. They need to know - **THEY** have your undivided attention. A customer will often be undecided as to which product they fancy - a friendly serve can help this along.

Example. 'Hi there, sorry to keep you waiting, my name's Michael - what can I get you?' The customer might ask about a red wine. You can say, 'Let me help you with that' - on you go. Helping steer a customer through a sale adds **VALUE** all round.

Warning. If you know sod all about red wine, you're going to be about as useless as a chocolate fireguard at that point.

You've set the scene. You have the premium products. You've somehow persuaded the customer to enter. Now here they are standing in front of you - like a lamb to the slaughter.

Everything now hinges on HOW you serve!

Seal the deal

How many times are you served; not just in licensed premises, but anywhere you care to mention in general retail and not thanked? When you're out and about, notice how the person serving **YOU** finishes their transaction. I have been watching this trait for some time now. You may be surprised at the size in percentage of times you are left wanting.

Fundamental. Every single time a customer makes payment, in whatever form that may be - they must be thanked. Whether it's 40p for a box of matches, or eighty quid for a food bill - thank them. If you **FAIL** to say thank you . . .

Opportunity to ADD VALUE will be missed.

Customers waving money

Beware, beware the customer physically waving a note at you. They usually present in the form of two different disguises.

Pricks and bigger pricks!

Why? The smaller prick might be just that, but only if **YOUR** service is tip top. The bigger prick will **DEFINITLY** be trying to rip you off. They'll wave and wave a twenty pound note so everyone in proximity will notice. They'll order a round of drinks just under a tenner in value, at the last minute swapping the twenty for a ten. They will hope you've been brainwashed into thinking it **WAS** a twenty. If successful, you'll proceed to give them back the change from a twenty. At this point you will be down a tenner, and they'll be laughing – **IN YOUR FACE**.

AAAAAGGGGGHHHHH!

Tip. It might explain a ten pound note being found in the twenty pound note compartment when it comes to cashing up.

Furthermore. If you haven't fallen for their trick, they might still immediately accuse you of short changing them a tenner. It will be **YOUR** job to discredit that claim. A mate (another prick) might butt in at that point backing their friend up. You will be left in one hell of a corner. Loud heated arguments at the bar in front of **NICE** customers; licensee called in to do a cash check on the till; new custom walking in and leaving straight away in case it **ALL GOES OFF**. One big shower of shit.

How can you avoid this carnage?

Acknowledge the note

When some twerp is waving a note in front of you, let them order what they like and serve it up as nice as. Whatever denomination of note they hand you, turn to the nearest team member and get them to witness the colour of the money.

Vocally say the amount at the same time!

End game. The server will have a witness to the transaction. The fraudster will go off with their tale between their legs. You will still have your sale, all money intact – **HO HO HO**. If you haven't another staff member on the bar at that moment; acknowledge the note with the customer. Get them to agree **BEFORE** you open the till, that they have given you e.g. '**A TENNER SIR**' whilst waving it in the air. Other customers and your very own CCTV might both pick that up. On top of that: keep the note in hand until the customer physically puts the change back in their pocket. Strictly speaking – that's the point of no return for them. You might have to acknowledge waiting customers that you'll be right with them though.

Do your staff acknowledge the note?

Scooter boy story

It was the opening night of a refurbishment completed on my unit. The place was packed and an atmosphere to die for. The bar was three deep, with my new crew under pressure - no more rehearsals. There was this guy waving a twenty pound note in the air. He waved it until he was served - by me. He'd not been waiting long as we had only just opened the doors. I served him his pint and took his note. As if by magic it was a tenner. I gave him his change – of a tenner. He immediately pulled me up in a loud, brash manner and accused me of short changing him. This is the last thing I wanted to get into five minutes after opening. I wasn't really focused on catching thieves at that point, my head still spinning from the previous weeks of blood, sweat and tears. His attitude was shite. I was 100% certain he gave me a tenner; there was no way I was backing down. I told him he was trying it on and to back off. I informed him that if he persisted - I would ban him, simple as that. There were so many people waiting, I just had to serve someone else. He was now getting aggressive and swearing at me across the bar. In that moment I opened the till after serving another - to find not a twenty actually in the till.

Finale. Much to everyone's entertainment, I took the opportunity of removing his drink from the bar and informed him of bad tidings. His drink went down the sink and he ran out with me chasing him. After that, it so happened he would drive around that area on a scooter. From time to time he would run in with his helmet on, swear at whoever was behind the bar, run back out and scurry off on this scooter.

I could have avoided all that by SIMPLY acknowledging the note!

Whatsisname?

In most cases, regular customers absolutely love being called by their name when served. If delivered in a natural manner, it can add **VALUE** for both customer and server. It might provide a sense of belonging, a unit family vibe. Be proactive.

Assuming drink choice

Big Derek saunters in after a long hard day at the office. You pre-empt the scenario by pouring his usual pint of lager at £3.80 a touch, all ready and waiting for him. This would be fantastic customer love; apart from the fact that **BIG DEREK** has developed a bad case of the pox, which he caught from that cow he met in here three weeks ago. He's on antibiotics for two weeks until normal service resumes - nasty.

Lesson. Never assume the product choice of **ANY** customer. Always get them to confirm what you anticipate, by vocally asking: in this case – 'the usual Derek?'

Why? Losing £3.80 will cost **YOU** between five and six quid.

Why? A double negative: not only have you lost the £3.80 that would have been generated by the sale, you have also lost the stock value to replace that pint - extremely **NASTY**.

Personality clash with customer

Not all humans like each other - sad but true. A member of staff falling out with a customer – is a problem. Having to tell a bartender to back off is embarrassing; other customers witnessing the whole charade even more so. Not to mention how you then deal with the customer, who regularly puts £150 over your bar every single week. Does it happen? It happens.

Again - doing nothing is not an option!

In the event. You cannot pretend it isn't happening, it will just make things worse. If you personally witness what has gone on, tell the customer you will have a word with them in a minute. Pull the staff member to one side (preferably outside). Find out what the hell is going on. If **PRICKLY JIMMY** and you are the only ones on duty - that will prove difficult. If it turns out to be a clash of personalities, you will have to remind your touchy bartender - **WE** are all there to provide a **SERVICE** to **EVERYONE**. Whether we like them or not, matters not one iota. If a customer is frequently, blatantly rude - that is one thing; if the bartender has a personal problem, albeit historic or whatever, that's **THEIR** problem - not yours.

Solution? I can't tell you the right or wrong way to deal. In the back of your mind, the seven and a half odd thousand pounds that customer spends in your place will be distracting to say the least. If it's a case of abuse from the customer, the money should always come second. You must however, obtain **ALL** the facts to make fair judgement. I have lost staff over this. If you have a big enough bar with lots of staff, it might mean you can get the customer served without **PRICKLY JIMMY** having to make contact. Make the customer aware of any plan.

Warning. If the **GRUMPY** one develops a habit of falling out with customers, you may have a more deep rooted problem. Personally, if a bartender was completely out of order, I wouldn't hesitate issuing a verbal warning - and demand they apologise to a customer with immediate effect. You might well lose that bartender at that point, but just make sure of the facts before slinging any stones. You don't want to end up in a tribunal arguing the toss about a complete load of shit.

Managing staff - can be a pain in the ass!

Dealing with complaints

Let me confide in you. Some members of the public **REALLY ARE** a complete pain in the arse. I would link serial complainers to serial murderers; only difference being – you might be the one contemplating murder at the end of a confrontation.

Mostly. Complaining only occurs if a customer actually feels utterly compelled to do so. I would guess the majority of complaints one receives at the bar will have some legitimacy. This will usually mean that . . .

A human somewhere in your delivery chain has made a cock up!

Put yourself in the shoes of the customer. When was the last time you complained? What was it that drove you to make a fuss? How was it dealt with? Did the server make you feel like a million dollars at the end of the story, or did it leave you with a nasty taste you're unwilling to forgive - let alone forget?

Bad news. Complaining customers are often looked upon, and treated with disdain and suspicion by a receiving staff member. Therein lays the problem and answer all in one neat trick.

Instead. Think how much investment you will have made in the battle to persuade a customer to cross your doorstep, parting with their own hard earned cash on your premium products. The mere fact they're standing in front of you, should indicate you've done an awful lot of things right.

That's a whole lot of effort - right?

So why on earth would we make a complaining customer, feel awkward - as if they're a piece of shit on your shoe?

Astonishing! Why would we even think of blaming a customer for what has more than likely been one of **YOUR** errors? Why would we want to make a customer feel anything but . . .

Better?

A wild guess. You might well be thinking right now, 'that doesn't happen - I don't make a customer feel like that'. I've got news: this is exactly how we make a lot of customers feel.

This is when you SHOULD be wishing you'd spent more than a fiver on training!

You're aim should be. Turn the complaining customer into that prized possession called – a **RETURN CUSTOMER**.

How? Embrace the complaining customer. I don't mean hug them, but something subtly similar. Be genuinely interested in what has gone wrong. Give them your **FULL** attention. Make them feel #1. This is what working the bar is really all about. Whoever is dealing with that person needs to commit to not only solving the problem, but leave that customer feeling an awful lot better than when they felt **FORCED** to complain.

The customer journey. Customers don't generally walk into a place and look for the nearest thing they can complain about; that is the last thing on their minds. What they really want: is to enjoy the ambience of a unit and turn off from their everyday life for ten minutes. They might **NOT** have been expecting; to find a long blonde hair in the meal they've just waited forty minutes for, a jagged edge on the rim of a £6.20 250ml glass of Merlot, or a soft drink full of ice when they did request on ordering - that no ice be put in.

Above all: say sorry as many times as you have to and . . . MEAN IT!

A way forward. Implementing my suggested premium service equation, combined with continuous on-going training - will mean fewer mistakes. Fewer mistakes mean fewer complaints. This has to be driven by **YOU**. If you're not on site all hours of the day and night, it will need to be carried out by the person next in line. It will still need to be driven and checked by **YOU**. It's not complicated; the more you practice a dance routine, the better the outcome (well that's the idea). It also harks to the quality of person you recruit in the first place.

Bonus. If you deal with a complaint in a cool, calm, apologetic manner, and look as if you mean it; a customer can only admire those qualities. Not only that: so will other customers listening and watching it all play out, whilst recording it on their bloody phone. Free advertising word of mouth is a hard won prize. Next time you have a complaint at the bar . . .

How are YOU going to turn that around?

Irate customers

It's all well and good berating a customer losing it **BIG STYLE** at the bar as the result of a complaint, telling them to calm down or else. I can tell you categorically - shouting at them to calm down will only **INFLAME** the situation.

Try asking yourself instead. What the hell have we done to wind them up? Who is responsible? Can I turn this around?

Prediction. I would bet 95 times out of a hundred it will be the unit to blame and who's in charge – that'll be **YOU** then.

Example. A chap comes in at twelve noon for his dinner hour with some mates. They order separately. He orders his drink, which is poured and then proceeds to order a meal. At this point he is told that food orders are taking about 40 minutes.

A very bad start. Having watched the group enter, and knowing there was a forty minute wait on food, the bartender should have first inquired whether the gentleman and his mates were planning on ordering food. In receipt of that knowledge, the customer and friends would at least have been given the choice to move on - to somewhere that might serve them in the customers allotted timeframe.

Dilemma. Now the gentleman has been poured a drink which he'll be obliged to pay for and will already be stressing about time management. This is not what he expected when entering. The gentleman takes a glance at his watch and decides to gamble on an hour and a bit for lunch. He orders fish, mashed potato and peas and joins his mates. At twelve forty-five he starts to feel a tad uncomfortable and approaches the bar. He enquires how long his meal will be and is told they will find out pronto. The staff member returns and shouts over to him that his meal has just been put on. It's now twelve fifty. At that point he's between a rock and a hard place (pardon the pun), bloody starving and riding lady luck on time having paid for his meal fifty odd minutes ago.

Drum roll. Five minutes later the meal arrives and he digs in. Two minutes later he approaches the bar and bangs the meal down on the bar in front of the server. The peas and the potato are cold. The server enquires if everything is alright?

End result? The shit hits the fan. The chap starts flying expletives at the bartender about the way he's been treated. The manager is called and without asking staff what has occurred - proceeds to ban the gentleman from the premises. If he doesn't leave right now they'll call the police - **BRILLIANT**.

A fine way to boost trade sir!

Consequences. The bloke came in with three mates. For starters, this could have got really nasty, that's **SHITTY NASTY**. Secondly, those four ex-customers and others present in the bar will tell **ALL** their friends what happened. It'll end up the worst advert you never paid for – but **PAY** you will. Think of income lost from the four guys over the next twelve months, never mind the **CAT SPRAY** damage to reputation.

Question. How can we as a trade be angry at a consumer who's done nothing but bend over backwards to spend money. How dare we put customers through this kind of shenanigans? This could all have been so different. One thing for sure . . .

Asking an irate customer to calm down
who has done nothing wrong whatsoever, but be subjected to your gross negligence . . .
Might act as a trigger sentence – to HELL!

What to do? **APOLOGISE** and keep apologising until you can think of what to do next. I can't tell you every word you might say, each of us will have a different approach, but it's your job to regain **CONTROL**. Find a way of placating the customer and bring the whole sorry saga to a satisfactory conclusion for all.

Advice. On more than one occasion I have been stood in front of a raving mad customer, knowing my supply chain has completely cocked up, feeling an overwhelming urge to throttle at least two of my staff – all at the same time. A customer would rather hear the truth every single time, than spun some false politician bullshit. Being told the truth in this age can be reasonably refreshing. After all that though . . .

Find out what went wrong and make sure it - NEVER happens again!

Rude customers

You just can't ban a customer for not saying thank you; after all, they may not actually know the meaning of the word. But, receiving a multitude of complaints from either staff or other customer's, would without doubt warrant investigation. The measure will be in the form of a question . . .

Is this rude shit costing me a loss of takings or staff?

If the answer to that question is yes, it's decision time. Do you pull them to one side and preach the new rules, or have they got to go. Not dealing will mean it boiling over at a later date.

Warning. I lost a great member of staff through my inability to deal with a really rude bastard. It took that loss to focus my full attention on the problem - by then it was too late. I dealt with a lot of things differently after that.

Harsh lesson. Not only did I lose an original team member in whom I had invested a lot of time and training; I had also lost someone whom was just a superb human being. I hadn't recognised that this lady was the glue that held my crew together. I don't think we ever regained the teamwork that endured that period - takings dropped as an extra kick in the balls. When I finally came to my senses; Terry Tit did leave the building in spectacular fashion, but I remember not feeling the usual elation on ejection, just remorse in my inaction.

Trouble brewing?

Mixing alcohol with humans can quickly become an anything can happen experience, at **ANY** time of the day. Being alert is fundamental, not **JUST** in the name of service.

Watch out. Bartenders have to be switched on to receive any little signs; that Terry is about to wrap that pool cue around Desmond's head, or out of the blue; Mavis - normally the most docile pet in the box, has just thrown the best part of a pint of lager all over some bloke whom nobody has ever seen before. Mavis's husband Clive would like to know as well. Front line troops need to make **YOU** aware of any probabilities ASAP.

On-going. It's just as important to train staff in dealing with all this crap, as it is pouring drinks in the correct manner. Sometimes the mere act of calling in the guvnor will suppress an oncoming altercation. Other times; it will still go off, but having been called - **YOU** might be around to regain **CONTROL**. Luckily for us humans, if you can tune in, there's a sixth sense available on all this bollocks. Prevention is the tidiest cure.

Waiting time on food

Linking back to a previous example of an irate customer: If food orders **ARE** backing up in the kitchen, it will be **YOUR** problem, not the customers - please don't share the burden. How would you personally like to be treated in that situation?

Warning. Never **PROMISE** that which you cannot fulfil. Make customers aware before taking an order – it **ADDS VALUE**.

Menu knowledge

Any member of staff taking a food order, should at least possess a basic familiarity of every item on a menu. Without that - smooth service is simply unobtainable.

Why? Slow and unsure service will create an unsure message subconsciously to the customer. They will, without even realising; be alert to any misgivings of ongoing service.

Truthfully. I have thrown boys and girls onto the bar, giving them a quick glance at a menu and pointing out where they can find the food menu on the till. Sometimes, being thrown in the deep end can be effective, but I really must have been suffering from **HUMAS** to believe this was a viable long term staff training policy. How many customers did I lose as a result?

How to instead? Start the day you decide to offer the job. Hand them a menu and tell them to take it home and study it. Inform them you'll be quizzing them on the content when they start work. Tell them if their knowledge is up to scratch, you'll pay them an extra hour as a bonus. Let's be honest, it'd be worth it - wouldn't it? If they're really keen, they'll know the thing inside out on their return. It'll be hard enough steering their way round a new till system, let alone which of the five breakfasts the customer requires, where the no tomatoes button lives, taking the money − then finding out you don't actually serve breakfasts after lunchtime.

One-on-one. Stick to this **APPRENTICE** like glue. Introduce the server to the customer. Customers generally don't mind being used as a learning curve, as long as the novice is accompanied by an **EXPERT**. They will not appreciate being served by someone who hasn't got a clue and isn't supervised.

> # Time conscious customers, mean that lunchtime is probably inappropriate for an initiation in taking food orders!

About you. The headline story will be how well you train your team. That generally means that **YOU** need to gain some experience before entering this trade. How can **YOU** expect to communicate the job in hand, if **YOU** haven't got the first clue?

Taking a food order

Having ascertained whether food is required at the beginning of service, and as mentioned, the importance of making the customer aware of any length of wait; can I also suggest the habit of repeating a food order back to the customer. You may have other customers waiting, but let me explain why . . .

Ordering food as a couple, or in a group of family or friends, it is customary to eat together. The food ordered must be delivered together.

That means at the same time!

Not only that. The food should be exactly what has been ordered in the first place. This won't be a problem if before finalising, collecting payment and thanking; the server has repeated the order back to the customer. A simple check takes seconds. Here are two examples of what can go wrong . . .

People like to eat together story

I witnessed an older couple order food at the bar. They sat down, made small talk and sipped at their accompanying drinks. After about twenty minutes their meals arrived. The gentleman had a steak on a sizzling platter that was indeed sizzling away and very impressive – it smelt gorgeous. The lady had a leg of lamb that was again very attractive on the plate. The waiter delivering this mouth-watering order, proudly announced the steak meal and passed it to the gentleman; followed by announcing the leg of lamb directed at the lady, only to be greeted by silence and faces a gasp. The gentleman had ordered lasagne for the lady - definitely not a leg of lamb.

AAAAAGGGGGHHHHH!

The lamb was duly whisked away with a promise of the lasagne to follow. The chap got on with his meal and so would I have. As he eat, he kept apologising to his partner. They had a conversation that centred around what had happened and how **THEY** could have got it so wrong etc. etc. Ten minutes later, out popped a lasagne and madam tucked in. By this time though, the fella had finished his meal and the conversation had turned to total criticism. Last bit I over-heard, was the chap saying they wouldn't bother again; it's just as nice down the road and they always get nice service down there. Two or three times they mentioned they hadn't actually been apologised to. I personally didn't hear an apology. When the gentleman paid at the bar, he settled the bill with another member of staff, who had clearly not been told of the scenario just taken place. My heart was in my mouth as the customer sort of hung on slightly, to see if there was any kind of apology forthcoming. Of course there wasn't, and he walked back to his wife looking very unhappy. Put yourself in the shoes of that couple. Take their journey and imagine what effect that had on them. How many people will they tell that story to? Word of mouth can be damaging. The moral of this story is . . .

If customers wanted to eat separately, they would have sat at different tables!

The customer journey at that point was totally buggered. They might just as well have stayed at home, enjoyed beans on toast together, at a twentieth of the price. Repeating the order to the customer at the bar, could have prevented this upset.

Apologise? The waiter should have been on his knees begging for redemption!

What should have happened? Huge regret should have been ushered on the couple in question. The second meal at least should have been made complimentary. The moment the shit hits the fan, you are in damage limitation mode. Forget how much profit you were on and focus on escape. I would have made both meals complimentary; a scrap of dignity recovered from a double negative. At least when they're slagging you off to all and sundry, they'll have to finish their tale of woe with the fact they had a free lunch. I would have offered a pot of tea or coffee on the house with the express apologies of the management - to **SEAL THE DEAL**.

Prevention. I reiterate: verbally repeating the order back to the customer and issuing a receipt that clearly prints out the meals ordered - should avert most blunders. More importantly, getting things right first time will add to the smooth service we all strive for. It will create less tension in the kitchen and less of a blame game within the team – a plethora of **VALUE ADDED**.

Cold meal story

My partner and I with our new addition, went for lunch at a highly regarded independent pub/restaurant. There were no cheap meals on the menu. It was a busy midweek lunchtime session, only a couple of free tables available. After visiting the bar to collect drinks, we made our order with the waitress. The food was some time in arriving, but we were in no rush - busy ogling our new born. The meals duly arrived after about forty minutes and we both tucked in. My meal was cold. Luckily for the unit, I was still in chilled out mode, what with recent events. I had also just started to get to grips with this project, so was interested in what might happen next.

Showtime. What I presume was the owner, came over and performed a disappearing trick with my sweet'n'sour chicken. Now call me old fashioned, but I really have a problem with this particular action related to the serving of a faulty meal.

Why? Whilst my meal was being **TAKEN CARE OF** (as the owner put it), I could only hazard to guess they might be trying to **REHEAT** it. To be honest, it spoilt enjoyment of the meal when it finally arrived. I couldn't make out if the chicken had been reheated and fresh rice added. I was left in the dark.

Tip. If you do have to cook someone's meal again, do them the justice of leaving it in view; **ANYWHERE** as long as the customer has reassurance that that very meal will be cooked from scratch - how jolly refreshing that might be.

Finale. The food was nice and I wasn't charged for my meal when settling up. My main bones of contention? I wasn't kept in the loop, the chap didn't really apologise and I think he felt it was all a bit of a nuisance.

What should have happened? He should have apologised profusely. He should have made me aware immediately my meal was **ON THE HOUSE** and left the cold one where I could see it. He should have then sent a waitress over to ask us both what we would like to drink, whilst waiting a further 20 bloody minutes – **WITH THE OWNERS COMPLIMENTS**.

On reflection. I think this fella has such a strong business; we were just a pin prick in his big picture. It was an intimate setting with lots of customers sat close by. He didn't make too much of a fuss of us; he didn't want the people sitting around us finding out he'd served a plate of faulty goods - his version of damage limitation. He'd also completely forgotten . . .

People like to eat together!

Hot plates

If you're serving hot food and want to give it the best chance of staying hot - serve on a hot plate, it **ADDS VALUE**. All staff should be fully trained and aware of current health and safety issues connected. Do you need to write risk assessments?

They say things happen in three's story

I stopped off for a mixed grill with my partner in a national chain eating house. My partner ordered a burger and I a mixed grill. We took a bottle of wine back to the table to await our meal. The glasses were absolutely filthy and were replaced. We opened the wine to find it had gone off and smelt like a bag of sick. To add insult to injury, the hurrying waiter carrying my meal, tripped whilst climbing some steps - leaving my mixed grill spread over a wide area (will we ever get to eat together?) I'd have liked to have seen this unit's stock result - bloody hell.

Out on the floor (you can still ADD VALUE)

Next time you're out and come across staff walking toward you; do they get out of **YOUR** way and apologise whilst smiling, or do they steam toward you expecting **YOU** to shift? I know what I think should happen – what do you think?

'Is everything ok?'

It really is nice, to just touch base with the customer once in receipt of a meal; it lets the customer know **YOU** care. A natural obstacle remover – it **ADDS VALUE**.

Warning. Delivered in a couldn't give a crap but I've got to say it anyway manner - chips away at the customer journey and puts you in the relegation zone. Be genuine, it's a free hit.

Cutlery

Unless sitting down to a laid table, it really is fundamental to have wrapped a knife and fork in a serviette ready for the customer. How often have you ordered a meal, paid the money and not been informed where the cutlery lived? After finally locating some grubby plastic container full of non-hand dried silverware, you'll continue to leaf through the items until deciding on the least tarnished choice. Is this acceptable?

Grave warning! How many men will leaf through that cutlery after just taking a piss and not washing their hands?

AAAAAGGGGGHHHHH!

Staff not busy? Point them in the direction of the cutlery and remind them where the serviettes are. Always keep more cutlery than you need - so as never to run out at busy times.

Condiments

Personally. If anyone thinks after purchasing hot food, waiting patiently for it, then being forced to negotiate a load of sauce sachets **IS** any fun at all - they must have a few loose rivets.

Why? Smooth delivery of premium products, delivered in the correct manner, is only as good as its weakest link.

Example. Your customer can have a big breakfast costing £7.95 delivered after a fifteen minute wait. It'll be a good idea if that breakfast **IS** on a hot plate, cause' by the time your customer has found the sachets and navigates tearing them open - they'll now have sauce all over they're pinkies. This will mean using the one serviette that came with the cutlery - to wipe they're hands on; requiring another flaming visit to ask for another flaming serviette, there being none provided on the condiment table. I'm glad I got that off my chest.

My personal choice. Use bottles every time. It involves a lot more graft and commitment, but faster and cleaner in delivery of the condiment. It really is **HUMAT** to suggest otherwise.

Smooth service = VALUE ADDED!

Clean condiment decanters

If you do choose bottles or plastic containers to decant your sauces, they'll need daily attention. What use is an empty, or near enough empty sauce container? Let me tell you . . .

It's BLOODY USE-LESS!

On receipt of a meal; the smooth journey I bang on about, means the customer should simply reach out and use a fully stocked condiment container - in the blink of an eye.

Do you offer that standard of service?

Advice. Laborious though it may be; before topping up a sauce, wash the bottle completely by flushing any old product out. Immerse the damned thing in boiling hot water, including the bottle top which can be a pain in the ass.

Tip. Perhaps when interviewing new kitchen staff, you can mention this requirement. In other words you might be able to cook, but do you mind the crap jobs? Personally, I found little jobs like that respite from playing in the lunatic asylum.

Essence. This is what putting the customer #1 is really all about; finer details completing the puzzle can make all the difference. You may have your own preference, or perhaps no choice in the matter, but thinking thoroughly through the customer journey can reveal the most avoidable obstacles. Reach out and pour, it's a no brainer. I've told you what I think.

You must make your own mind up.

Setting the scene

Don't wait for events to start, before moving tables and chairs to accommodate any forthcoming event. Not only is it lazy, but stupidity in its thickest form. Just like prepping a kitchen, bar or money before service - you must prep the room itself.

Why? Firstly: it's a free marketing opportunity. Signalling something's happening, can encourage customers to stay a while longer. Secondly: if for example you're expecting people for a live footie game; you might want to set your furniture facing a big screen, still leaving avenues to visit the loo and access for clearing tables of all weapons (glasses). You may want to leave a space at the front - it being too close to view.

Warning. Failure to set the room up may leave it difficult for customers to move once entrenched; even more problematic for staff to clear tables. Once customers start arriving in droves, it may be too late to leave the bar and **YOU** will look the cowboy you really are - playing catch up as usual.

Example. My second pub (opposite a train station), was a hybrid live music venue, come business and commuters during day times. After the lunchtime session on Thursdays and Saturdays, three quarters of the furniture in the unit would have to be moved and a stage wheeled in with carpet laid on top. This would set the scene for everyone stopping in after that, sending the optical message - there was music tonight. As soon as the band had cleared away their gear at the end of the night, the room would be put back ready for the daytime custom - as if there had never been a band there at all.

Lesson. Setting the room up was **KEY** to the success of that venue; a fundamental slice of the carrot meal at the end of any marketing we'd put in place - increasing capacity at the same time (legally of course).

Be creative. Don't be afraid of changing furniture around to fashion something that works for you and your particular unit; especially for live performances, big screen and T.V. sport. Be careful about moving gaming machines, there might well be a stipulation on your license that states exactly where these machines have to be. Always take into account fire exits and clear space for access to toilets. Move furniture out altogether and create a dancing area in front of the live act. Dim the lights, people are shy to start with. Think out of the box.

Prep the scene – it ADDS VALUE!

At the end of the day

How will the cleaners in the morning hoover efficiently with the furniture in the way? Stacking chairs on tables as you shut down the bar can also signal to customers in a subtle fashion - it's **TIME TO GO**. Of course you can't stack chairs if it damages certain table tops, but you could put chairs to one side of the room. The cleaning crew could hit the clear area first, placing chairs back as they go. This is the evening crew prepping the way for the next session – it's called teamwork. Perhaps that might create another ten or fifteen minutes to spend in the loos - now that might be highly beneficial.

Chewing gum

Just as I wouldn't expect a bartender to be chomping through a plate of chips whilst serving me, neither would I expect them to be chomping happily away on gum. Certain standards of hospitality just have to be adhered to. I chew gum all the time, but this is one of those fundamental yardsticks . . .

What do you think?

Long story cut short

This chapter should demonstrate the complexity of working the bar. The first draft of this chapter was over a hundred pages long, including over eighty subjects. That didn't include the pouring of drinks, which is clearly best taught real time. A bartender making the job look easy is no accident. Trained by someone who can actually **TEACH** not **TELL** . . . a barrel of patience and a whole lot of time spent behind a bar more like.

You might NOT have the luxury of time!

I make no apology for repeating and reiterating certain points. Nearly all the subject matter links in one form or another, like a cobweb trapping no other goal than a satisfactory customer journey. Repetition is the nature of the job; customers the hand grenade that makes it interesting. Preparing staff is fundamental. However, I will admit you can only learn so much before being thrown to the lions. It's tricky, but I'm a firm believer you make your own luck. Cultivating a great team to carry out all these jobs is a massive task, but it **CAN** be done. You probably think I live in never-never land in my expectancy of staff. Believe me, through awful choice - I have had some **SHITE** staff. I've then had to endure the pain of that choice until they, or I moved on. Your ability to delegate staff to take care of all these jobs and more - without prompting, is a tall order, but again – it **CAN** be done. Training really is the key to the lock; the right recruit certainly helps. I hope this chapter highlights the magnitude of the job in hand and the consequences to the smooth running of **ANY** unit.

Marathon runners have got sod all on successful licensees!

19 TILLS & FLOATS

Most of the money feeding your business will filter primarily through your tills.
The secondary source will be the machine take, though this might still be fed to some extent from your tills.

What can I learn from taking the money?

Take note. Every single penny passing through your tills must be accurately counted and accounted for, in order to measure performance and pinpoint problems. All cash from this primary source will be inextricably linked to your stock.

Example. If you carry out a seven day stock that says you're down by £300 – **WHERE'S IT BLOODY GONE?** Accurate till counts are the first line of intelligence gathering. One glance at the till counts might indicate a total loss of £150 in those seven days. That's good and bad news. Good you have accounted for half the money, bad because; you, one or several of your staff have cumulatively lost or stolen £150 in seven days flat. The other £150 could be just bad housekeeping on your part - it not being hard to lose £150 a week in stock.

Where did the cash go? It's a process of elimination. Exactly when did it go missing and who was on duty at the time? Did you as a rule complete a cash check between staff finishing and starting service? Who counted the tills? If you work for a managed estate you'll have some idea what I'm on about. If you're an independent you might think I'm talking double Dutch. Counting accurately is a science in itself. If things don't add up – you need to know why? It's called – **CONTROL**.

Standard till layout

Staff will get used to however you lay your tills out very quickly. If new to retail and never been near a till, ask someone who does have experience. How do they arrange their tills?

Tip. Whether you have one till or twenty; duplicate the layout. It'll be easy for you - universal for the team. Label each tray and drawer. You'll always know at a glance, which till draw will correspond with the till reading you have in front of you.

Counting

I find it astonishing when entering retail of any kind, no training is ever taught on the protocol and importance of counting tills. Fundamentals learnt, you'll command a far stronger position to recognise problems and recipes for solutions. In the process you'll be prepping for the following session, banking and daily reckoning of all monies in the safe.

Where should I count a till? One of only two locations usually. If you are lucky enough to have an office, this is ideal. The other on occasion will be at the back of the bar, when a cash check might be required on an individual till.

Why would that happen? Usually a customer discrepancy, claiming for example - they handed over a larger note than change given, or if you have cause to do an on the spot cash check in the process of trying to catch a staff member **AT IT** (see *STAFF AT IT* chapter).

Warning. Please don't tell me you count the tills in the bar when all the customers have gone. You may as well just stitch a target on your back with a sign attached saying – **ROB ME**. I'm going to take it for granted you have an office. Quite honestly, I just can't imagine or bear the thought of you not.

Tip. Try and shut the door whilst you are counting tills. Sometimes, after a whole day listening to all sorts of crap on the juke box - you'll be glad to shut that door.

Warning. Whenever you leave the office, **ALWAYS** shut and lock the door – **DON'T** say I haven't warned you.

Tip. In certain situations, it may be appropriate to lock whilst inside. A sliding bar on the inside is a great idea, making life a tad easier – **FOR YOU**.

Manual counting. Even if you possess scales, these can malfunction. In your office; your desk should be completely flat with smooth edges, so you can pull coins off the table into your hand. If the table is worn, purchase a cheap piece of hardboard and secure shiny side up on top of your table.

Shiny is easy to drag coinage across.

Counting scales. I only started using a set of weighing scales in my last unit. As if by magic, they just arrived one morning. I can't remember whether it had become company policy, or was due to a marked upturn on the back of banning 176 assholes in three and a half months since arrival. I didn't **HAVE** to physically count coins or notes from that moment. Superb for speed and accuracy, it also added up as it went along. If you're turning over less than 5K weekly, I don't know if you could justify buying a machine like this, but certainly anything over 10K will make an investment of £100 - £300 a must.

Paper roll calculator. No licensee should be without one. Using a normal calculator, if you make a mistake half way through counting, you have to start again. With a paper roll job pressed to print mode, it will print each item. If you get distracted, or make a mistake - counting change twice is history. Yippee.

Till float

Each draw should have enough change and notes to see you through the first part of the day. A £100 just won't cut it.

Why? If your first customers all pay with big value notes, it'll begin to decimate smaller denominations almost straight away. If the next few customers do the same, and you've two people giving it large on machines – you might only have twenty pound notes and few (if any) pound coins left (let's just hope the guvnor's not gone into town with the safe keys).

What size till float? I would advise a float of at least £300 as a working tool, that's each and every till. I personally would go for £400, providing comfortable headroom. If that sounds arrogant – I have sympathy. Running a unit only taking a few grand a week, it would be hard to justify that size till float, but moving any business forward, means relegating competition to exactly that. In attempting to raise the bar in the level of service, the last thing you want - is staff shouting requests for change every ten minutes. All this does is slow service down.

Service that is smooth and professional is usually no accident!

From a customer perspective, nothing should appear a problem. By removing all possible obstacles in the customer journey, you increase the odds of success. Flip that to running out of change and having to ask the customer if they've got the right money – and you **WILL** have **FAILED**.

Security. If I said to an experienced licensee I was planning to put £400 floats in each till, they'd probably say I was stark raving mad. First comments might be directed towards the security of this money, several swear words included.

My retort would be. You'd be stark raving bonkers not to. After you've been open two hours, most units in question would **ALL** hold at least £400 in a till. What's the difference?

> You're either in this to be the best or you're not.
> # Get your fundamental bricks into place and start building your business!

House floats

It doesn't matter how big your operation is; if you run out of change, you can officially wear a clown's hat with pride. Other expletives are at the forethought of my mind. You should have enough change in your house float to see you through the busiest times, no matter what. My own preference for three tills on a busy day would be: £600 in fivers, £1800 in pound coins, £150 each of 50p's and 20p's, £100 each of 10's and 5's, fifty quid of assorted 1's and 2's, the other fifty quid in odds. That's a total of £3000 as your float. Your requirements may differ and that's a lot of dead money – but **FUNDAMENTAL**.

End of day cashing up + floating tills back up

It's the end of the evening session. You have three tills. You remove till tray three for counting. Whilst still standing at till three, you print off a till summary declaring what the contents of till three should amount to. Before departing, it'll be a quick bend down to check inside the till casing for any notes and coinage spilt, or notes planted for **STEALING**. Off you'll trot to the office, leaving staff clearing up debris of the day.

Example of how to count a till. The following is a ball park scenario - there are many. The float in this case is £300.

1. Start by counting your 1's, 2's, 5's, 10's, 20's, 50's, pound and two pound coins. Let's say your total comes to £126.51 in coins, with ample small coinage left in the till.

2. At that point - remove the rest of the money, including card receipts (PDQ's) and put to one side. Call this the pile.

3. Remove £1.51 more from the draw to leave £125.00 in the till tray. Add the £1.51 to the pile.

4. The even figure in the till leaves you a foundation to work from. Remember that as well as counting your till, you have to leave £300 in that draw for the next day.

5. Next add say £75 in fivers and £40 in ten's back in to the till from the pile. You now have £240.00 in the till.

6. Add 3 twenty pound notes from the pile (exchange for bags of pound coins). Till tray three is now floated up for the next day. You are left with the pile, which should add up to somewhere very near what the till summary says.

7. Do not open any fresh bags of coinage added to any till in floating back up (in this case pound coins), until you're happy **ALL** the till counts and safe check are present and correct. If you've already made a mistake, you don't want to complicate things. Move till tray three to one side.

8. Now count the pile. The notes, PDQ's (card receipts), cash lifts in envelopes, and your £1.51 will give a figure. If that total figure you have is very near (and I mean pennies) to the till summary figure you printed off - put that money in a tray/bag in the safe and move on to count any remaining tills. Even at this point – do not mix this cash and PDQ's with the contents of the safe. If you find a discrepancy along the way, you'll have to solve this straight away before proceeding to count more tills. This will be far easier and quicker if kept separate.

9. Remove till three from the desk and put it in the safe (please tell me your safe is big enough to fit your trays in).
10. Proceed to count the next till, or both tills.

Aim. In an ideal world, all tills should be floated up and ready to slide straight back into work the next morning. After checking the total PDQ summary is **EXACTLY** the same as all the PDQ slips added together from the three tills, the takings can be added to the safe ready for banking and change requirements, with a final safe check before bedtime.

Advice. Being two steps in front all the time will become a habit. If two staff ring in sick the next morning, or your food delivery arrives just when you're going to open the doors, along with the plumber to fix that infuriating leak that's leaving a lake sized puddle - is when you'll be glad you squared everything last night – tills ready to go.

Warning. If you're a manager and get a walk in stock or audit the next morning, you'll be only too pleased to be a trifle in front of yourself. Sporting a hangover and opening your door to one of these scary bastards can put the fright up anyone.

Be prepared – be very prepared!

A word in your shell-like. If you have three tills for example: come ten to midnight, you might get into the habit of removing two of your tills towards the end of opening, in the vain hope of an early bath. This creates problems. Firstly: if you have three staff on separate tills (that have been using separate tills all night long), for the last ten minutes they all end up using the same till - it negates all accountability.

What on earth would be the point of that?

Secondly: you might have delivered supreme customer love all day long. At the last hurdle, you might destroy that standard and keep customers waiting with only one till left in operation, or a till bereft of change - all to save a poxy ten minutes.

Advice. If you're open till twelve, provide a full service till twelve. Opening times are exactly that. **OPEN**.

Opportunity. More focus should be shown at this point than any other. You've stripped customers of all their cash; this is prime time to seal it with a kiss basically. Truly successful units of the future will leave customers inspired to return.

> ## 'We've had your money – now EFF OFF, needs kicking into seriously long grass!

Designated tills and checks should be the 'Norm'

Before every session a bartender starts, their till should be pre-counted and henceforth - not touched by anyone else. This is an ideal of course. What actually happens is: the boss, the assistant manager, or any staff for that matter - steam in at busy moments, even on occasion just to serve themselves.

AAAAAGGGGGHHHHH!

This particular brand of incompetence haunts the trade. It makes a mockery of the term – **CONTROL**. If you have enough tills and ratio of staff to match that number, separate tills are sensible – more especially when you're not there.

> ## Accountability is not just the prize possession of those in charge - it is imperative all the way up . . . and DOWN!

Smooth service tip. If you only have one or two tills, acquire spare drawers for each; float up with the usual amount and keep ready in the safe. On handover, print a sub-total, slide the used drawer out ready for counting, check the empty tray and put the fresh drawer in - a speedy handover solved in seconds.

Control. Sometimes, a small amount of understanding of what exactly is going on in-house, is better than none at all.

Example. There are units that may have six or seven staff on duty and room for only two tills - I understand that. You could put three on one and three on the other, with the guvnor flitting between the two. It does make a pig's ear of it all, but might narrow down any shortcomings in a particular till.

Flipside. In the same bar on a quiet Wednesday afternoon, two staff on duty – you **COULD** and **SHOULD** implement separate tills; any shenanigans easier to spot and investigate.

Poles apart. Although normal till checks and emergency cash checks are similar, I have deliberately kept the subjects apart. The first should be completely normal etiquette; the second is usually a forced scenario. In prepping tills for incoming staff, you will have already to some extent - narrowed down the plot lines for any discrepancy during a session.

Emergency cash checks

Should there be any discrepancy on the bar requiring a cash check, you will **ALWAYS** (in my opinion) need to do this on the back of the bar in front of the customer. Lugging scales from your office into the bar area along with the power supply, is a bit **OTT**. Simply grab your **PAPER ROLL CALCULATOR** and print a till summary relevant to the till in question (basically a sub-total of all transactions registered in the till to that point).

Check the till drawer. When you extract the till from the casing, bend down and look inside the casing. Are there any notes or coinage laid in the base of the casing? If there are, you have a problem. Either money has accidentally fallen into the base of the drawer, been moved by pixies, or the member of staff using that till is building a stash ready for withdrawal at some point. In the trade, this is generally called – **STEALING**.

AAAAAGGGGGHHHHH!

The only other possible explanation; the money lying in the base has been there for some time. When the till has been full to bursting on occasion, cash might well have spilt over the top into the base. That might explain previous till shortages.

Options at that point. You can leave the money in there and not indicate you have noticed money in the casing. Tell the staff on duty not to go anywhere near that till whilst you count the contents. Watch the bartender's actions whilst you do so. Are they looking nervous, or are they nonchalant? A human face can tell **YOU** an awful lot. The other option: immediately hook the money out from the drawer and add it back to the till. Either way you'll still have to count the flaming contents.

Big lesson. **ALWAYS** check the empty drawer for cash. From that moment onwards, you'll know that any cash left in the casing could only have come from the present session. It **ELIMINATES** one explanation from the frame.

Count the contents. After fully informing the customer of what you plan to do and safe to do so; count the till on the back of the bar in full view of the customer. Be as nice as pie. A quick comparison of the totals should tell you how much the till is either up or down. It'll be time to hand them back the tenner you owe them or tell them to sod right off (only joking).

Why count on the back of the counter? If someone has a genuine claim, it'll require solving with the minimum of fuss, in a manner that keeps both parties integrity intact. It adds **VALUE** and **TRUST** for the customer. By removing the till to an office behind the scenes, you remove all sense of transparency.

Finale. Of course give them the tenner back if you find it, but it may not be the end of the story if the till does appear to be correct. If you happen to have made a cash lift earlier in the session, you must check the money you have lifted and deposited in your safe is correct. If you have to disappear from the trading area, keep the customer fully informed – **BE NICE**. This really does make a case for putting any cash lifts in an envelope, marking it up with the amount, what till it was extracted from, and not touching until you are counting that tray at the end of the day's session. In doing so, you will have not mixed it up with any money already in the safe. If the lift isn't a tenner up, you might have floated the till up the night before with a tenner too little. That would explain for the till to be correct, and not have a tenner too much on first count.

Still with me?

The only way to check that would be - a second safe check. If the till is correct, the cash lift in the envelope correct, the safe spot on, and you haven't borrowed a tenner out of the till and forgotten about it - the customer has been mistaken.

Tip. If you have numerous cameras on your CCTV system (please tell me you have), you would **OBVIOUSLY** have a camera aimed at each till wouldn't you? Why not make this first port of call. If this proves conclusive, obviously you can't let the customer in your office (security being reason alone), but you may have the facility to replay in your trading area.

An idea. To save embarrassment, have you the means to send the customer a video to their mobile phone? Just a thought.

Relaying bad news. Failing to find validation of a claim, won't mean you're right. It will only indicate failure to validate. Communicating bad tidings after a long wait is never easy.

> **If a customer goes absolutely bananas at that point, it's probably odds on they might not have been lying at all.**

AAAAAGGGGGHHHHH!

If a customer has made a strong case, it might be more trouble than worth, but you can't spend all day handing back tenner's can you? It'll be decision time – for you. It'll also still leave you a conundrum – what was the true story on the tenner?

The customer journey. Customers don't expect to be short changed. If it was me – I'd be pretty angry, quite rightly too.

Adding up an emergency cash check

A cash check is not a time to fart around. More often, a customer will be pacing around in front of you awaiting good news. You won't be changing the till up or lifting any notes . . . Just count the whole damned thing as **FAST** as possible. Every single penny and PDQ . . . Add it all together. Simply deduct how much float you carry in the till and you'll end up with a figure. Compare this figure with what the till says you should have at that very moment. If it's a tenner up, I would just check the till once more before handing back the money, apologising with the offer of a freebie to compensate. Using a paper roll calculator will make this last check the quickest operation – figures to compare with.

Cash lifts and adding change

Key staff might **HAVE** to use all possible tills, if for no other reason to keep them changed up. They might **HAVE** to perform cash lifts to remove all excess notes (what a wonderful thing). If you cannot trust the team leaders to carry this out, why are they a team leader? Train them up and delegate out.

Before making a cash lift. It's no good removing all large denominations of notes if a till is short on coinage and smaller value notes. Quickly pulling out the same value notes as the change is delivered, is a no brainer. That ten second job after glancing at the till, will prevent running out of change and leave the rest of the larger notes for lifting.

Tip. When lifting a wad of notes from a till, always count the amount there and then. If you have the facility on the till pod to register a cash lift, it will immediately deduct that amount from that till. If you haven't - leave a written note in that tray of how much you've lifted. The note must be intelligible.

Why? If you, or another line manager is called on to do a cash check on that till between then and close of play, it'd be a bit of a shock to find the till four, five or six hundred quid down.

Tip. Already touched upon: do not mix any cash lift with **ANY** other monies. Put it in an envelope or a cash bag. Mark up what till it came from and how much you reckon is within. Throw it in the safe until counting at the end of the day, not before. If you've casually mixed two or three cash lifts in the safe and not recorded amounts or source, you'll be buggered.

Why? Should a discrepancy occur with any count or cash check, you will have no way of checking the amount lifted. Just because you say you lifted £440 from till two, doesn't mean it to be true. If you have an envelope in your safe that you can open and check, it will solve any query fast as.

Voids and No sales

I covered speed of service in relation to no sales and voids in the last chapter, but a tills fundamental roll is simple. It is your very own recording machine. A calculator, mini safe, change provider, a stock controller's best friend, and yes, a tool to assist in the detection of staff on the take. If you have stock loss of any kind and were able to talk to your tills, you might ask them – 'listen gang, I need to find out what the hell is going on here; can you help me please?' I have news . . .

Tills should already provide that service!

An all singing, all dancing, modern till/stock system; should provide all this and a whole lot more. Not being in full control – you might as well be wearing a blindfold. As far as trusting staff is concerned: if you've made good choice in employing a human and trained them properly, there will be times a till might be brimming with notes, and you don't trust them to void an item off? It makes absolutely **NO** common sense.

What then? Ensure there is a facility to measure voids and no sales. If I was to glance at this figure and realise 41 no sales and 17 voids had taken place in one session, I'd probably cardiac arrest there and then. Never mind alarm bells ringing - this is dancing with pixies territory. I'd be checking the audit trail I had in place and exactly who was responsible for said transactions. I'd probably do a full stock take the next morning and build a bloody bonfire, to burn some little shit later in the day. Designated tills and personalising key-fobs, so each server cannot use another till, are the crucial ingredients. Ample supply of change protects speed of service and adds **VALUE** for the customer, revealing the real answer . . .

Accountability from the rear end!

Example of an audit trail

I had a query from a customer about a PDQ (credit card) bill. It was something like £41.25. This guy was a regular midweek visitor and had noticed an irregularity on his bank statement. The same amount had been debited twice on the same day. I asked him the date and told him I would investigate it pronto. I found my copy of his PDQ receipt within 5 minutes. I only found one PDQ receipt for the day in question, which indeed was for £41.25. I then looked at the previous day's PDQ's. Sure enough there was another transaction for exactly £41.25. I then went in to my back office system (computer) and retrieved the sales data from both days trading, scanning five minutes either way of the times recorded on the PDQ receipts. I printed these off, providing the names of the two different servers responsible for those transactions and the exact times of those transactions. I quickly found the customer, explained he had been in on the previous day, who had served him and times he had been served. He promptly apologised and made some joke up about going to see the doctor about his memory. He left happy and continued to be a lovely regular customer.
Lesson. The right tools for the job save much grief all round.

Training scenario

You and all key staff need to be able to count a till within a time frame of three to four minute's tops. What's more, it needs to be completed with supreme accuracy. As part of your training; put a till out with say £511.01 and see how many different totals your gang come up with. Use a stopwatch (included on most smartphones) and time how long it takes. How do you think your team would cope?

End of week

If you haven't the resources to fund the size of house float suggested, you may consider end of week on a Saturday. That way you have Sunday's takings to convert pound coins to notes for banking on a Monday. Banking bags of pound coins is crazy, having possibly been charged for the privilege two days previous. Purely for accounting purposes you'll need an end of week; plus - how else would you **MEASURE** performance?

Long story cut short

Quite honestly, tills do all the adding up, and by definition should be – penny perfect. Only humans destroy that equation. Smooth service relies on efficient management behind the scenes of the monetary supply chain. Accounting for every single penny taken and protecting the house float, is a never ending battle of wits. The more organised you are, the easier it should become. All tasks mentioned should run like clockwork. They are fundamental chores that shouldn't be hard work. If it's hard work – you're doing it wrong. Address hiccups. Methodical it may be, but methodical works. Almost every task involved with money is repetitive, the need for concentration crucial. No wonder the person in charge of the money feels knackered at the end of every shift. Keep as big a house float as you can afford, and as bigger till float as you can stomach. The message I'm trying to hammer home is . . .

Prep your financial tools in the same way you'd prep your kitchen or bar!

One final tip. Never walk away leaving a till draw open. A tray brimming with notes is a visual orgasm to an opportunist thief.

20 THE OFFICE

There are three engine rooms that will drive your business. The first will be you, the other two being your cellar and office. In managed houses there will be a fourth, a mystical home of sorcerers and witchdoctors called – **HEAD OFFICE**.

If your office is a cubby hole with a bigger space available - bloody well move it!

The office **SHOULD** be where you count all the money, work out stock results, do accounts (either by hand or by computer), watch CCTV for any thieving that might be going on, order wet and dry stock, and make business calls that require focus. Ideally the location of your safe, it should be secure and alarmed. All communication lines will be piped into this room. Last but not least – it should always furnish a comfy seat.

Personally. I wanted to have forty thousand volts of electricity rigged to the safe handle, but apparently this facility wasn't available (I'm joking by the way – well mostly). I expect I'd have been burnt to a cinder anyway (terrible memory).

Structure

Advice. An office needs to be clearly organised. Anyone who has to work in that office, should be able to understand where exactly everything is, and where everything should go at a glance. This may be key staff, assistant manager (plural if you're very busy), stock taker, boss, ABM, BDM, auditor and holiday relief. Whichever way you set your office up, shouldn't need a team of code breakers to understand what the hell is going on ok - a clearly organised framework.

Why? An office is your base tool. That tool is the link to a hundred **DIFFERENT** jobs. They'll be important jobs, fundamental in the smooth running of the unit. You'll often need to get in there and get out of there fast.

Tip. Get rid of anything and everything from your office that has no connection with your current needs. Just like your bar, de-clutter the whole space and keep it that way. Everything you'll need on a daily basis should be to hand. If something holds you up, why does it? Deal with that obstacle immediately so it never holds you up again. Start as you mean to go on.

Example. If you run out of a product you swear you had delivered, you'll need to check the invoice. If you walk to your office and after twenty minutes still can't find it, you'll have wasted all that time, become demoralised and **FAILED**. If you enter the office and reach straight for a clipboard where you know you put it, you can get on and check the trail - **EASY**.

Advice. A nice big table area is essential. You'll be counting a lot of tills, room enough to fit all your change containers at the back ready to float the tills as you go. I used to use ex-plastic ice cream containers that were nice and thick and could hold say £200 in 50p's easily. The table mustn't have a lip; you'll need to count coins off it into your hand. Even if you use scales as a rule, there will always be a time you might have to manually count a till, especially if they break down. If there are shelves above the table, safely hang clipboards and bulldog clips for all your weekly data. If you haven't got enough shelving, take whatever crap is on the walls - off. Put some up, you need shelving. I can't remember being given advice of how to set a back office area up. I roughly copied the template of where I was trained in Aldershot. I made the rest up as I gathered more experience and fine-tuned the engine.

You will need clips for the following . . .

- A clip for weeks/period wet invoices in order
- A clip for weeks/period dry (that's food) invoices in order
- A clip for your bank paying in book that always seems to hide itself when needed
- A clip for weeks machine invoices
- A clipboard for the staff rota
- A clipboard for staff hours completed reference wages
- A clip for all house expenses in order
- A clip for all house promotions in order
- Two clips for PDQ keep and send invoices
- A clipboard for daily house safe check book
- Clipboards to house health/safety, fire record sheets
- Any other item unique to your unit

Aim. At the end of each week, most of these clips should be empty, clear and ready to start a fresh week.

End of week envelope. All this information should be placed into an end of week envelope. The envelope should then be marked up with the inclusive dates and stored within the office. You'll need easy access to this envelope.

Why? If there's a query about any past transaction, invoice, or payroll - it should be easy to hand. If a stock taker needs an invoice, you might be paying them by the hour. If it takes ten minutes to find the flaming thing — that'll be a costly ten minutes. Stored on a shelf in order is an easy find.

Measuring performance

Constantly under pressure working too many hours, it's easy to lose track of how things are going. How are you going to notice that when you're tired and beaten up?

Answer. A wall graph in your office. If you can notice at a glance that food sales for example have dropped in the last two weeks, you can investigate. Is there a problem in service standards? Is there a supply issue? Is it a staff issue? Why?

Action. A quick meeting in the kitchen might reveal a hidden problem. All this from a wall graph in your office.

Example. If you notice machine income has been taking a clear and visible slide downwards, you would need to investigate which machines are dragging you down. A quick call to your machine provider could arrange replacements.

Warning. Bear in mind your machine provider may not be able to action this straight away. It may take two weeks to line up and deliver different AWP's. The sooner you notice any downward trend, the sooner you can instigate a solution.

Question. I wonder: how many units have disappeared with no one actually pinpointing clear and obvious misgivings?

Long story cut short

Not being in control of your car travelling at seventy miles an hour means – it **WILL CRASH**. Not being in complete control of your business means – it might well **FAIL**. The office will be your hub. It will hold all the confidential information about your staff, suppliers and financial records. It should remain confidential. It will on occasion, hopefully hold stacks of cash. **NEVER** ever leave your office unlocked. Not for one second, not for one minute. Called away in the middle of counting a till? Put the whole lot back in the till and place it in the safe – for safekeeping. Again – **DON'T** say I haven't warned you.

One last thought. Don't supply keys to the cleaners. Clean it yourself and get rid of spiders – they **WILL** set the alarm off.

21 MACHINES & COLLECTIONS

On entering the trade, I had no idea machine income could be an important slice of the weekly takings . . . Silly me. Just one problem – nothing is simple. However many machines you decide to cram in will all be taking up space. **YOU** will be paying for that space, plus a variety of licences and rental on each machine. Each machine has to pay for itself. Each machine must have a **POSITIVE** effect.

Quick guide

AWP (Amusement With Prize) is basically a gambling machine. They are the cash cow of todays licensed premises. Used correctly, your business will benefit greatly from these alone. They deserve your full attention; learn every facet you can digest. SWP (Skill With Prize) is a machine which may give you a quid or two back if you're bloody clever. Football table, pool table, pinball, any other arcade type machines, will all fall under the banner of machine income. Juke box too, although I have covered this subject extensively in other chapters.

Advice. Before taking on any unit (manager or independent), ask to see records of the historical machine take. What do those records tell you? Is your share in credit or deficit? What has been the trend in the last year? Can you improve the odds?

Managed houses. Will generally contract a single company to supply and maintain all the machines in their units. All the unit manager will have to do is keep an eagle eye on how those machines are performing, possibly liaise with a dedicated machine manager at head office, and sign for the money at the weekly/two weekly collection - easy peasy huh?

An independent. Will need to do homework. Ask several different operators to come and visit you. Get them to totally explain the machine world. Listen carefully for those little gems of information. Ask lots of questions. Make lots of notes.

Pertinent questions

- How do rental prices compare?
- What is the percentage of pay-out **YOU** will receive?
- What is the proposed pay-out to the customer?
- Does the operator take care of all the legal and licence requirements?
- Does the operator supply the latest up-to-date machines?
- If the latest machine is unaffordable, what's next in line?
- If an AWP has a malfunction, or a dispute occurs with a player, how long will it take for an engineer to attend at your premises? Will there be an agreed response time?
- Will there be a person within that company **YOU** can develop a working relationship with?
- Will **THEY** have time to talk to you when you ring and be pro-active in advice and support of you?
- Will it instead be someone different you talk to every time you ring, who has no idea who you are, what your unit even looks like and might not give a damn?

Be careful. A lot like signing up for a mobile phone contract; once you've scribbled on the dotted line, it'll be too late to start moaning about the crap deal **YOU** agreed to. You need the best available deal, offering the best chance of profit. What will be the quality of customer love you can expect to receive? Remember: in this case - **YOU** will be the customer.

Warning. Check you have **ALL** necessary licences to operate **ALL** machines and pay the required duty. If part and parcel of any deal with an operator, check this is so. **COVER YOUR BACK**.

Change

More often than not, machines come equipped to receive and swallow bank notes in several denominations. You'd think this solved the problem of having to carry quite so many pound coins, but beware; most machines will be intelligence programmed. If they run low on pound coins, the note acceptor might turn itself off automatically - ensuring customers only use coins to play. Great theory, but not being geared up with an appropriate in-house float when 'Fruity Frank' arrives next morning, requesting change because the note acceptor has gone in to intelligent mode means - **YOU** might lose 'Fruity Frank' to the betting shop next door. If the note acceptor does stop working, inform an engineer ASAP. It will inevitably hint an adverse effect on takings; perfectly reasonable to request immediate attention. It will nearly always mean; the hopper (bank) is in dire need of coinage.

Remember. You're the customer. If a machine needs topping up with coinage - that's what you pay rental for. The operator may try and pan it out till next collection day. Stand your ground; losing even one customer might prove expensive.

Tip. Spotting 'Fruity Frank' waving a twenty pound note for change, it might be wise to just slip Frankie the coins before the person you had already acknowledged and queued next. It might only take seconds to solve. You could end up with one unhappy **GAMER** pouncing up and down, behind a new customer you've gone to an awful lot of effort to impress.

Take into account. 'Fruity Frank' might also be at a precarious point in his playtime, afraid another gamer might jump the same machine he's just pumped a hundred quid in. Serious gamers can be like spoilt children. It'll all be now, now, now. If it's doable - pile on the customer love.

Measuring performance

Warning. If you notice on the printed dockets the operator leaves on collection day, a particular machine is producing a negative return - it probably means it is losing **YOU** money.

Another equivalent of burning cash!

Tip. Carry out a weekly review of every single machine. Produce a graph. Even a primitive affair will help. Put it where you can't ignore, on your forehead if you need to. Spot any downward trend developing, way before the negative strikes.

Advice. If you need to change a machine ASAP, the operator might try to sell you - it will take weeks to order up the next up to date alternative. Better then, to opt for an interim replacement than leave the shortfall culprit in place. There's a good chance the operator will still be making money, even if **YOU'RE** in the negative zone - you are not a charity.

Get the knowledge. Make sure **YOU** are the one managing your machine income. Manager or independent: get to grips with the essence of machine income. Invest time to understand each aspect. If you don't at least have a basic knowledge of a subject, how the hell are you going to manage it? Just signing for the money doesn't mean you know a rat's ass about machine income. Can you decipher each machine docket? Do you know what every single figure represents?

Example. One of my AWP's showed a minus of nearly £300. Its income had been dropping, but never been in the negative zone. Before I signed for the money, I asked the collector to make a phone call. We had mistakenly been charged nearly £500 for some licence which was refunded two weeks later. The machine should have been £200 in profit.

Can YOU read every single machine docket and recognise anomalies?

Machine money collection

After reading every single figure on every single docket; **WITHOUT EXCEPTION** count **EVERY SINGLE** coin the machine collector leaves you. You will have to sign for the money. Once you've signed, you cannot suddenly claim the collector left you a quid short in various bags. It did happen to me, it could happen to you. Once counted – **NEVER** take your eyes off the money. You simply cannot move until done. Watch like a hawk.

Cash/change machines

If you have one of these, empty it every single night without fail. If the money is left in the machine and you become victim to a break-in – it's just the easiest of targets.

Example. Do you leave the money in overnight and only refill it every few days like I did for three months? I found out quite by accident that I was responsible for the dosh should there be a break in. Five hundred quid to be precise – **WHOOPS!**

Warning. In delegating key staff to refill your cash machine, I suggest it safer to carry out with doors locked before and after trading. Once again – **DON'T** say I haven't warned you.

Machine volume

This will vary in different genres of unit. You should be able to dictate the volume at which each of your machines is set. If the noise of a machine is too loud, it might detract from the image you are trying to project. On the other side of the coin this may completely suit your offer. Just know this is an option.

Pool tables

Never ever Trevor, let any customer at any time, stand a glass of any kind on the lip of a pool table. Have a notice displayed. Your machine operator may be able to supply one - ask them.

Why? When a drink is knocked over, that table will need recovering. YOU might have to pay for this, you might not. Either way, it will cost revenue in the interim until recovered. It will look awful, and be a total lack of control ON YOUR PART.

Showtime. If after asking a customer to remove their glass from a table, they continue to be a pain in the ass, YOU need to become a pain in their arse. There will always be an element of people who think they can do what they want, when and how they want, within the ever more spoilt society we now live. This is still a no-brainer. You are completely justified in asking someone to remove their glass from a pool table. If they give you any attitude whatsoever – BAN THEM! Ban them for life. Believe me, if they give you attitude over something that is plain common sense - YOU do not need THEM in your gaff.

Warning. Being in complete control of your unit and not putting your life at risk will be a dilemma you may face on occasion. Remember though, they'll be holding the pool cue and there exists no real persuasive deterrents in this country for killing or hurting someone really badly. Please STAY SAFE.

Scary. Some of the scariest moments I had in pubs involved pool tables. As I gained more experience, I learnt to handle these moments with more affirmation.

How? Noticing a glass on a pool table, I would berate loudly, so every single person in the pub could hear, 'Would you please remove that glass from the pool table – thank you'. This embarrassed the offender, whilst at the same time somehow diffusing the scene (that's the clean version anyway). I must admit, I probably came across as some kind of psycho, never backing down or backing off - it didn't mean I wasn't scared.

Pool credit notes

You'll need a relationship with your operator that covers refunding the odd quid. They should credit without malice.

Consequences. If not agreed as a matter of goodwill, the customer journey can be reduced to shit. It will mean shutting down that table, taking the punters name and phone number, ringing the engineer to attend – all for a quid. If it's your only table; interrupting the customer journey and breaking that magic spell, the customers might take the sixty quid they would have spent on liquor and pool – somewhere else. **OUCH.** Not only will you lose money, so will the machine operator. It's a give and take situation. Negotiate a working relationship from the start to limit damage. Pay the quid and get a credit.

Warning. Happening regularly by the same customers, they'll more likely be taking the piss – out of **YOU**. This will spoil trust built with your pool operator – too many claims a bad recipe.

Have you trained your bartenders to recognise a problem in the making?

White ball stuck?

If the white ball does get stuck in a table, do not let a customer lift one end of the table - only to drop it in the expectation this will magically solve the problem.

Why? There is a slate underneath the cloth that is quite expensive. If you don't think this can break, take your head out of your arse and listen up folks – it **CAN** and **WILL**.

YOU might well have to pay for replacement!

Advice. When you spot some idiot picking up one end of your pool table - feel free to shout at the top of your voice, why it would be a very bad idea to drop that bloody table. It may well save you a few bob, once again preserving what might up until then have been a good relationship with your pool operator.

Tip. Eliminate, by carrying spare white balls behind the bar.

Rip off merchants

Be wary of groups around machines, they may be robbing it. They might be trying to stop **YOU** seeing **THEM** up to no good.

Advice. Ask your machine engineer/technician to give you the lowdown on current tactics used against their machines. If that doesn't work, speak to that person who promised you could ring them, **ANYTIME**, **ANYTIME**. Your operator will have a vested interest in any money stolen from machines they have on your site. They should be more than helpful. If you're a manager; ask pertinent questions of your appointed machine manager, or indeed ask colleagues at the next available area meeting for tips and advice. You may be surprised at some of the antics and methods used by robbing little shits.

Machine claims

There should always be someone on duty, fully trained to deal with problems arising from machine hiccups.

Example. A customer approaches the counter complaining the AWP he's just pumped the best part of a hundred quid into, won't pay him out the eighty five quid it's now displaying. This customer has chosen to throw his hard earned money into one of more of your machines. You've already succeeded in the main part, in winning them almost as a prize yourself. Gamers don't usually drink an awful lot; they're just there for the thrill. They deserve the respect you would pay to anyone willing to spend a hundred quid. At least they're not falling all over the floor wanting to fight the bouncers at the end of it.

How? After listening intently to the customer, inspect the machine and take note of what is displayed. Immediately ring your machine helpline. If you have a wireless pub phone, you can do this standing right next to the machine and customer, displaying direct action on their behalf. The helpline should take control of the machine aspect at that point. Follow their instructions closely. Remember, **YOU** are their customer. **THEY** should be trained up to the fact that - **YOU** will already be suffering from sleep deprivation, stress from staff not turning in and will more than likely have some gamer staring at you like they want to dig your eyes out with a spoon.

The customer. Inform directly of what will happen next. You may be advised to turn the machine off; an engineer to attend within a given time. Take their mobile phone number. Promise to ring them when the engineer arrives and is still on site. Ask them if they would like a tea or coffee on the house. Do not forget to ring them - that would be unforgiveable.

Validity. If it be a genuine claim, the customer will have done nothing wrong. Therefore, **YOU** must do all you can to repair the damage - even if a customer is irate. As long as they're not threatening bodily harm, you've got to expect a certain degree of unhappiness from their end. Customers in this state will deserve your patience up until the point they don't. I'll leave you to decide what that line in the sand is.

Beware! Same scenario, but not a genuine claim. The world is full of scumbags. Just like rats, there'll be one near you.

Showtime. If you've already spotted a fraudulent allegation, still deal in a professional manner. Ring the helpline and request an engineer attend – it will still require investigation. Do not appear condescending or matter of fact. Kill them with kindness. Cover your back (you can always be sick in a bucket once they've gone). Take their mobile. When you have the engineers report, ring them back later with the bad news. I used to worry like hell about awkward situations. Should I just have paid that fella the fifty quid, he seemed so genuine.

AAAAAGGGGGHHHHH!

What a load of old bollocks. By the time I moved in to my fourth unit, I could spot a tealeaf at a thousand yards. If it does turn out to be bogus, it will go away all by itself. You won't know it, but as soon as that individual walks out your door, they'll have moved on to their next target. When you ring to inform them the engineer couldn't find a single thing wrong, they'll struggle to even remember who they're talking to.

> **Unless an engineer leaves you a credit note – you DO NOT refund any money whatsoever – GOT IT!**

Positioning and switched on?

Are expensive to rent machines in the optimum position? Are they accessible to players 100% of time, or are they where a live act sets up, preventing use pre, during and after performance. If live music nights are busy, preventing use is a form of self-harm. Also; when preparing to open, make sure every machine is switched on. You won't even pay the rent on a machine - if the delegated person is half asleep at the wheel.

Staff usage of machines

One sure fire method of alienating gamers; is for the landlord, after watching 'Fruity Frank' throw ninety quid away – to wander over, bung in a fiver and walk away with fifty quid. Most of these selfish arrogant bastards will have no idea the damage done with such behaviour. Unless they've the training of a cold war spy, that knowledge will not stay secret for long. Firstly, the dim shit might actually be bragging to regulars. They in turn, might be casual users who make up a big slice of weekly machine cake. They might think twice before slotting that odd quid left in their pocket in the future. Secondly, the news always carries to serious gamers in the end – a big loss.

Story. I witnessed a bartender literally running over to an AWP, as a chap whom must have pushed in at least £200 left the building, probably to jump off the nearest bridge. This guy left customers waiting at the bar whilst he put in about a tenner. Consequently the machine spewed out at least a hundred quid. Three customers walked out, tired of waiting.

AAAAAGGGGGHHHHH!

Solution. Ban **ALL** staff from using AWP's. Machines are for **CUSTOMERS**. You gain revenue; let customers enjoy the thrills.

Clean machines

Clean and polish all your expensive toys daily. Shiny machines are attractive to the eye. Remove another obstacle.

Long story cut short

Taking machine income for granted is arrogant and lazy. Simply switching them on and signing for the money won't cut it. Of course the money is important. I would bet that many bars and clubs only survive through machine income, but . . .

Machine income should be the icing on the cake - not a shoulder to cry on!

Every dog and his duck seems to have a machine of some kind plonked in the trading area. From fish shops to café's, machine arcades, coffee shops and what seems to be the biggest predator – the flaming betting shop. What can you offer that all these can't? Why should they choose to play in your house? There is only one way to increase machine income.

Put the customer #1

Of course bartenders need to be switched on to what makes machine users click. They need to be alert and able to tune-in and tune bloody out when need be. But, putting the customer #1 for **ALL** customers, not just gamers - will improve footfall. Improving footfall will inadvertently increase machine income. The only way to achieve that, is recruiting the right personnel in the first place and targeted on-going training by a highly motivated coach (that's you by the way). Machine wise; a healthy relationship with your operator will certainly help oil the wheels. If you're doing well, it's in their interest too.

Success breeds success!

22 STOCK & ORDER BOOK

What's the point?

Question. Do you have a photographic memory?

Why? Whether or not you are blessed with such a gift, can I suggest the merits of a stock and order book?

Why? Checking through my diaries, I realised I'd kept a daily hours worked record from early on. Monday to Wednesday inclusive, the average hours worked was thirty six. That's in the quietest three days, including my supposed day off. A photographic memory won't prevent tiredness and mistakes. Your time will be precious. It should be easy to walk round the cellar and spirit store compiling the week's wet order, in preparation for a phone call or transfer by computer. If it's not easy – you're doing it wrong. A stock and order book is the vehicle and point of reference to boot.

Make it easy. Line physical stock in the cellar and bottle store to match the stock and order book (or vice versa); thus being able to walk along a line, product by product, eliminating travelling corner to corner in pursuit of stock.

Example. In your spirit store, set your product page up as you look at them from left to right. I can't tell how easy this job becomes, once you've done a bit of moving around and writing sheets out. Your time is valuable, be organised.

Example. Write your keg/barrels list as they are laid out in your cellar. From left to right, it couldn't be easier.

Suggestion. If you have a computerised stock system, is it possible to duplicate the product list with the way your physical stock is stored? Think out of the box and simplify.

Stock & order book

Think of an A4 ring binder with a product card inserted at the front on the left hand side. All products will be listed down this card, a smaller column on the right of that card indicating how many cases/barrels you would normally stock to prevent running out of this product. This is your **ORDER TO** figure. A sheet placed underneath will have two columns (S) and (O) to record each consecutive order. Write the date on top of that.

Example. On the morning of your wets supplier weekly phone call, haul yourself into the cellar and bottle store area. Mark down in the stock column (S), how many unopened cases/barrels/individual spirit bottles you have left in stock (not including stock in fridges, shelves, or optics on the bar). Comparing this with your **ORDER TO** figure on the product card, will determine how many cases/barrels/individual spirit bottles you need for the coming week. This becomes your **ORDER** figure, duly written in the column (O).

Tip. Make sure you do your order – after you've bottled up and not before. You need a line in the sand.

Example. If you've two cases of mick's bottled lager left unopened in the cellar, your **ORDER TO** figure normally being ten; you'll need at least another eight to make sure you don't run out by the same time next week. You order eight cases.

Example. There are four unopened 1.5 litre bottles of vodka left in your spirit store. Your **ORDER TO** figure is twenty four. Therefore, you've got through twenty 1.5's of vodka this week. You might order twenty 1.5's or four cases of six.

Warning. Be careful not to order twenty cases instead of twenty individual 1.5's. Stipulate exactly what you require if it's a phone order. An expensive mistake – it happens.

Example of product card and order sheet

Product card ↓   Order sheet ↓

Product	Order to figure	S	O	S	O	S	O	S	O
Lager 22's	10	3	7						
Vodka 1.5ltr	24	6	18						

Spotting trends

As well as making ordering easy, there is a bonus. By quickly glancing back at ordering behaviour; glitches or spikes in sales of particular products - should stick out like a sore thumb.

Example. If you have no stock left of Micks bottled lager, other than a few left in fridges on the bar, it will require changing the **ORDER TO** figure to a larger quantity. This might creep up on you over a few weeks. The ability to re-evaluate and run with a positive trend, is like having your finger on the trigger. Do not run out of a key product, losing valuable trade **YOU** have successfully developed and failed to notice.

Overstocking. By the same token, you need to identify a drop in sales of products. Negate the chances of being left with loads of stock you can't get rid of. A stock and order book can act as an early indicator for a tired human. Being left with dozens of out of date product isn't that appealing.

Example. Identifying a non-selling product you've eight cases of, plus another two dozen on the bar all close to their best before date, can be a costly affair. You'll need at least to retrieve any money laid out for that stock - and fast.

Action. If the bottles cost you a pound including VAT, with a normal selling price of three pounds; as long as you have a reasonable amount of time, put them on a promotion for half price - two for the price of one. If you've only got a week it'll be panic time. Sell them off at a pound a piece and get shot.

Consequences. It will produce an adverse effect on any future stock result, dragging your GP down in the process.

To rectify. When promoting this offer, ask bartenders to print off a receipt on every sale of said item. Claim the difference in monetary value as a promotion, in theory protecting both GP and stock. Managers would need permission to undertake this course of action. Persuading staff to print off a receipt every time is no easy task however. Good luck with that.

Long story cut short

Managed houses should have the ordering structure down to a tee. If you're new to the trade; a well thought-out stock and order book, matching how your cellar and bottle store is laid out - is a no brainer. If nothing else, it really is the quickest method of composing your weekly order.

P.S. If you lose your delivery sheet, at least you'll know what was ordered and when it was ordered. Hallelujah - It happens.

Running out of any product is unforgivable. Done right - a stock and order book should put paid to that.

23 WET DELIVERIES

What's it worth?

Scenario. You go to the bank for a car loan and borrow ten grand. Loan approved, a bank clerk enters and presents you with ten thousand pounds in crisp twenty pound notes.

Question? Do you count it before leaving?

Answer. You bet your life you do. Every single note until completely satisfied. You'll sign in receipt and hope in hell the **PUB** you're taking on (car what car?) is worth it.

Point. Let's say for example you make a 100% mark up on all your stock. A smallish unit turning over 6K a week would mean deliveries amounting to 3K a week on average. That stock will be worth six grand to you, not the three you pay for it. Checking the quantity and quality of the produce, is not only fundamental, but vital in your ability to gain maximum **YIELD**.

Tip. Do not mix the new stock in with the old, until you've got the whole delivery in, checked it with a fine toothed comb and are completely confident of signing the delivery docket.

Why? Once you have signed that docket, there will be no disputing any missing cases, barrels, or 1.5ltr bottles of spirits.

You won't have a bloody leg to stand on!

Advice. **NEVER** leave the cellar during a delivery for **ANY** reason. Whether it's your boss, the Pope and the President of the United States, in a car driven by the English Prime Minister dropping in for a pub lunch – they'll have to frigging wait. With all due respect to delivery teams: would you leave six grand in cash with someone you might never have met, whilst you pop to the loo? It just wouldn't happen - **HUMAT**.

Tip. Purchase a cordless digital phone system for the unit. If there is an important call you **MUST** take, a member of staff can bring the phone to you. You can still watch proceedings.

Tip. Check every spirit bottle, even in unopened cases. There could be broken product within, the box having dried out. You can usually hear the tell-tale sound of broken glass crunching.

Tip. Always wear protective gloves to move barrels and cases. Premium service at the bar; does not mix well with blood, cuts and plasters. Wash hands afterwards - gloves tend to smell.

Tip. If draymen are inserting barrel's in position for you, ask them (if you have room) to leave a foot between the old stock and the new. In the event of you wanting one last check, it might just provide a moment of clarity. Move them up later.

Tip. I got in to the habit of counting for reference, all the barrels I physically had - before the dray arrived.

Why? It's so easy to lose focus during a delivery. There are a hundred and one things to distract. On several occasions I almost had a panic attack, believing I'd been short changed an eleven gallon keg, or a twenty two of lager – simply horrible.

Tip. Do not unlock the spirits store and add the new stock until the bird has flown. Keep your eye on the game.

Advice. Always be friendly to your draymen/women. Offer tea or a staff squash afterwards, a bad back can strike at any time.

Long story cut short

For those new to the trade, think of this like any home delivery from your supermarket – except a shitload more valuable.

SECURITY, SECURITY – think of your delivery as wads of cash!

24 CELLAR MANAGEMENT

Strong advice

Don't even dream of taking on licensed premises without attending an in-depth cellar management course. You would have to be brain dead to contemplate commencing the trade without this knowledge. Read as many books as you like, it still won't be as effective as taking a course real time.

Tip. Make sure that course is based within a working cellar, or at least a simulated scenario. Find a course with **NOT** too many pupils at one time, six to a dozen tops. You'll need to get hands on. You'll need to ask as many questions as it takes. How will you do that if there's forty candidates all vying for attention?

Please. Don't just let your uncle (who runs a pub the other side of town) show you how to change a barrel and the gas, then walk away thinking - 'that was easy.'

AAAAAGGGGGHHHHH!

Of course a recognised qualification with a certificate hanging on the wall is advantageous. What really matters is the ability and the knowledge, for you and your team to work efficiently and safely within the cellar. For you in particular, to maximise performance of what is in effect – your very own engine room.

Not only do you need at least the basic knowledge, you need to fully understand that basic knowledge. No, you can't possibly know it all straight off, but yes you will pick the rest up as you go along - usually learning from mistakes that lose **YOU** money, or from equipment malfunctions. An efficient organised cellar is the infrastructure that will drive front of house, joined by its own umbilical cord – literally.

It can be a trifle intimidating viewing a series of lines, pumps and the deafening noise of the cooling fans for the first time, but . . .

Don't be afraid of the cellar.

Must have basic knowledge

- **How to change a barrel/keg.** Covering **ALL** the different types of fitting for the products you plan to sell.
- **How to manage and harvest cask ales.** I would advise attending a specific course for this alone. If you're serious about providing cask ales, it will save you money in stock loss and enable delivery of products that actually present and taste like they're supposed to.
- **How to change the gas.** Safely for **ALL** products
- **Co2.** How to store and secure gas bottles safely.
- **How to change the bag in a box.** Syrup product.
- **Find out the correct cellar temperature.** When you see staff pouring a lager with a head they can't seem to quell; it may be the lines are dirty, maybe the gas pressure is wrong, or it may be a sign that the cold room where the barrels live is way too warm. If the temperature is incorrect, it will lose **YOU** money all day long.
- **Health and safety.** Cover your flaming back. Cover the employee's back. Find out all the relevant posters you need to legally display in your cellar. What training needs to take place for an employee to legally be allowed in the cellar? What risk assessments need to be undertaken?
- **Cellar security.** Look at all aspects of securing products.
- **Alarms.** What alarms are required to ensure your safety?
- **Line cleaning.** How the hell do I do that?

Change the locks

Manager or independent. If I was taking over any licensed premises, I would immediately on accepting the keys and the stock - change the lock on the cellar door, spirit store and any padlocks on any access gate. This stock will now be **YOUR** responsibility, and frankly – **WHY** take the risk? How many people have had access to those keys before you? Add this cost to any business plan. **DON'T** say I haven't warned you.

Keys. The thing about keys is, you'll lose them all the frigging time. It will be the bane of your life. I've spent hours looking for keys, again probably reducing my life expectancy. Do yourself a favour; designate a little hiding place within the cellar to place those keys until you leave. Put them in the same place every time – it'll save you hours and hours.

Warning. When entering the cellar, if you need to lock the door behind you for security, inform staff where you are going. Have a spare key with a trusted member of staff, in case you have an accident within the cellar whilst the door is locked.

It may save your life!

Tip. Never take the cellar keys out of the unit. How in God's name will **ANY** of your staff gain access to change a barrel, or the gas, when **YOU** have disappeared up town for the whole afternoon? One last thought about keys . . .

Never ever leave the cellar unlocked!

Stock management

As broached in the last chapter: match the layout of your cellar and bottle store products, with either the stock and order book, line check menu, or both if possible. Why wouldn't you?

Cold room

Place **TWO** thermometers in the keg/barrel area. From bitter experience, one thermometer led me a merry dance for about two weeks, till I finally realised the damned thing was kaput. I thought I was losing my mind, not to mention the amount of lager I was losing at the pump; the room running a few degrees the wrong direction. Cheap as chips – an easy check solution.

Hose down

Do yourself another favour - **DO NOT** buy a cheap hose for the cellar, it will continually crease in several places and you'll end up wanting to ring a psychiatric help line. Hose down the cellar every single day. Keep the smell neutral, the lingering stench of dried stale drink is a trade killer. Make sure the sump pump is working as it should be in the drain. If not, **WHY NOT?**

Clean! Clean! Clean!

First in first out

Another reason to keep new stock separate on delivery, relates to best before dates and your own in-house supply chain. First in first out, doesn't just apply to what you place on the bar, it applies to every product you store. Upon delivery, you can't just throw cases on top of existing stock. You might think you're being efficient, but this caper can only end in tears. Finding out the case on the bottom went of date six months previous, will be down to lazy management – **ON YOUR PART**.

Example. You have one case of Micks lager left. Move the one case away and put the four cases you've had delivered in its place. Replace the one old case back on top of the four new ones, thus ensuring – **FIRST IN, FIRST OUT** of the cellar.

Bag in a box

If you use syrup boxes, insist double boxes are fitted to each product. When empty, it will automatically change itself.

Penalty. Failing to do this will cause an interruption to customer service when a box runs out. It will remove a staff member from service to change the box, possibly leaving a customer waiting for their top up (taking for granted the possibility there is anyone available who actually knows how to change the bloody thing). A daily check of the boxes will ensure you never run out on a busy session. If you're getting through more than one box a night, you'll probably be in the Bahamas on permanent holiday anyway - hallebloodylujah.

Stock loss. As a box runs out and you're adding mixer to a vodka; it might still be working visually to you, but when the customer sits down to enjoy their vodka and whatever - it'll taste like **SHIT**. You will have to replace and apologise profusely, damaging reputation and losing valuable stock.

Remove the obstacle. Fit double boxes to ALL syrups and check daily!

Gas supply

If you use CO2 bottles; same as bag in a box, have double bottles fitted. The moment you realise the pressure on the pumps is dropping; a quick visit to the cellar, opening the valve on a new bottle and pushing the lever across, will again be a quick fix (may or may not apply to you). Make sure every bottle stood up is chained to the wall without exception. All spares on the floor should be chocked each side to prevent movement.

Safety first, even in a rush!

Backcovering

Bleed valve. When changing a barrel, you'll have to fill a chamber on the wall relevant to that barrel, with product from the new barrel. You do this via a bleed valve. If you forget to turn that valve back afterwards – the whole barrel will bleed over the floor and down your drain. I did it once. Seven years later a staff member did it. Both times, I nearly **SHIT** myself.

Accidents. Keep passageways and walkways completely clear of any debris and obstacles. The last thing you want is being taken to court for a fat slice of compensation. It takes an awful lot of backbone to enforce, but clean as you go is fundamental.

Protocol. If really organised, create and tailor your own cellar protocol list and hang it on the wall - in the cellar.

Spare bulbs. Keep spare bulbs for every single fitting in the cellar. Don't store these somewhere else in the unit, keep within the cellar. If the strip light in your cold room has gone, reaching for the new one stored on a shelf is an easy fix. You'll have to do it imminently, so just get on with it. It could prevent an accident - that really would be a poke in the eye.

Freezers. Many cellars have enough space to contain food storage freezers; keep these locked at all times. Apart from the security aspect, it will ensure the flipping thing is definitely shut once you've finished in it. It might save you a freezer full of stock thawing overnight through negligence. It might just save you the odd bag of chips being transported to a staff member's house. How trusting am I? It happened to me.

Tech services. Keep a list of all relevant phone numbers in the cellar as well as the office. Identifying a problem is better dealt with immediate effect. Make the list intelligible; it may be a relief having to call, make it an **EASY** solve.

Cask ale

It may cost to enrol in a quality course, but it will cost you a fortune in stock if you don't. Cask ale is a great product, but if not treated with the respect it demands and needs - you'll end up getting your ass kicked really badly.

Just one tip. If you develop a problem pulling cask ale through to the bar, don't just pick the barrel up **THINKING** it might be empty; dip with a measuring stick first. I quickly learnt the hard way on that one and lost at least half a barrel by **THINKING** it empty. Measure before and never assume.

Cleaning the lines

If you're lazy and don't clean the valuable supply lines to dispensers; products they emit, will themselves start to taste like shit. On a Friday night, a boozer packed to the rafters thinking to yourself; how clever you are to have got away with this time wasting, stock losing chore for two weeks now, is I suggest - **NOT** the wisest decision. Various automated cleaning systems are available now. If you have to carry it out manually like I did, get someone to show you who is qualified to do so. There are **NO** short cuts and it takes an age. Done wrong, it could end up with a double page spread in the local rag; how your customers ended up in hospital – **BLOODY HELL**.

Example. I had a pint of cider recently and could taste the cleaning fluid from obviously newly cleaned lines. I was very happy to know that the lines in this boozer were being cleaned, but not that impressed having to taste the evidence.

AAAAAGGGGGHHHHH!

Tip. If there exists a course on cleaning lines – take it. If there isn't, could someone please design one? A fundamental must.

Tip. Before taking on **ANY** existing business, find out the state of the supply lines and cold room cooler's. Ask to see relevant historic invoices. Who has been looking after this equipment in recent years? Secure names and numbers. Speak to these people. Get the dirt on two vital pieces of expensive kit.

Warning. The last thing you want, is finding out three days after you've signed a ten year lease; the lines need completely replacing and the coolers have seen better days. Is this down to you? Even if it isn't, you may find it a long slog persuading the brewery, or company responsible to shell out thousands of pounds after the event (nigh on impossible). All the while, **YOU** could be losing a stack load of product, cash and regular customers whilst problems persist; leaving you loading up another credit card and a fresh prescription of Prozac.

Advice. Knowledge gained pre-signing any binding contract, could give the leverage needed for an altogether better deal. Independent's in particular; find out your-self what needs sorting. Don't trust an ABM, BDM or whatever they call themselves telling you everything's hunky dory. I suspect all **THEY'LL** be interested in at that stage, is how much bonus **THEY** might be receive when - **YOU** sign on the dotted line.

It'll be too late then!

Long story cut short

Think of the cellar as the engine room that drives the conveyor belt. If the engine only fires on two cylinders instead of four, the products you deliver will suffer before you've had a chance to work some magic at the other end. Invest in quality training vehicles; the greater the knowledge - the smoother the ride. Above all, make it safe for all employees – **DO THE TRAINING**.

25 STOCK CONTROL

If I arrived to train you on stocktaking and found no EPOS (Electronic Point Of Sale) system, invariably linked to a BOS (Back Office System) for monitoring stock and transactions; the first thing I'd do is tie you to a chair, gag you, walk casually over to the till, take five twenty pound notes and set light to them – I'm pretty sure I'd get your full attention.

Tied and gagged? You may as well be. You'll have no way of confirming if the stock you physically consume on a daily basis matches the income derived from the sales you register.

Why burn the money? No controls, bar a yearly visit from a stock taker in conjunction with yearly accounts, is equivalent to driving a car with a blindfold on. You could literally be burning money all day long and be totally unaware. Understanding stock loss provides opportunity to make good any leaks in the bucket. No control severely restricts indication of any repair needed. No repair will lead to **BIGGER** holes. Even a fairly ordinary EPOS/stock system is an investment. It will **MAKE** you money by detecting loss. And before any bright spark asks . . . No I haven't got shares in an EPOS related company.

Aim. To police stock and maximise revenue.

Example. If a bottle of lager costs you a £1 to buy inclusive of VAT and you currently sell it for £3; losing one will cost three quid in cash and a pound to replace the stock - four flaming quid on one little bottle. If you pay £1.50 inclusive for a pint of lager wholesale and sell it for £4.00, **YOU** will lose five pound fifty if the barman slips their mate a freebie.

How will you know if this is going on?

Easy answer. You probably won't - unless you have a mechanism in place to track stock going walkies. An independent new to the trade, may be more worried about how much they will actually **TAKE** this weekend, than how much stock they might lose. In total contrast; an organised managed estate will of course be targeting sales, but in the same breath be identifying stock loss in whatever form it may reveal itself, solving issues on a daily basis. Whilst one business is working double hard, seemingly shedding stock without indication, the other will steam along, gaining momentum, gears to spare. The essence of stock control to identify loss.

Accumulation of stock loss in a smallish unit

Example. If you're doing between six and eight grand a week, that'll still equate to a fair few 22's of lager. It's very easy to get into the position of losing eight or nine gallons a week. I frequently watch staff pouring lager with too much head. What do they do? They pour and pour until eventually attaining a visually sellable product - another half a pint in the drip tray.

AAAAAGGGGGHHHHH!

Where does that lager in the drip tray go? Down the bloody sink I expect. If you're not around to clock what's going down, then lose you will. You may be paid for the pint you sell, but what about the half a pint in the drip tray? If that half pint cost you a quid wholesale and you charge two on the bar, any profit on the pint sold alongside is largely cancelled out.

> You're not only losing the stock - you're losing its worth!
> Are you getting the picture?

Also. You might have a tealeaf on board feeding mates the odd couple of lagers, not charging for mixers, or dishing a double for the price of a single - a **VERY DIRTY TRICK**.

Also. You might have a clever bastard who tops up their wages by at least twenty quid in cash every session they work. I call these people – one for me, one for you merchants.

Also. I've watched staff drinking softies all afternoon straight from the gun. This is probably one of the most profitable items you'll be selling and therefore cause **YOU** great expense.

Consequence. Eight gallons of lager a week (from one single product), a hundred quid in cash by not ringing it in, fifty quid in freebies and staff consuming free stock items is probably in the region of £450 a week. Not to mention; ullage in drip trays from all the other pumps, line cleaning, genuine breakages, wrong products poured and the guvnor drinking their regulation eight pints on a Sunday night without seemingly **EVER** ringing sod all in the till.

Armageddon. Suddenly you're losing five to six hundred quid a week without actually having any idea it's really happening. Thinking sensible, or just desperate; an independent struggling to pay rent every week might opt to cancel their three monthly stock take, pushing it to six months instead. At the end of that long awaited stock take, the stock taker will sit there at their laptop scratching their head and duly inform your loss of roughly thirteen thousand quid – consternation abound.

AAAAAGGGGGHHHHH!

Failing to implement a system putting you in total control of stock, relegates you to being buried whilst still actually breathing. Understanding that system may be a big ask, but for me it's a no brainer. No one said this was easy did they?

Efficiency. This issue highlights the difference between a professional managed house and an independent having a bash at their dream job. If a managed house can prevent stock loss to a major degree, they'll already have a head start before the off. This is just one issue. Take into account all the other important facets of running licensed premises. How far behind is the sole operator before the starting whistle blows? I'm not trying to put you off, these are hard truths. Learn fast and box clever. You need to know the facts before stumbling in to either a career move, or a determined financial gamble. Of course you're not going to be an expert at stock taking, the cellar, or any other aspect of the licensed trade, but hopefully reading all this will deliver the heads up on issues that might have taken you years to pick up.

Personally. It took me at least five years to begin some joined up thinking. I was the hardest worker, but crap at delegation. You actually need some staff to be able to delegate. That means raising turnover. Raising turnover is punishing on the brain and body, but with stamina, commitment and a few ideas - you can raise the bar. Without knowing what was happening to my stock, I'd have been on a hiding to nothing.

What does the ability to line check give me?

After adding all deliveries into your BOS (back office system, otherwise known as an in-house stock program linked to every transaction on the tills), EPOS will automatically subtract each item from your stock as it is sold.

Example. A barrel of lager runs out in the cellar. This provides perfect opportunity to line check a keg product. There will be no arguing the toss about how much you estimate is left. The barrel is empty at that point - it's a line in the sand.

Action. After checking barrels left in the cellar, of which you find four 22's, you spark up the BOS and tell the system you have 88 gallons left in stock. If all your deliveries are entered into this system, the BOS will deliver a perfect result of either a loss or a gain on this lager. It might indicate you are 0.7 of a gallon up overall. In laymen's terms, this means seven pints up. If this is the result after three months and you clean your lines once a week losing three pints per week in the process - that would be a bloody marvellous result and a pat on the back. If you're 11.3 down, that's a loss of 91 pints – you're in the shit.

Cumulative loss

Go to the bar. Order three hundred and sixty four pints of lager and line them up. Pay the thirteen hundred odd quid and instruct the staff to throw them down the sink.

This would officially brand you as stark raving bonkers wouldn't it?

This is the damage losing 7 pints a week of only one single product can do to your business in the space of a year. Oh and by the way, this doesn't take into account replacing that stock.

AAAAAGGGGGHHHHH!

Last time I looked, it was a legal requirement to fill a pint with no less than 95% of liquid – the rest being froth (that's a head start - pardon the pun). Taking into account weekly line cleaning; a quality, not illegal head gain, should always achieve a plus result on most keg products, as long as you eliminate loss. The better the training, the more you sell, the better the gain. Just recently I've discovered keg cider with not only a head, but a long lasting head – another obstacle overcome.

Prime examples of stock loss

1. Disaster. The lager goes. The first you get to know about it is when the dispenser explodes at the bar with froth and gas. This will probably lose the drink you were pouring and at least another pint once the barrel has been changed, after pulling the lager back through of unusable product - **AT LEAST!**

How and why does this happen? As a keg of lager runs dry, the chamber (FOB) sitting above the barrel should empty. Inside that chamber will be a floating plug. As the chamber finally empties, the plug should fall neatly into place cutting the line off dead. The supply line should remain full of beer instead of filling with foam. Off to the cellar, change the barrel and refuel the chamber (remembering to turn the bleed valve off afterwards – or else you could lose the whole barrel). The plug in that chamber will sometimes rise of its own accord, but normally have to be released manually by **YOU**. Manipulating a lever on the chamber, the plug will then rise out of its resting place and float back to the top of the chamber until the next time. Before returning to the bar, there will be one last job . . .

You have to manually reset the FOB!

Failure to reset - means the next time a barrel goes, it will NOT cut the beer line off automatically. It will instead - drag whatever's left in the barrel through the line at incredible pressure - as a foamy nuisance. It will forcibly explode . . .

All over the server on the bar!

On the cellar course you **ARE** going to take; ask as many questions as it takes for you to understand the whys and wherefores of the **FOB** – it might well pay for the bloody course ten times over! There are some half decent videos on social media – **WATCH THEM ALL!**

2. Communication. Staff experiencing problems pouring a product, where the head is out of control and not passing this information to management - **IS** head up my ass territory (**HUMAT**). Not only are you in a stock loss situation, speed of service will be interrupted. Unless truly telepathic, train **ALL** staff to communicate pouring problems as a matter of urgency.

3. Theft. Detecting stock loss on a particular product would alert my suspicion to a host of possibilities . . .

Example. Which of your talented crew drink this particular brand of poison? Keep an eagle eye as to what is happening when these people are on duty. Do they seem to stay at the end of their working hours and drink the seven pints they claim were bought them in their three hour stint?

AAAAAGGGGGHHHHH!

Warning. If you think this doesn't happen – **THINK AGAIN!**

4. Scum. If losing stock: how many no sales or voids happen during each day's trading? Narrow it down to specific sessions. Who is working those sessions? Who deals the no sales? What system do you have in place to identify individuals? What is the total value of voids carried out by your team on a daily basis?

Are they pocketing the cash?

Deal in the dark. It might not be prudent to make them aware by stopping no sales and voids.

You'll need to catch the little shits!

Set a trap. Upon identifying the problem, send in someone not known in the bar to catch them red handed. Mark the notes you give your mate to pay for drinks. Match it up with CCTV and get the evidence. What you do then is up to you.

Warning. Before accusing anyone be - **110% SURE**.

5. Staff drinks. What is your policy? Are staff entitled to specific drinks they're bought that session? How do you know they've definitely been bought that particular drink? Do you let those drinks be carried over to their night off? Do they print off a receipt every time they're bought a drink for claiming later?

AAAAAGGGGGHHHHH!

I've worked all the possible equations concerning staff drinks. Unfortunately, in nearly all of them you're wide open to abuse.

Reminder. These people are coming to work aren't they?

Example. Working in a supermarket, you don't get to the end of your eight hours, casually walk up to the drinks aisle and grab the four pack of cider you claim was bought for you by a customer at 7.15 that morning - it just **DOESN'T** happen.

On the other side of the coin. Staff working late evenings is by nature a tad more unsociable, this is the hospitality trade after all. I would actively promote staff accepting drinks. Many customers would view this as a given. All genuine sales help oil the wheels don't they?

Warning. Drinks should **NEVER** be carried over full stop.

Find a system that works, with penalties for abuse. If you want to show gratitude to staff at the end of a really busy night, just pour a round of drinks, ring through the till, print a receipt and claim it back as a promotion. Check with your accountant for viability. A manager might not be allowed this facility, so if up on a particular product - that's what you offer. Manage it.

The moment you put in place a leaky staff drinks policy will mean exactly that - leaky.

Whatever policy you impose, make sure it's BULLETPROOF!

6. Recording loss. Breakages behind the bar occur. You **MUST** have a book to monitor loss, including the total amount in drip trays. If one specific drip tray has a couple of pints in every night, that's a big hole in a bucket; it would stick out like a sore thumb to me. How many times has that been emptied down the sink that day? When a stock taker informs you of a loss, at least you can explain some of it away, learning lessons as you go. No record – no explanation - no lesson learnt.

7. Over pouring. Even products that appear to pour perfectly, I watch staff over-pour - **ALL** the time. In the smallest of boozers to gigantic managed houses. In wine bars, social clubs, sports clubs, hotels - it's all I can do to prevent myself from leaping over the bar shouting at the top of my voice.

Stop . . . Stop . . . Please stop!

How does this happen? Often, a lack of concentration. Some pour the perfect pint, only for the customer to watch a perfect head disappear over the side of the glass, as the server takes their eye off the ball. Wine way over the line printed on the glass. Way too much spirit mixed in to a cocktail making it too strong to taste, not worth serving at the new reduced level of profit. Not only is this lazy, but bloody irresponsible.

AAAAAGGGGGHHHHH!

The next time someone remarks to you that anybody can pour a pint, do me a favour and put them right – **THEY CAN'T**.

Who's to blame? More than probably **YOU**. You have to train people properly to pour a pint, or any other product for that matter. If you haven't spent sufficient time chaperoning staff, training and continually monitoring what's actually happening real time - you'll be the one scratching your head looking at a stock result, wondering what the hell's going on.

Personally. I don't believe staff intentionally set out each day to see how much money they can lose. **YOU** need to supply **THEM** with the skills **THEY** need to do a good job. You also need to fully explain **WHY** you should do it like this, and the consequences of not; once again - **TEACH** not **TELL**. The art of pouring product comes down to how well you have trained each bartender live in situ, no book can teach you all that. I didn't plan to parp on about all this stuff in the stock control chapter, but in essence, this is what stock control is all about - 100% of stock returning 100% of the selling price.

Erasing loss can transform your business!

8. Flat pouring. If a pump product is pouring flat, you'll end up shaking the glass as it fills up. Over shake and you end up with a three inch head once again – a bloody nightmare.

Advice. Teach all staff that finding yourself with a big head means **STOP POURING**. If other drinks have been ordered, let that settle whilst getting on with the rest of the round. At least you'll stand half a chance on the second or third visit. Meanwhile, the flat pouring problem will have been communicated to **YOU** or next in line for solving **WON'T IT?** You have to find solutions, it **WILL** drive your business.

However. I had a keg of flat product for which I had a credit awarded. Tech services couldn't raise it from the dead either.

9. Cold room temperature. If two different gauges in the cold room are exhibiting two different results – buy a third.

Warning. Products should pour perfectly within reason. If they don't, you need to put that right. Do not stick your head in the sand, or go out for the day instead, leaving the rest of the crew to send your next stock result east. It will be a constant battle – but one you must win for the most part.

Without EPOS

If all your deliveries are legit, all your takings declared true; I guess a stock taker would be able to load all your deliveries and cash declared into a software program, giving some indication of a result. This is dangerous terrain to be in.

Personally. Whilst writing this book, I have wasted weeks of my life trying to fathom out certain issues. For the life of me I cannot think of any advantage in **NOT** employing a full blown EPOS/BOS system, other than how much time it takes to learn and understand stock control. Weekly, sometimes daily line checks on products that I was losing hand over fist. Weekly line checks of my top selling wet items. Complete wet stocktakes every month, with additional walk in stock takes by the man in black at any given time. That's not to mention a weekly/two weekly dry stock without fail. I didn't understand the first thing about the stock process. Even after a couple of years I dreaded stocks. Trouble is, when your job provides the place your family live, you cannot simply run away and hide. Sometimes, you have to face your demons – and learn. Slowly I began to realise what a fantastic tool stock control is. I must have thrown so many stupid questions at stock takers and colleagues, they must have thought me thick as a plank.

Huge advice. Managed houses will **ALL** have these control systems in place. Without means – gambling on **BULLSHIT**.

Upshot. An EPOS till system linked to a BOS should provide total control. It will pay for itself, time and time again.

> ## If the cellar is the engine room . . .
> ## An in-house stock control system is the very beating heart.

Independent traders

Search for a system simple to use. Do your homework, ask your stock taker. If you know other landlords, ask what they use. If they don't use one and bang on relentlessly about why you don't need one, feel easy in the knowledge that that person has no control whatsoever in their business. Unless employing no staff, they are talking **BOLLOCKS**. You're aim is to limit the damage of stock loss, end of. Understanding this system will be a long and painful process I'm afraid. No pain, no gain.

Warning. EPOS systems can crash. Make sure any system you employ, has a standalone feature letting you carry on using tills, even if the whole system is having an unannounced holiday. It will always happen at the busiest moment. You may need a contract providing on the spot phone diagnosis. If you do, make sure that helpline does what it says on the tin.

Advice. When you're system does go down, customers waiting and no way of even opening the till, you'll probably want to run away – I'm not joking. It really can be the most frustrating and infuriating experience all rolled in to one. You'll need to know from the outset how to navigate the fastest solve. **DON'T BUY ANY SYSTEM WITHOUT THIS KNOWLEDGE**. Many times I wanted to rip the whole thing out and throw it through the nearest window. I would still advocate it being a no brainer.

Miscellaneous stock control wisdom

Calculating tenths of spirit bottles. If you're bloody awful at estimating tenths of spirits, keep an empty bottle of each major brand. Fill with water, pour into ten even glasses, pour back in and mark a line at each point. If an optic, don't forget to mark the bottle upside down. Laborious - but effective.

For all. Learn as much as you can from your stock taker, they are experts in their field. If you're lucky and get the right kind of person, it can help dramatically. Treat them with respect. Always keep them dosed up with tea, coffee and the obligatory bacon sandwich (buy the contents yourself, not from stock).

Managers. Your stock taker **SHOULD** be there to help and support you. Yes to bollock and send the fear of god into you on occasion, but mostly as a tool to improve your stock control. Companies don't spend a stack of cash training you up and moving you about to want to sack you over silly mistakes. Mistakes are lessons. Lessons are profitable. They will **ALWAYS** want to sack the very naughty or thoroughly incompetent.

Learning to count. Learn to count in different multiples. Dozens, sixes, twenties, tens, tenths of a spirit bottle in an assortment of sizes. Whether it's your first stock or hundredth: if you don't understand what a stock taker has just done, stop and ask - life's too short to **FAF** around. Knowledge can improve dramatically within a short period. I can now count fluently between varying multiples as if I was riding a bike. At school maths was my weak subject. If I can do it - so can you.

Independents. If taking over an existing business, do not take on the last licensees stock. Inform the owner to run down their stock, there will be **NO TRANSFER**. Of course you need stock and will have to purchase, but why buy second-hand?

Why? What guarantee is there that all this hotchpotch of products are legit and in date? **DON'T** even think about it.

Example. I was once told a story, that upon taking over a pub, the new people accepted all these barrels of lager - only to find that the four 22's in the corner were full of water.

The cheque had already cleared!

Tip. If this does happen to you, don't tell anybody. The last thing customers need to know is - the new guvnors an idiot.

Question. How the hell can **YOU** or **ANY** stock taker guarantee the barrels in your newly acquired cellar actually contain what they're supposed to? This really is **HUMAT**. Why risk it?

A word of advice for managers. Play it straight right from the start. If a company is good enough to employ you, be thankful for the opportunity, no one's forcing you to do it. Living upstairs, no bills bar council tax and being paid a wage to boot - doesn't seem quite so bad in the cold light of day.

Independent. I guess you can do what you like. Still bear in mind that giving away four pints of lager to your mates at £3.50 a go, will set you back the best part of twenty quid in total cash/stock loss. Not paying for those lagers in the morning will certainly leave you with a stock deficit and a headache; either imminently, at a later date - or both.

Long story cut short on stock control

The title of this chapter says it all. With no controls in place, chances are you'll be losing money hand over fist. In laymen's terms - it's a never ending battle. That battle being - 100% of the sale price you set is received. Liquor stocks falling way short of 100% yield are a huge obstacle. Defeating the ogre of stock loss, will make throwing the biggest scumbag out of your place look like a piece of piss. Think of it as your very own insurance scheme — for **ALL** of the products you sell. Losing momentum to bad stocks is lazy management.

Employ a system - become its master!

26 ENTERTAINMENT

In the 70's and 80's it was normal to have to queue at a social club on a Saturday night. Pubs were packed. It was almost as if, all you had to do was open the doors and hay presto - Ker Ching. In recent years, advancing technology has provided an entertainment choice never dreamt of - **AT HOME**. During this time the licenced trade carried on as if unaware of being under continual attack. The only shot fired back, being units with a strong emphasis on food and huge investment in marketing, but you know what? Technology ain't the crack – at least, not yet. You still can't acquire the social aspect at home. It's a reward, a break, a few hours away from the hum drum of life. A truly successful operation **SHOULD** leave customers entertained by degree after **ANY** visit at **ANY** time of the week. Every slice of your offer should enhance a visit, providing elements that make it a **TREAT**, something **SPECIAL**.

What would you class as entertainment?

Is it a disco on a Friday, maybe a live act on a Sunday teatime? Is it a karaoke night or a quiz on a Tuesday? If these are the first things that spring to mind – you're already clutching at straws. Whilst still a valuable tool, traditional entertainment **SHOULD** be the icing on the cake, more a reward for customers as part of your weekly offer. Take a long hard look at the bigger picture. What **ELSE** do you offer?

Example. If you visit the theatre to watch a play or a pantomime; you'll watch people act, but it'll be the backdrop, props and sound that complete the scene, providing maximum value to your senses and satisfaction factor you take home.

Showtime. Your backdrop - will be every damned thing a customer witnesses on approach, entering and spending time in your place. That's day in, day out. From the décor, to the music in the background, the products you offer and manner of delivery; how attractive the bar appears, the ambience of clever lighting, superb service and a safe, asshole free environment. These are the bedrock of your entertainment offer; otherwise, why the hell would people leave the safety of their locked doors, cold wine in the fridge, 48" surround sound TV, a thousand channels - all to witness **YOUR** pricing regime? Experiencing a truly sociable experience is currently unavailable on-line. Humans don't need that much excuse to go out, but it's your job to provide an incessant alibi to do so.

Providing maximum value to the customer journey IS your entertainment offer!

Opportunity

Humans live a fast, furious life, working all hour's to pay bills and keep afloat, but goal posts are moving. Takeaway food is a shitload dearer. A decent bottle of wine is loads more expensive in the supermarket lately, and food in general has rocketed in price. TV technology has vastly improved the ease of recording two or three programmes simultaneously, to watch whatever, whenever you damned well choose. All are obstacles **REMOVED** in preventing **THEM** from visiting **YOU**. Prospective customers might be sick of watching crap TV. Most people have watched every film ever made three times over.

Life is getting bland – people are bored. HUGE OPPORTUNITY!

Wi-Fi

High on the pecking order will be a superb WI-FI signal. Advertise free Wi-Fi. Supply the code, or free log-in info' on numerous blackboards. Wi-Fi is essential to most human's, it's like a disease we've all signed up to. In providing Wi-Fi, you are effectively cancelling out one of the benefits of staying at home, putting the customer #1 - another obstacle down.

Wi-Fi will become way more significant than live sport on TV!

Tip. Don't make people have to ask for the code, it interrupts the customer journey and stops a member of staff from serving. Make the Wi-Fi easy to access. Why would you offer something then make it hard to get? Remove the obstacle.

Blackboard that code!

The future. Any new communication technology will sure as hell encompass Wi-Fi or similar. If you decide a TV package is too expensive – keen sports fans can watch live football or rugby on their phones and tablets, via Wi-Fi supplied in-house. Picture 50 customers staring at their phones watching sport. Sad but true. This is only the start, but improving customer love beyond measure, may prevent redundancy – **FOR YOU**.

Kids. It is completely normal now for parents to produce a couple of tablets (non-prescription) providing a perfect anecdote in keeping children happy whilst awaiting a meal.

Warning. Not providing Wi-Fi is like saying you're closed for business. A fundamental service, just like providing a knife and fork for a meal, it should be of high quality, able to furnish many customers phones, tablets and laptops. Slow Wi-Fi is a negative and will deter custom – you have to **ADD VALUE**.

Live entertainment

Split into two categories: bands and solos/duos; the following applies to both. Up and above the service you already provide, it is possible to create extra income from live music, but merely opening doors and expecting people to flock in is naive. **Market the news.** Unless you're taking thousands a night, don't even think about newspaper advertising, it being way too expensive to be financially viable. Sign up to the local rags free **WHAT'S ON** page. People will actively search for this page, but may miss a paid advert with ease. A small fee will secure listings in a local gig guide, distributed widely, free for perusal.

Has your venue got its own social network site? Set one up straight away, make it straightforward. If it's not easy, it won't work, you simply won't be able to spend half a day twice a week updating. For a licensee, time is your enemy. If it's Facebook, just use Facebook, it's an effective blackboard. The more friends you add, the more you notify of this week's act, starting time and special offers. The better the act, the better the comments - better the **VALUE** all round.

How? If you've four hundred people signed up with a live act on this Sunday at 6pm (after the football), post a specific message at the start of the week - again at dinner time on the day to promote that act. Why wouldn't you do this? You would have to be a complete numpty to disregard this opportunity. Post again just before the act is due on. Potential custom in a bar down the road will always be sneaking a look on their Facebook app – on their mobile phone. Quite honestly it's hard to get people to look away from their bloody phone, let alone have a conversation with them. It's almost like it's attached to their body. You need to tap into this. It is here and it is now. It is **FREE** and it's staring right at you – bloody well use it.

Texting. Same as above, but be careful - keep the list confidential. Sending 200 texts is easy though, it might just provide that excuse to visit the pub – Ker Ching!

Table talkers. Placed on every table they will hold a card advertising the following month's acts. Change every two weeks and supply A5 paper copies for customers to takeaway.

A-boards. If safe to do so, place an A-board outside the unit solely advertising up-to-date entertainment information.

Flyers. Still an effective weapon in delivering the message locally - live music is on offer every Thursday from now on and you are very welcome. Going door to door is time consuming, but at least you'll know for certain the leaflets you have spent time and money on, have actually been delivered and not binned by lazy staff or promotion companies. Get out there, meet people, make friends and create some magic. Of course I don't mean door to door every week, but if launching live music, a quiz night or new menu - include leafleting local housing and businesses as part of your attack.

Posters. Can an act provide posters for your frames?

TV messaging. Nowadays, every licensed premise seems to think it applicable to plant a television on every wall available. During the day I would have appropriate music on at a sensible and workable volume via your juke box or similar. Many units have all the tellies on, the sound down. Instead, use these tellies to promote live acts and forthcoming events. Plaster information on these all day long. Having them on daytime TV is wasted opportunity, it **DESTROYS** social interaction. You're in a game specialising in social interaction, **THEY** can watch the bloody telly at home. You'll need a gizmo to programme this facility, but in house advertising is free - **FREE!**

Advice. Turn all TV's off when a live act is performing - people will look at the TV and not interact with the act, or each other. How can you create an atmosphere in a confused picture? Why spend money on an act to condemn to wallpaper? Used wisely, TV's are a weapon, don't effectively dumb audiences down.

Local press. Begin a relationship with a local music journalist. Not sex, just an email, or call to let them know you are starting live music. When booking a quality act, notify and invite them down, buy them drinks and hope for a favourable review.

Staff. Your boys and girls need to be clued up with all relevant information should a customer ask a question. What time the band starts on Friday. What sort of material do they play? Are they any good? Are they on Facebook? Here's an A5 flyer telling you all about them and future events. One of your biggest marketing tools will be your staff. Get them on board.

Story. With friends, I was in a pub in a major British city during the day. We asked at the bar whether there was live music on tonight. The bartender didn't have a clue, nor did his mate; there was no indication in, or out. That night, we passed by with the sound of a band playing and a fiver entry fee.

AAAAAGGGGGHHHHH!

Set the scene. Already covered, but fundamental; create a setting that promotes something's happening tonight.

Live bands

Firstly, check out legal requirements specific to your unit. Will you need doormen? Will the council allow the noise? What time can you operate till? Consult your local licensing officer for advice and guidance. Be nice. It may all seem like bullshit to you, but sometimes you have to play the game.

Warning. Booking live bands is not about **YOU** and what you like; it's about putting the customer #1. What do **THEY** want?

Example. Take an indie band. After playing their demo you might chuck it in the bin, and on the night absolutely hate their brand of music, but - has that band got 5000 people clued into their Facebook sight? They might pack your place out, providing **YOU** a healthy return. Four bookings a year and you've only got to find another eleven acts providing the same level of interest; suddenly you have a live venue all year round with great profit on entertainment nights.

Example. A social club may want to be a little more adventurous, but with an average age of fifty, can I suggest the local heavy metal crew may not be the answer.

Cost. Whatever you put on must be the best quality your budget can afford - it's a problem. Obviously you can't pay £500 for a band and only take £800 on the night over the bar. Before very long you're going to be in deep doo doo.

Example. Anything less than a ratio of 6 to 1 upwards, would be a bad result. That means, if you pay a band £300, you need to take at least £1800 to start feeling at all comfortable.

Charging on the door. Even if you were to charge a couple of quid on the door as a token admission, at least this would pay for your two door staff, meaning one less bill at the end of the night. A name band or popular tribute act might mean you can charge anything you like on the door – check legalities.

Warning. What is the capacity you can legally admit? Ask the door guys and gals to keep an eye on numbers entering and leaving. Click them in and out. You may also need walkie talkies for communication between the door and you. An extra expense maybe, but once you've got them, you've got them.

Story. I had one particular act that seemed well established on the UK gig scene. Everyone and his dog told me to book them. When something sounds too good to be true, I get a little twitchy. I rang and asked how much they would charge. I was quoted something like £300, plus ticket's at something like £12 to £15 a go, which they would send through. I would sell these tickets behind the bar - they would get all the money. This guy literally guaranteed me they would sell out, no problem. I weighed it up; £300 was my end of the deal, plus two door staff. This was to book a name band that would give the venue heaps of kudos. It wasn't the greatest deal, but might attract other bands to get in touch. My unit would be featured on their UK gig list raising **OUR** profile. I took the bait. By the Tuesday before, I had sold all the flaming tickets – incredible. The band got the cash, but I took about three and a half thousand quid on the bar and didn't lose my job. Bands came out of the woodwork from everywhere wanting to play the pub. The ratio was just above 11 to 1 with regard to takings.

Warning. As time went on, the gigs would all sell out with these fabulous bands (mostly tributes), but sometimes I wouldn't take the money. A full house is an achievement, but you can be victim to your own success. If people can't get to the bar, they just won't bother. They'll enjoy the act, two pints and then bugger off. Lesson being: you **CAN** take more money with a few less people in the gaff - than stacked out.

Consider. Staff you choose to work these nights have to be able to adapt, you won't always be able to hear what people are asking for. Encouraging customers to point can be really useful, I kid you not. I certainly improved my lip reading. Don't complain about the noise. Basically, as soon as a drummer sets their kit up - you know it's going to be noisy.

What to book then? You're attempting to offer something customers simply can't access at home. Look at your customer base, or what you'd like it to be. Only **YOU** can decide what to book; but, not seeing an act before doing so leaves you wide open for a smack in the teeth. A reputation for quality live music is only as good as its weakest link. If customers don't like an act, they'll leave - along with your so called reputation.

Story. I booked a band I hadn't seen. By the third number they'd half cleared the building. They weren't just awful, they were diabolical. I had to ask them to stop. I still paid them, but all the work I'd invested reputation wise, took a hefty kick that night. If you book a **CRAP ACT** – only **YOU** can take the blame.

As a general rule of thumb, live bands should provide exactly what it should say on the tin – ENTERTAINMENT!

Tip. Don't ask a live band to play all night. Two 50 minute spots will showcase an acts strongest set. Bands aren't machines - any longer than that and you dilute the quality. On top of that, when people are watching or dancing - they aren't drinking. Leave space around the performance for plenty of that, opportunity enough to witness your superb service.

Tip. Don't pay **ALL** acts the same money; pay them what they're worth. Save on one to pay another more.

Advice. Make the act aware that an invoice will be required.

Tip. Tape up coin slots on your juke box to avoid upsetting customers firing money. Do it way before the act starts. Ask an act to play backing music beforehand. Ask the act to put music on immediately they take a break and when they finish. Avoid sharp silent spells, it kills ambience and sheds custom.

Solos and duos

A unit may not be big enough to promote bands profitably, or cope with the noise factor. You may just want to bolster your all round offer to include a solo act for example. It might not break the bank. It might be more an ingredient.

Why not think of entertainment as a thank you note in your weekly curriculum.

What to book? A solo that gets everyone singing and dancing. A saxophonist in an eating house might provide that live ambience. An acoustic solo or duo can be perfect.

Tip. Solos and duos are cheaper to book between Monday and Thursday. Friday and Sunday will be dearer, with Saturdays dearer again. You may **HAVE** to put a live act on a Saturday, but if busy anyway, choose a quieter time to boost trade.

Warning. There are some really great solos and duos out there, but also piles of steaming shit. I repeat - a bad act can clear your place in ten minutes flat, with only **YOU** to blame.

Tip. Book quality acts with a quality sound system. If you use an agent, make sure they've actually seen the act in question. What sort of agent hasn't seen its acts? Is it **WORTH THE RISK?**

Tip. Most quality acts will know other class acts.

Tip. Don't clash live acts with sport. If you sign up for an expensive sports TV package, plan your act to start when it finishes, not before. Look at fixtures in advance, be organised.

Let's get something straight. No pub or club will go bust spending between a hundred and fifty to two hundred quid a week on a quality solo act. Bankruptcy mostly happens because **YOU** will have failed to persuade the general public to enter and stay – **MOST OF THE REST OF THE TIME.**

Live entertainment bottom line

I am a great fan of quality live music, but live acts actually need an audience to perform to. Creating ambience needs human interaction – that's before the act even starts. I visit units all the time with a live act setting up, there being no more than a dozen people in attendance. I'll ask the bartender, where is everyone? They'll say; it's the weather, they're all on holiday, there's a party on down the road, it's the end of the month, start of the month, they're saving for Xmas. There will be no indication on any blackboard inside or out, no inclusion in the free **WHAT'S ON** page and positively no use of social networking. Truth being, the unit isn't busy at **ANY** time of the week. If a unit is making a bunch of fundamental mistakes in just one aspect, how many other mistakes are being made across the board, crucial to creating profitable conditions?

AAAAAGGGGGHHHHH!

Persuading customers to leave their out of this world computer games, TV production making even crap look good, and an all singing, all dancing broadband package, necessitates **YOU** pulling a few rabbits out of the hat. Avoid booking sub-standard acts and set the scene beforehand. As technology has advanced, the last three decades have seen a gradual decline in the numbers of truly talented superstars, working their apprenticeship in the pubs and clubs of this country. They're way to busy learning how to text at lightning speed, than learning guitar or lugging drums around. Combine this with units shutting all over and you have the perfect storm, which has culminated in almost no new acts appearing on local circuits. Plenty of karaoke kids, but no pure spellbinding talent.

Bloody hell, how sad is that?

Pub games

Skittles. An alley in house can be a real boost for quiet nights, providing competition and a giggle for people of all ages. You need to be proactive in attracting different teams for different nights - space is expensive. Lay food on, claim as an expense.

Darts. If you have room for a board then use it. Some units have a thriving darts community involving many teams and leagues. Again, provide food, a quality board, spare darts, rubber mat, a chalk scoreboard on the wall and generally set the scene. Listen to the players for any other requirements.

In general. Liaise with the secretary of the relevant local leagues to fill you in with all the necessary. They'll probably be only too pleased to encourage new avenues, and **YOU'LL** need **ALL** their advice. This goes for crib, dominoes and any other skilled game. It's all entertainment and a tool in the box. Whatever you promote; understand it, do your homework.

Warning. Running a pub team takes an awful lot of commitment on your part. Neglecting or taking them for granted will be spotted very quickly – by the team itself. If you're going to run a team - do it properly, or not at all.

Quiz nights. People love a quiz. I ran a very successful midweek quiz in two units that put a lot of bums on seats, but you have to have the right person running the show.

Question. How is it that one landlord can take 12K a week and within weeks of them leaving, the new guvnors takings have dropped to half that? It's the same with a quiz.

Answer. Ask two people to share the responsibility, what if one goes sick? Ask the locals for nominations, preferably with an entertaining character. A retired person might love a crack at that. Pay them twenty quid each for their trouble.

Tools of the trade. This is where investing in a quality sound system starts to pay off. You should have the facility to put a microphone through the speakers that sounds perfect. If it sounds awful, the quiz will be awful. Your one chance to promote a quiz night will be the first - don't blow it. Make sure in advance that everyone will be able to hear the questions. Initially finding and persuading all these quiz types to make the effort on a cold winter night is one thing; not to be organised and able to deliver - will prove demoralising all round.

Advice. Ban the use of mobile phones during quiz time.

Live sport on TV. Have the sound from the TV wired in to your sound system. At the flick of a switch you can transmit all the atmosphere of the ground and the commentary to particular zones in the unit. If rugby and football fixtures clash, can you screen these in different zones with sound to match? For a recap on zones; refer back to the **ATMOSPHERE** chapter.

Astonishing. I visit units obviously paying bags of money for a sports package - the juke box still pounding out tunes clashing with commentary - pure **HUMAT**. Think ahead; tape the juke box slots up, or turn the damned thing off.

AAAAAGGGGGHHHHH!

Live sport. In signing up to a sports package, you are by definition making a statement - of who you are and what your customers can expect. Use that weapon and set the scene. Why would you pay all that money and not bother? Set all tables and chairs in front of a big screen facing forward.

Warning. Keep a spare bulb in-house for the projector. Before buying a projector, demand instructions in how to fit one. That bulb will always go ten minutes before the biggest game and you'll just want to - **RUN AWAY**. Been there, done that.

Free juke box

Some thrive without, most can only benefit from music.

Personally. Entering a unit without music is like attending a funeral and accidentally farting during a really quiet moment, praying nobody noticed. Music is part of your backdrop, it sets the scene. In my experience, revenue gained from a juke box is minimal. Why not provide several tablets around the room letting customers choose tracks for free.

Advantages. You can load music that fits your business model, even changing choice of genre to suit morning, teatime and evening clientele. You can command what volume you set throughout the building and adjust as required. Set the system on random play, eliminating silent moments. At the same time as being in complete control of a slice of the ambience you provide, the customer will feel rewarded. Word might spread.

You can't just take, take, take – you've got to offer something back!

Disadvantage. Cost, you'll be getting nothing directly back, whilst still having to pay music licences.

Alternatively. Arrange an evening where the juke box is free. Housing the best juke box in town is all well and good, but what do you do to promote it? Arrange with the supplier to make it free on the quietest sessions; you're paying the rent on the flipping thing, so make it happen. Customers love this sort of freebie, it makes them feel loved. One unit I tried this in doubled the gross weekly juke box income in weeks.

Warning. Whilst I believe silence in the majority of units is a business killer, the wrong choice of music at the wrong volume, played through a substandard sound system, is an even worse crime to commit a customer's ears or senses to.

Discos and Karaoke

Never disregard how much a quality disco can bring to an evening. Couple this with a themed fancy dress night and you now have an occasion instead of a plain disco. Ask staff to dress up. Even if the first bash doesn't get the locals on board, don't give up. Give prizes for best costumes and all that.

Slowly slowly, catchy money!

A hired disco **SHOULD** provide a superb sound system and entertaining DJ. What's the point of a disco sounding like a muffled megaphone and some moron who doesn't say a word all night? Make sure of a great light show and not the regulation four lights on a bar. There is no excuse for discos not to provide a quality lighting show. If you pay a hundred quid, you'll get a hundred quid's worth of shite. Pay a bit more and witness what they offer before unleashing them in your bar.

Karaoke. You don't have to be the greatest singer, but popular TV shows continue to encourage all and sundry to get in front of a microphone. Hold competitions. Employ a professional who can compere. Go and see them in action.

Legal

Ensure **ALL** entertainers have their own public liability and PAT testing schedule. Provide **THEM** with safe electricity sockets.

Other options

I haven't enough pages available to cover all the possibilities, but the list is endless. Race nights, comedy nights, a book club, dance classes, a beer festival, pool teams, charity fundraisers, casino nights, private functions, gaming machines - are all opportunities to strengthen your entertainment offer.

Entertainment long story cut short

There are only two types of entertainment – **GOOD** and **BAD**. One will actively promote the cultivation of regular return custom; the other will drive both new and existing customers away in droves. Invariably, a successful unit will be firing on a combination of winning cylinders. The emphasis has moved to the overall value of **ANY** visit to your premises. In this fast changing world, people are noticing the inadequacies of bad service, inexcusable hygiene and how much value your unit will deliver in return for **THEIR** money. Forget the competition: if your customer service is 500% better than anyone else – you'll already have the required head start. Customers don't analyse for hours, they make snap decisions. Live act or not; if the service is shite, the ambience unpleasant with no sense of warmth - off they'll trot, telling all and sundry on their travels. Superb service and a welcoming atmosphere **ADDS VALUE**. People like busy vibrant places. Live acts in particular thrive on busy places. Without a warm bed to lie on, a live act will struggle, just like the unit they're performing in.

Superb service is entertainment alone . . . By STEALTH!

Everything a customer witnesses will affect how long they stay and ultimately spend. Your capacity to translate what the majority of the middle ground in your targeted market would not only appreciate, but thrive and multiply on - is **THE KEY**. Creating from the tools at your disposal, the ideal customer journey and replicating that 99.9% of the time, is your challenge. For you it will take stamina, organisation and imagination. It will be completely bloody knackering. **EVERYTHING** away from the home should be entertainment.

27 MARKETING YOUR UNIT

The ultimate marketing tool for any licensed premises will be . . . YOUR STAFF!

THEY are the key to unlocking what the customer requires. **THEY** are the delivery lorry and purveyor of good vibes, enticing the customer to stay as long as possible. Everything **THEY** do, from the preparation of service, to the customer leaving will be crucial. **THEY** are the people you will have chosen to work the frontline. **THEY** will make or break any of your conjured up business plan. How efficiently **YOU** train them suddenly becomes alarmingly critical.

Warning. Taking on the wrong staff, with the wrong attitude, will undo any amount of effort you put in. They will turn every positive negative. They will eat your business from inside out.

AAAAAGGGGGHHHHH!

Example. You **HAVE** to build a customer base. You don't necessarily have to be the cheapest, maybe simply offering a better all-round service. If a pint is 50p dearer next door, but service and ambience consistently 500% superior, well guess what? I'll leave you to work that one out. Combine superb service with a strong offer and you have a potent weapon.

For you, marketing will mostly be about EVERYTHING a customer witnesses with all of their senses, leaving an overall impression and satisfaction score on exit!

Opportunities

Three stick out like a sore thumb. How the unit presents itself externally, internally, and how to communicate your existence to humans not actually in the building – effectively and economically. To a major extent, they are all linked to the performance of you and your team. Everything I have rattled on about in previous chapters comes together . . . **NOW**.

Externally upon arrival

DOES the unit look **INVITING** or does it look shut? At the very least it should score as neutral, although you would have to be quite lazy not to improve on that impression.

IS the outside area free of litter, or are there a thousand filthy butts like an advert for a government stop smoking campaign?

DOES anything stick out that might **DETER** a customer? Broken or dirty windows, badly kept garden, distorted music?

ARE your A-boards in good condition? Can you read what's on the board from the other side of the road, or is there way too much information crammed in? Is that message going to generate or promote income? Does it add **VALUE**?

Inwardly upon entry

- Is the music appropriate and at the right volume?
- Do your crew appear to be busy? Nothing worse than three bods; one with arms crossed staring at you, another reading the paper, the last fiddling with their newly fitted ear stud. How do your staff come across?

- Does the bar itself look impressive and organised?
- Are the bottle displays attractive? Take a trip round town and pinch ideas; this is **YOUR** shop window.
- Is everything on the bar either for sale or for service?
- Are the tables and chairs in natural positions and tidy? Continued and regular tidying of chairs, in tandem with clearing and wiping tables, will set you apart from the rest. Customers absolutely love seeing this sort of caper.
- Are the pumps clean?
- When you lean on the bar, is it sticky? Why is that?
- Are the lights all working in your bottle fridges? If not, why not? Fridges without lights working indicate that you don't give a crap. Carry spare bulbs.
- What bottled products supply the biggest profit? Display them on the top shelf of your fridge, it's an angle, try it? If it hampers fast service, you'll have to weigh it up.
- Are all blackboards up to date? Do they attract the eye? Is the message uncomplicated for smooth perusal?
- Are all your glasses super clean? Are all your shelves cleaned at least once a week? If not, why not?
- Can you take any single wine glass and be absolutely positive it is shiny, clean and ready for use? Do it now; pick a glass, hold it up - does it pass muster?
- In-house, ashtrays have disappeared, but blank tables look bland. Make use of beer mats, menus and table talkers. **TREAT** customers to frequent wipe downs.
- Have enough glasses. What's that got to do with marketing? Queuing to get a drink, only to be told you can't have one for the lack of glassware, is a really bad advert for your place. It's relevant and it happens.
- Is the Wi-Fi code advertised freely throughout?

- Are your bartender's uniformed and smart? Dirty or smelly uniform is a really **BAD** idea. Have **YOU** supplied your staff enough uniform for three days work?
- Do your staff go the extra mile, adding **VALUE** to your premium products, or do they serve like a blank page?
- Are **YOU** smart and presentable?
- In-house posters should deliver a message you **NEED** communicating. Is the poster in that frame increasing the chance of greater profit, or is it not?
- Refrain from hand written signs **ANYWHERE** within the unit. It comes across as amateurish and shoddy.
- Between -10 and +10 how would you score ambience within and the welcome you offer? Mark from a customer's perspective – not your own.

Yes we've mentioned most of these points time and time again in past chapters, but each fundamental point is a slice of the cake that paints an attractive picture - or **NOT**. Nearly all subjects covered in this book are intrinsically linked to one or more other subjects. Being apathetic or just plain not understanding how to complete a simple task, could mean it affects different parts of your business all at the same time. Every detail of your unit and every single action by all staff members will ultimately be judged by the customer. As they leave your building at the end of their visit, **THEY** will decide how well **YOU** have marketed your offer and whether you will be seeing them again. I visit units all the time that seem to actively work at driving custom away - how crazy is that?

Removing obstacles that put a customer off is as strong a marketing tool as any!

Think – mobile phone

Website. Try logging a pubs name in to a search site. It will generally lead you directly to other sites listing multiple units in the area. Seldom do you find a pub, bar, social club, or hotel for that matter, with its very own website. **WHY NOT?** If you're not in it, you can't win it. Compared with regular newspaper advertising, a website is cheap as chips. A marketing base linking social network sites, flyers, business cards, menus and all conventional marketing tools - is a smart move.

Tip. Keep the site simple but informative. Feature photos of the unit promoting your strongest selling points. What are you **FAMOUS** for? If it's great coffee and croissants during the day, a live solo act in the evening - focus on your 4K coffee machine and solo acts with people dancing. **FLAUNT IT!**

Tip. Put the address, how to get there and what you're famous for on the **HOME** page. I go on to sites all the time, where I simply **CAN'T** find the address or current phone contact. One hit on a phone is **ALL** it should take. A one click, mobile phone friendly, instant advert, is a **FREE** opportunity. Second only to your staff, mobile phones are the obvious conveyor of marketing; most humans seem surgically connected to the bloody things. If attracting new custom is crucial, ignoring the use of the largest marketing tool in the world would be silly. After the initial cost of a website and yearly hosting fee, it can work quietly in the background 24/7 – **FREE** to the customer.

Warning. If you state on your site; nipple piercing from 7-10 every Wednesday, then bloody well make sure someone's there every Wednesday to pierce some nipples; nothing worse than customers turning up for an event, finding out on arrival that actually - karaoke stopped three months ago.

Tip. Produce a sight you don't have to update every two weeks, this will prove expensive; be professionally vague.

Example. If you have a live act every Sunday teatime after the football, don't list who's on week by week, just state you have a live act on every Sunday teatime. Promote this week's act and start time on your social network sight, a blackboard inside, an A-board outside, table talkers on every table, and secure a listing in the free **WHAT'S ON** page of the local rag.

Example. Don't list your whole menu and specific prices, this might change at regular intervals. Instead, state an overview of your offer and the quality of your products and hygiene.

Cost. £500 to a grand. A yearly rental of no more than a hundred quid to host the site and you're on the map. It gets costly and complicated if you change things all the time, a website programmer will charge by the hour every time you want to change this and that. Think carefully about content and try to end up with a low maintenance option.

Marketing the website. I wouldn't bother playing that game. Paying other people to try and get you up the top of the page is futile in this instance. The name of your unit and where you are should be suffice, and probably available to you. If somebody hears about you by word of mouth, it should be an easy hit. A prospective customer can view directions at a glance and images of what they might experience. A website isn't an easy option, but done right can tip the balance.

Function rooms. Featuring a photo gallery of a live act or disco with people dancing, spreads of food and facilities offered on a dedicated website is a no brainer. Matching your facilities with highly trained staff who actually want to be there is fundamental. No amount of expensive bullshit marketing will work, unless the customer perceives **VALUE** for money.

Word of mouth

For all your hard work, this **IS** the bonus. If you spend nothing at all on outside marketing, but provide superb hospitality, paying infinite attention to detail - your business **WILL** grow. Sales growth will provide the vehicle to afford enough staff to deliver premium service. Humans will always tell other humans of a great experience, but too many ways to communicate that experience make word of mouth all the more critical.

Warning. Bad reviews on social networking sites extend the reach and power of word of mouth. If your service is rank . . .

Everyone will get to know how SHITE you really are – FAST AS!

The magic wand. Customers used to be drawn down the pub or the club by the social aspect – that hasn't changed one iota. A pack of women all giggling and gossiping, a bunch of blokes all taking the mick out of each other, laughing out loud, watching an act, a romantic meal, celebrations – none of that has changed. **YOUR** job is to provide the setting and service fuelling their happiness within a safe environment. **THEY** will provide more word of mouth than you ever dreamt possible.

Re-launch

If sales are crap and you're not paying the bills, look at what you're not doing. Retrain your staff, give the place a makeover within a small budget and put a better offer on the table. Don't just sit there waiting for Xmas, you might not make it that far. Set a date for your re-launch and hand deliver leaflets telling everybody and his dog. Use all the marketing mentioned, but remove the profit obstacles mentioned throughout this book.

Marketing story cut short

The first sentence I used in this chapter is my biggest piece of advice on marketing. If I'd have been brave, I'd have stopped writing after the first page.

The ultimate marketing tool for any licensed premises will be . . . YOUR STAFF!

I don't know of a licensed unit that doesn't sell a strong range of products. Most units will have something about them that works. Of course use all the tools in the box; social network sites, business cards, flyers given away at **ANY** opportunity, attractive blackboards in all disguises, reward cards, a text library for informing latest offers and upcoming entertainment, in-house posters, TV's relating messages, money off vouchers and whatever else you can think of, but . . .

The strongest marketing vehicle will still be the one you already pay for . . . YOUR STAFF!

If your staff add value to your premium products, you will almost automatically have an overall premium offer. I don't mean 'Would you like crisps, nuts, or one of our lovely chocolate bars with that?' before actually **ALLOWING** someone to pay and get on with the rest of their bloody life!

That's patronising and utterly - SHITE!

Showtime. A well trained, conscientious, non-condescending team; will not only deliver all the marketing you need, they'll **ENSURE** customers beat a path to your door for next to no extra marketing cost . . . **WHATSOEVER!**

28 WINE OFFER

**Humans drink vast amounts of wine . . .
Not necessarily in licensed premises!**
A massive market and huge opportunity continually
staring at you every second you open.

Am I the only one who finds the selection of wines offered in
bars, unattractive, unapproachable - an expensive **GAMBLE?**
The blundering manner served, I can only describe as more
self-harm, scoring way into the negative. Good wine **SHOULD**
add class to your overall offer. If bartenders aren't trained in
the art of serving wine, how do you increase **VALUE** for the
customer? Why do we treat customers with such disdain?

**Walk toward your bar with customer's
eyes . . . Is YOUR wine offer crystal clear,
or do you need a degree in TELEPATHY?**

Competition

Offering inept service and products the public clearly find
either, unpalatable or puzzling seems widespread. This
incompetence leaves supermarkets by default, the only clear
competition - another perfect storm. Supermarkets devote
huge areas of massive aisles to wine alone. The average bar
sells no more than a dozen choices covering the whole gamut.

**Competition? – We're not even in the
same ball park as supermarkets!**

Reality

Mostly, you can forget this pathetic excuse that supermarkets somehow damage your trade. **THEY** offer goods which people buy and take home from a warehouse type building, with minimum customer care and attention extended. You **PRESUMABLY** offer premium products from a building full of character and ambience; delivered with oodles of customer love and attention by trained members of staff, waiting hand foot and finger on every last whim (at least that's the idea). Both retail, but no other similarity between the two equations. Personally. I love a glass of dry white or a smooth red. I'm no connoisseur by any means, but can immediately tell you what I don't like. I've watched wine experts on TV talking double Dutch; neither the patience nor memory to take in - who has? I find it challenging and tiresome locating something to my taste in a supermarket. It is purely by chance I'll stumble upon an attractive product (classy label) and find it tastes surprisingly passable - a lucky gamble basically. I'll then stick to that brand until some bright spark changes the label, or removes it from sale just to annoy me. Over a tenner and I won't gamble, but at least the big shop has a plethora of choice.

Put yourself in the customers shoes

There now exists, a huge army of wine drinkers all based in their own homes. With the benefit of no baby sitter, no taxi, no need of a purse full of money and a seemingly compulsory sixty quid paid every month to rent a TV package - **WHY** would they want to leave the house? This is the wall we have to climb.

How are you going to tap in to this market and crowbar these customers back?

Answer. You're not trying to reinvent the wheel. Simply offer products the customer might already consume at home, but add value way and above the price paid in a shop; otherwise what's the point? Try asking customers **THEIR** preference.

Example. After successfully persuading a customer to enter the building; acknowledgment is the first hit, even if the server is busy, that'll already be **ADDING VALUE** for them. Upon service and asking for a glass of red, a clued-up server should be able to pinpoint a small selection of products that narrow the search. Further genuine enquiries to find out what suits the customer normally and it shouldn't be too much of a wild guess. Spending even a small amount of time liaising - is custom building. After pinpointing the taste of the customer in front of you and recommending a product, one could easily supply a dash to taste. If you personally possess enough product knowledge, you can steer a customer reasonably quickly towards a sale. Some houses might not consider tasting, stock control being paramount; I would see it as an investment. Predominantly, this action will take very little time and the cost minimal, but goodwill created might supply the biggest payback - a **REGULAR RETURN CUSTOMER.**

Don't knock it – lately they've been as rare as rocking horse shit!

Flipside. Failure to train bartenders with the knowledge to back up the service, you may as well put bottles in a vending machine and sod the niceties. You shouldn't have to pay staff more wages (unless you think they're worth it) to deliver this standard of service. This is where **ALL** bartenders should be and not an exception to the rule. I personally have never met a member of staff with these skills - have you?

The personal touch

When a customer makes a decision, enquire as to the size of glass they would prefer. I personally love a 250ml glass flashed in my face, but maybe they would like a 175ml or 125ml. If the customer purchases a bottle; serve in a cooler as bare minimum, an ice bucket even better. Make it special, a treat, **ADD VALUE** - people positively love being indulged. Are **ALL** your wine glasses spanking clean? Do **ALL** your staff check each glass at eye level before even thinking of pouring one drop of what the customer might perceive – an expensive choice?

Warning. Large attractive wine glasses add kudos for the customer, but glasses that are way too big can make the portion size seem diminutive when purchasing by the glass.

Choice

I'm not suggesting you offer a large selection, it's clearly impractical. Think about what people currently enjoy at home and expand your entire offer from that position. If the current rage is Pinot Grigiot - offer several choices. Plan from there outward instead of one token Pinot plonked in the middle of an expensive collection of stooges gathering dust. Compliment with a choice of bubbly and sparkling wines at varying prices and a selection of enjoyable reds, with the emphasis being on enjoyable. Forget the snobbery of wine; supply product's customers will love and return for. Consider subtle products, easy on the palate, dare I suggest – middle of the road.

Why? At home, the average human might down a couple of large glasses of wine and think nothing of it. The next day, just like you; they still have to bring home the bacon so to speak and generally not be too affected by a 12% volume product.

New build, bad taste story

I visited a new build pub and took advantage of a two meals with free bottle of wine offer. The wine was rancid, I can't remember the meal. I can only recollect how bad the wine was. It wasn't off or corked, it just had that familiar rancid taste, which emanates from a bargain-basement product wrapped in sheep's clothing. This place must have cost a million to set up. I chose the freebie after combing the wine list, unable to find anything worth the gamble. I still lost.

Therein lies the problem: a gamble with small possibility of discovering a winning horse. We have to change the way we sell and promote wine. How difficult do we have to make it? Put the customer #1.

It needs to be the norm' to taste before decision – not a novelty, awkward, or rushed request made in desperation!

Short measure story

I visited a brand new bar and grill late at night. I stood at a beautiful bar and waited. Three smartly dressed bartenders stood behind, none of them facing me. In-fact; it took the manager who by chance, was stood by my side chatting, to notice I was waiting - there were no other customers in sight. He alerted the staff and off we went. I decided on a glass of dry white and the bartender held a glass up to check before pouring (10 out of ten for that). I asked for a 250ml and he picked up a 175ml measure, cockily poured my short measure and asked £6.95 for the pleasure – the price of a 250ml. Serving mistakes are easily made, impressions irksome to lose.

Long story cut short

Yes I've slated what is currently on offer and I would stand by that, but this creates massive opportunity. If you're thinking of entering the liquor trade, learn all about wines beforehand. That knowledge will help translate what the customer actually craves, toward a more profitable outcome. If creating a wine menu from scratch, be careful about spending £500 on menus; you may find that half the products you've chosen - simply don't work. Far better and economical to use table talkers and easily altered card templates, alongside an attractive blackboard. Make sure products are kept at the correct temperature. Spring clean glasses at every opportunity.

Pick nice glasses . . . Be bloody nice!

Why? Two customers meeting once a week after work and sharing a bottle of wine at £12.99 discounting holidays, adds up to just over six hundred pounds a year, with no food, snacks or a second bottle taken into account – **BLOODY HELL!**

A sure-fire certainty. Superb customer love will always increase custom. A professional delivery by motivated staff aiming to please and people will beat a path to your door. Word of mouth is hard earnt, but always the strongest tool. Even teaching the basics could elevate your team head and shoulders above the competition, if for no other reason at present – there is **NO** competition.

Hold tasting sessions – for your STAFF!

Get your staff on-board, provide the knowledge and continually train and encourage. If there are units delivering high quality wine and service I apologise profusely, but I don't see any evidence of that I'm afraid. By any standard, this is another **HUGE** opportunity.

29 COFFEE OFFER

It's a no brainer

Fact. Pubs and clubs are shutting at an alarming rate all over this country, but one particular chain of coffee shops has just opened its tenth branch within a short reach of the city centre where I live – a small city. Someone is doing something right.

Advice. If I were opening **ANY** manner of licensed premises from here on in, I would include serving coffee to a very high standard. You would have to have had your brain removed not to embrace the current trend in coffee consumption. Look at any new builds of licensed premises - they'll **ALL** have adopted a strong coffee offer. During the day, a modern bar can have as many customers drinking coffee as they can alcohol, a kind of self-marketing dream team. Not so weird they mesh so well (ask the French), one wonders what took so long. Subtract coffee from that equation and call me Shirley if it didn't make a severe, if not fatal effect on takings in those same units.

Why do we love coffee so much?

A coffee shops product range is minimal, yet there they sit in prime positions on a high street near you, right now. How can they afford to be there? Think about it. Think about it a lot. I bet there are an awful lot of people in **ANY** town centre that will think about nipping for a quick coffee. Alcohol is too extreme sometimes, whereas a coffee can be a nice fix. Licensed premises used to be on the receiving end of that reward scheme, now coffee shops have taken that crown and capitalised on it **BIG STYLE** – a change in culture maybe?

Opportunity

Most licensed premises will already possess facilities the average common and garden coffee shop would die for. Think about developing a food offer based around hot drinks. Muffins, Victoria sponge, cookies and chocolates, just like a coffee shop. You might not want to serve hot meals, but have enough kitchen space to expand your menu. Freshly prepared salads, baguettes, club sandwiches, bowls of fries; this might give the average pub a big advantage against a coffee shop, whose products are mostly pre wrapped and won't enjoy the luxury of space, or wage budget to offer this extra choice.

Advantages. People often like scooting to the pub for their lunch, but get put off by long waits for hot food. A cold selection with coffee or hot chocolate at the press of a button is a faster alternative, minus the cost of an expensive chef on your wages budget. Why not offer takeaway coffee and tea at a price that blows away a coffee shop. The mark-up will still be there, but might drag custom in to see what you're all about. Hand flyers out in the streets, **CULTIVATE** word of mouth.

Warning. Quality coffee is a powerful tool, but if you want to attract a coffee clientele, you can't have loud mouthed drunks shouting **F's** and **C's** at their mates across the room at **ANY** cost. If you plan to invest in a coffee machine, I would suggest you have already made your decision to go zero tolerance.

What goes around comes around. People might tire of the same old ambience a coffee shop delivers. The one chain I particularly like is slightly different, but delivers lukewarm products – what bloody good is that?

Advice. Ensure your products, facilities; ambience and customer service are way ahead of anyone else. Word of mouth alone will probably take care of the rest.

What type of coffee machine?

The USP (Unique Selling Point) of a coffee shop, is the authenticity and aroma of making the coffee in front of you. I don't think you can compete with that style of delivery.

Why? These machines are extremely expensive and high maintenance. Most baristas are highly trained individuals; you will not have the luxury of that impression, or the time it takes to produce each cup. Authentic though it may be, waiting in a queue as a barista works away can be excruciating. You need a fast option producing a quality product - **EVERY TIME**.

Advice. I would opt for an automated bean to coffee machine, able to make at least 300 cups a day, including hot chocolate as an extra. Make sure it caters for take away size cups. This is a press the button and the product pours job, with you refilling milk and flavours as required. It will need to be plumbed in, cleaned constantly and meticulously maintained on your part.

Cost. In the region of five grand installed, with the first year of service agreement all in. A yearly service cost of a machine like this is roughly £600 - £1000 for an all singing all dancing repair deal, but I don't really see a way round that. My only beef would be a guarantee of how long it will take from time of call, to an engineer arriving on site in a breakdown scenario - trade slowly disappearing down the road.

AAAAAGGGGGHHHHH!

Tea

Whatever happened to tea in this equation? Can I suggest a spanking clean white mug, served at the strength requested, just like a steak. A huge market - just an idea.

Female friendly

In a social club for example, is a coffee always available? What can you offer a lady not requiring alcohol? How many soft drinks can one actually stomach in one visit? If a lady wants to go, she'll take her man with her – **HOME**, taking his wallet with him. Attracting both sexes is key to a successful venture. A well-dressed coffee offer might open up a whole new market and is sometimes blindingly disregarded as an **OPPORTUNITY** for **ANY** licensed premise.

Long story cut short

If you decide to go coffee; simply plonking an expensive machine on the bar, without investing in display trays for the counter, ample cups and all relevant pieces of the jigsaw simply won't cut it. Visit every damn coffee bar in town. What are their strengths and weaknesses? Draw up a business plan. Cover every angle and don't shoot unless you implement with conviction. As with the rest of your business, put the backdrop in, set the scene and hammer home the training.

Aim. Provide competition. Coffee fans now link patronage to coffee shops. Historically they won't remember having a great cup of coffee in a pub, but might remember the loos not smelling very healthy, the crap service, two drunks arguing and the juke box thumping noise that nearly drove them insane.

Do you get where I'm coming from?

The mark up on coffee beans and tea can be superb. The fringe benefits from both are attractive to say the least. Regular customers don't have to be **PISSHEADS** to boost profit. Sometimes you haven't got to be inventive . . . unashamedly jumping on the bandwagon can be a perfect fit.

30 SECURITY SECURITY

I only have the luxury of a few pages to cover security, but could write a whole book. What I really want to get over is the ethos behind almost every action you take as you weave through the working day. Imagine me shouting quite a lot.

The need to acquire security habits that in the end become purely natural . . . Is fundamental to keeping you, your building, staff and monies safe & secure!

Locks, keys, doors and money

Example. Every single time you leave your office, lock the door without exception. The first time you leave it unlocked, will be the day you lose the four grand you'd left on the table when called out to the bar to get rid of some asshole. Get into the habit. Get used to it real fast, or it **WILL** catch you out.

Lesson. Never leave 4K anywhere but the safe or the bank.

Living on the premises. Never leave the door to your quarters ajar or unlocked – **NEVER EVER**. Someone will break in. You and your **FAMILY** will never ever feel safe again as long as you live there. Not worth the risk or the heartache, your life will be hard enough without all this bollocks.

Locks. Make sure locks fitted to all relevant spaces are man enough for the job. If you think that one particular door is **IFFY**; sure enough that will be the one used for access – by **THIEVES**.

You have been warned!

If the locks worn . . . replace it.
If the door is rotten . . . replace it all!

Advice. Don't take chances and scrimp on what is elementary infrastructure. Actually being secure, allows freedom in your brain to concentrate on the other two hundred tasks ahead.

Warning. If somebody is that determined to break in to your office or quarters - they'll probably succeed. The least **YOU** can do is ensure they actually **HAVE** to structurally break in.

Advice. A night latch really isn't good enough for important areas; a credit card can open a lock like that in seconds. Back up with a mortise type lock at the very least and **USE** it.

Tip. If visiting a prospective site, inspect every damned lock and key apparatus in detail before you sign on the dotted line.

Nothing to do with locks is cheap!

Advice. If your office door is rotten and you lose eight grand as a result; a manager might have to pay that money back and/or lose their job and career in the process. Manager or not, point this out to the **KNOWITALL** ABM showing you round.

On handover of premises. It certainly would be as thick a shit, not to change the cylinders/barrels in **ALL** important doors. Even a manager should demand the office, quarters, main, safe and cellar doors to be sorted as minimum.

Keys. As per the cellar, the hours I've lost looking for keys is a real bug bear. There are certain keys you just **HAVE** to carry on your person at all times, but narrow it down. Once you've opened up; put door keys in the safe, in your locked office until shutting, or an easy access coded box on the bar in case of emergency. Lighten the load, feel less like a jailer and appear more professional, why wouldn't you?

Story. I was once told a story about a manageress who left her pub keys on the bar (before opening) and had a visit from her ABM. He found the keys left on the bar and put them in his pocket. He then went to the safe and removed an amount of money to teach a lesson - some lesson. True or not, I can't imagine a happy ending. If that happened to me, I'd probably have given that ABM a lesson in how to eat and digest keys.

Lesson. Never leave your keys anywhere but on your person, or in your locked office – a bloody nightmare.

Where money is concerned. Don't trust anybody: family, friends, staff, boss, nobody. **YOU** will be solely responsible for **ALL** monies held and taken. Your safe, is your safe. As you build faith in staff; of course you must delegate out, including access to **YOUR** safe, but never let your guard down – **NEVER EVER**. It is knackering, stressful and never-ending, but . . .

YOU will always take the fall for any loss whether it be monies or stock!

As a manager. Upon culmination of a safe check by a stock taker or auditor, **YOU** will be expected to explain the six quid missing and replace it before **THEY** leave. If it's eight hundred quid missing; you'll still be asked to replace it, shortly before a couple of significant phone calls to an ABM and other suchlike executioners, which might result in you being marched off the premises. And that as they say - will be that.

As an independent. You'll still take the full loss, but the penalty you pay for misdemeanours will more likely affect your pocket than the risk of a firing squad. Losing any amount of money is a real kick in the balls though. If it does happen to you, learn the lesson - wise up. Oh, and don't let the customers know - they'll think you're an idiot.

Money. If you're in the office counting a till, or floating back up and something does happen **OUT THERE** - don't leave the money on the workbench, put it all away in the safe first. Call me old fashioned, but I've heard of wackier diversion tactics.

Cash lifts. I did on occasion get in to situations where I had tills you just couldn't get any more notes in, but was too busy too sort, not enough staff to cope (a nice position to be in, but extremely precarious). If somebody leans over, helps their selves to a wad of twenties when the till drawer is open and runs straight out the door – it'll go from problem to **NIGHTMARE**. Being conscientious is a quality, but would you carry on serving until the boat goes down with you on it? What good is that? Even under extreme pressure, always lift excess cash. The not enough staff thing is a problem unto itself, but not clearing tills will be a problem **YOU** entirely own. Cash lifts are essential and fundamental. There can be **NO** excuse for not reducing risk for you and your staff; at the same time floating back up the change. If you're busy, no one will thank you for not having plentiful change available – staff or customers.

Break-ins. A likely time to be robbed, especially in your quarters - will be whilst you're actually **OPEN**. If you're downstairs, they'll know for a fact you're not upstairs. More especially, when the units packed to the rafters and your heads spinning - is opportunity time for thieves. Don't leave windows upstairs open when you're downstairs. Explain this to family members – **SPELL IT OUT** if you have to. Intermittently check round the whole gaff at numerous points throughout the working day. Exhausting - it will become purely natural.

This world is full of scumbags wanting a piece of what you've got!

CCTV

As previously mentioned; when in the office, always keep an eye on the monitor. Recognising a problem developing, you can quickly put tubs of money and till away in the safe, and be out there **BEFORE** the phone rings panicking for assistance. This type of multitasking will become second nature as you gain experience. Pre-empting problems with speed can save so much grief - not just for you, but staff and customers alike.

Outside lighting. What good is outdoor CCTV - if the lights either haven't been switched on or bulbs need replacing?

CCTV history. Keep as long a record of recordings as you possibly can. Choose a CCTV system that has the ability to record all data from the cameras to a data card. Memory cards are much cheaper now. Never throw them away – **EVER!**

Why? If an insurance claim is made against you or your premises, or for an incident on your premises; it might save not only a case full of money, but heartache, sleepless nights and stress - be your very own policeman before the fact. What's the point of only keeping a month of CCTV, if a person comes forward with a claim three months after – it happens.

It will have been worth buying this book for that little tit bit of information alone. I know a licensee who is being sued right now for an alleged fall on their premises!

Furthermore . . .

Make sure the time and date on your CCTV recorder is correct and corresponds with your tills, or go and find another job that demands way less of you!

Alarms

Big tip. Whoever the hell you are; on the day of handover, change the alarm codes for the building. I would bet that some alarm codes haven't been changed in twenty years or more.

Stupid Stupid Stupid!

Advice. Don't keep the code in your phone, what if it gets nicked? Keep in your head - a copy in the safe. If they're in your safe, they'll have already bypassed the alarm. Don't use the same number as personal cards – **PLEASE DON'T**.

Tip. If you part company with a key staff member, I would suggest you at least change the alarm codes, if not certain mortise locks too - is it really worth the risk? I'll leave you to be the judge and jury on that one. It's nice to **SLEEP** at night.

Door staff

Much has been documented about door staff from a door staff perspective. More important to **YOU** - will be how professional these people are and how they will add value to your offer. In other words, what is the **BENEFIT** to you?

Michael. There are some truly **GREAT** door guys and gals out there, who are a credit to the profession. There are however, individuals who will get **YOU** into all sorts of unnecessary shite. Just like crap service at the bar, every brick you lay – they will knock down. Picking the right door staff is a crucial piece of the jigsaw, the first point of contact for most customers; a welcome filter, cooler and your very own scumbag repellent jacket. For the most part, door staff provide an insurance scheme ensuring a smooth ride for customers purchasing your premium products, enjoying superb service and an ambience that **YOU** will have worked really hard to create.

Violent story

In my last unit (nicknamed the *VIOLENT SOLDIER*) I banned 176 people in the first three and a half months. I then went on holiday. I received a call on the first day from the relief, requesting permission to hire a couple of door staff in my absence. Trade had increased substantially, so that was ok. On return to work I was introduced to these two impressive looking chaps, went to a spare table and had a sit down which lasted all of sixty seconds. Hey presto I hired Brian and Ian, the best thing I ever did. It was my fifth unit and I was physically and mentally tired - I knew I needed some help hereon in. Those guys enabled me to focus on the real job of improving all round service and general atmosphere. In the next eighteen months I banned another 121 idiots, but maxed the takings. Brian and Ian had three mates who helped at Xmas; Tony, an Egyptian guy H and last but not least, Rocky. My blood pressure returned to **NORMAL**. Brian and Ian were exactly what I was looking for. Respected within the local community, they were zero tolerance delivered with supreme courtesy - bloody **BRILLIANT**.

Bear in mind. Credit where credit is due: most door staff will visit the gym two or three times a week, you won't be paying them for that. If they do a good job for you, genuinely thank them at the end of their shift - they'll respect you for that. Door staff should add value to the customer journey; humans enjoy feeling safe to let their hair down. Superb door staff will insure and boost takings – no question.

Big tip. Professional female coolers can be a real asset.

Are the door staff you employ, a positive or a negative to your business?

Security long story cut short

Running any licensed premises, means having to be alert 110% of the time. So many issues and chores to take care of, like juggling a hundred glass balls most of the day, every day. Dropping one might mean it smashes all over the place, creating another bloody mess to deal with. The ethos I mentioned at the start of this chapter, is all about developing systems and habits that assist the smooth path of the very difficult workload you endure. Just like removing obstacles in the ideal customer journey, removing security obstacles in **YOUR** journey - is imperative for your very own sanity. Imagine a parrot permanently on your shoulder, perpetually barking at you; did you lock that door? Shut that till. What are they doing over there? Pick your keys up. You need to remove that wad of twenties and tens from till two before someone does it for you. Did you shut the bathroom window in the living quarters? Turn the outside lights on. Did I download last week's CCTV to a memory card? She doesn't look old enough. A glass breaks.

AAAAAGGGGGHHHHH!

Quite honestly it's enough to send you completely bonkers when first entering the trade. You'll feel completely knackered ALL the time. So many things to take into account, at the same time developing eyes in the back of your head. My main advice would be . . .

Always keep a healthy stock of painkillers!

31 BANNING SCUMBAGS

Stern words with a typical asshole might just bring them back in to line, but do yourself a big favour - don't waste your breath on a scumbag, they are in a totally different league.

Who are they?

They might be the local bully or gang, who put the fear of god into staff, customers and you alike. They also might be the characters holding court and dealing customers - habitually doing drugs in **YOUR** loos and car park. If you think drug taking doesn't happen near you – I'm afraid you're probably naïve.

And what does that mean to you?

Scumbags are business killers!

Widespread use of pills and drugs is now part and parcel of everyday life. Every Tom, Dick and Harry seems to be growing something at home. For the life of me I cannot understand why the authorities of this land have to drag licensees across hot coals, when I regularly pass herberts smoking cannabis in the street and witness drug deals on my way to the local shop; these people never seem to get pulled. Unless licensees are in possession of a drugs dog, or can afford a security team to search every cavity of every customer's body, how can we stop drugs from filtering in? Pray tell us Mr Prime Minister!

Good news. You do get a nose for these things as you gain experience. I was green as grass about drugs before entering the licensed trade, that's naïve with a capital N. Now I can generally spot a drug dealer the moment I enter a room.

How can you stop it in your unit? Sad to say I'm afraid, I don't think you can totally eradicate it from your premises. **What then?** Be proactive. Train staff to be your eyes and ears. Regularly visit loos and deprive users of flat surfaces in cubicles (why anyone would spend twenty quid and pour on to a toilet cistern is way beyond my comprehension). Communicate a zero tolerance to all drug use on the premises. Make it known.

Story. I was recently openly offered a line of coke on top of a hand dryer. That hand dryer was thick with dust and dirt.

Michael. Politicians will talk for ten minutes on what they are doing about drugs and crime and not actually say anything whatsoever. They will say that crime is down, when it's completely obvious to the man in the street - crime is worse than ever. There seems no political will to stamp drug use out. There exists no deterrent, backed up with an ever decreasing number of police to carry out this war. Either politicians are walking around with their heads up their asses, or they just don't give a crap. Probably both of those I would guess.

Shocking. I'm amazed the government don't acknowledge a particular army of non-paid police that daily carry on one of the last great battles against drugs (that's you by the way). As if you haven't got enough to do, you will be expected to be an expert in the detection of drugs and crime on your premises.

AAAAAGGGGGHHHHH!

I find it galling that when a licensee rings the police for help it could count as a black mark against that licensee. **What a bloody cheek — the authorities can't even keep drugs out of our prisons! Hypocrisy on a grand scale?**

Pubwatch

Never underestimate the value of a quality pubwatch scheme. A pubwatch could ask the local drugs squad to attend and pass on vital advice, as well as co-ordinating the usual parade of lunatics banned from general consumption. Knowing who they are will aid identification as they attempt to pass your door.

Asking people to leave

Recent court cases in the UK in 2015 seem to have added confusion to the subject of either asking people to leave, or stopping them at the door before entry. As far I know to this day; you don't actually have to give a reason not to serve someone at the bar. Don't even get into that conversation. If they refuse to leave and you haven't got door staff on, surely you're going to have to call the plod? At pubwatch; ask both your local police and licensing officer if that's acceptable, or is that black mark territory. Clarify beyond question, what you can and can't say or do. I'm sorry to have to go through all this shit, but **YOU** need to know about the rancid side of life as a licensee. Even if you're built like a brick shit house, you can't apparently lay your hands on someone and eject them. Improving trade means creating a safe environment for all customers to enjoy the moment.

You might have to say no - an awful lot!

Licensing officer/police. Before taking on a unit, request a meeting with the local officials and ask pertinent questions about what sort of back up you are likely to receive should you have any problems. Be respectful, but ask the questions.

Warning. Bear in mind it would be a complete numpty of a licensee to call the police to attend for a silly reason.

Worst case scenario story

On one occasion, it did all go off. It was neither prudent of me to be seen ringing the **OLD BILL** – or **SENSIBLE**. I did take the phone off the hook, ring 999 and walk away. The call registered and the cavalry did come to rescue me. I'm not sure if this trick still works, but it might be handy to run past the local pub watch. The police should have the address of the number in question, be listening, and more importantly – **RECORDING** any scene/mayhem carrying on in the background.

Warning. Please don't use this trick unless life is in danger. The police will not thank you unless it is really called for. I used it twice in nine years – I'm still here to tell the tale though.

Where's the toilet paper?

Long story cut short and the effect on you

Banning people is not easy at the best of times. Try and ensure your staff and your own safety at all costs, not to mention the safety of your customers and premises. I had the experience of running a couple of very tasty units. I had literally dozens of scenarios occur that have left me with a very low opinion of certain characters of the human race. I'm reasonably well built with a strong resolve, but on several occasions definitely had to check the state of my trousers. Even the biggest, toughest licensee will swim out of their depth and wish they were somewhere else on occasion.

Nerves. Don't be surprised in suffering from shock when dealing with intimidating scenarios. Mostly I felt this after the event, shortly after breathing a private sigh of relief (with nobody realising, even though in a crowd). Your vulnerability will surface and reality will return with a thud. I used to shake.

32 STORIES & THE BAD TIMES

Drugs story

I banned this guy, but he came back – twice. He'd walk in to the bar through one door, pick up a bar stool, launch it over the bar towards the optics, then casually walk out the other door not caring what or whom he damaged - nice eh? The first time I put it down to experience; I'd upset my regulars, but he deserved to be banned – for life. The second time I rang his boss. He had rather a nice job and I brokered a deal to ensure it never happened again – it didn't. I will never forgive him for the stress and widespread unrest it caused. I remember the pressure seemed suffocating. No-one forces you to take drugs.

Pool cue incident

I had a group of guys playing pool in the afternoon. Something upset one of the troop; so much so, that as I peered through to see what the hell was going on, I witnessed him break a pool cue over his knee - that was all I needed. He was marched to the side door before he knew what day it was. As we got nearer the door, he began to realise where this was leading. I ejected him through the inner door and then an outer exit. He started to swear profusely and threaten me with violence. He hadn't noticed the two policemen standing six foot away. I knew one of the police by face. As they grabbed him I informed them he had just broke one of my pool cues on his knee and was no longer welcome in the pub – forever. I shut the door and the problem disappeared (that was in the days when we actually had police walking the beat). Humans often think they can do what they like, when they like – there is a line.

Bad conduct

I banned a whole family for bad behaviour and started getting abusive phone calls. After about three weeks of this, they threatened to attack my family in my upstairs quarters, even threating to plant a bomb. My company (bless 'em) agreed to fit iron railings to **ALL** windows upstairs. To be honest, I slept better than I had in years after that. Plod made a visit and the abuse stopped thank god, but I did get used to sleeping with a bat and consumed rather large quantities of brandy at that time. I remembered then what my first partner used to say . . .

"Come on, it'll be great fun running a pub"

Racial abuse story

I received a call upstairs from my assistant manageress, to say she had been on the receiving end of racial abuse and was concerned for her safety. I ran down rather swiftly to find a guy who I'd had problems with previously. I entered the scene to witness this abuse first hand; instinctively I knew trouble was only a short conversation away. I stepped in and instructed Melanie to ring the police discreetly from behind the scenes, so the guy wouldn't be aware the cavalry might arrive. This guy then invited me to come and throw him out if I thought I could, seemingly intent on causing mayhem. When he realised that I wasn't going to be drawn from behind the bar, he threatened to jump the bar and attack me. I duly informed him that would be his choice, but I would defend myself and my staff. I was secretly craving he would, but a bar is a formidable psychological barrier. It would take a total psychopath to actually jump the bar and attack, maybe aware of a number of customers witnessing this developing situation.

I knew that this would all be clocked by my CCTV, and I also knew the way he was talking and acting - this wasn't going to have a happy ending. He then paused and it flashed through my mind for a split second, he might have a gun. He didn't, and instead went on to threaten raping my daughter, who had come to live with me upon leaving school that year. He named her, and was really quite chilling in his delivery. To be perfectly honest, this did turn the tables on me and my bloody CCTV. If it hadn't have been for the cameras all over my bar, he would definitely have got his way, which is exactly what I can only presume he wished for. As he finally lost it, the police were able to listen to the last few threats as they came behind and arrested him. We all went to court on that one and he spent time in nick. What triggered it all? I have no idea.

Football fans

I had this boozer in front of Swindon railway station. A usually quiet Saturday lunchtime session, turned in to an hour and a half of living on the edge. I had one girly on the bar, whilst I took care of kitchen duties. About half past twelve we were rudely awakened by about 200 visiting football fans (West Brom I think). Before I knew it, they were through the door and fully entrenched. What do you do? I quickly turned everything in the kitchen off (sod the food), locked the kitchen door for protection, shutting bar flaps down as I came on the bar and checked the ice supply. I already had good floats on the tills (take note) so that was good news. I muttered a few four letter expletives under my breath, took a deep one and joined forces with my poor girly facing all these thirsty - football supporters.

AAAAAGGGGGHHHHH!

If you've ever been behind a bar, the whole unit in front of you stacked with football fans, and only two of you serving; it can be a trifle daunting, but when **ALL** of those fans start doing this chanting thing in support of their team, at the top of their voices - it can make the hairs on your neck stand to attention. Worry you will. The girly and me just about got away with it and took about fifteen hundred quid in an hour and a bit. No trouble, no assholes, a few requests for food but never mind, a rake of footy fans happy and on their way. I must state for the record: the fans were just so friendly and courteous - that is the only reason we **GOT AWAY** with it.

Lesson. If you're near a stadium of any kind; download the fixture list - plan ahead. After that though, we shut by police command - they didn't see it coming either.

Revenge

I had just finished an all-day stint in the kitchen (10am- 8pm) and was still in my kitchen blue check trousers and white polo shirt. The regulars were all in as usual and there was a jolly old banter flying about. I hadn't had a pint for a week and was easily persuaded to join the party. On my second pint, I noticed these three chaps sat at the bar - they were jumping. By that, I mean they'd definitely just done a line or two of something illegal. I sort of recognised the one in the middle who seemed to be their leader, constantly staring at me. I was right by them and leaned over. I said something like . . .

> **"I recognise you from somewhere, where do I know you from?" He replied "You banned me a year ago for fuck all!"**

That got my attention. I took one look at the two meatheads either side and knew I was in the shit; worse still – imminently. One of the guys had arms that had seen lots of gym. He followed me around the bar to the open hatch. He started laughing as he picked up a bottle on the bar; I knew exactly what he was going to do with that. In a flash, I slammed the bar hatch down, but couldn't prevent him hitting me square on the head with this bottle (come run a pub, it'll be great fun). I saw stars, but didn't black out. The whole pub just exploded like a scene from the Wild West. My ex ran out of the kitchen and kicked one of them (well done Trace). They escaped out the back door and down the back lane, leaving my white polo shirt with a new deep red complexion. That was how I entered the pub down the road - with police to identify two of them. I ended up with multiple stiches - it was a long night.

New job. I actually had an interview the next day for another unit within the company. I travelled to Newbury for this interview and was greeted with surprise, as HR had told them I probably wouldn't - too bloody right I did. The three people on the panel continually threw me funny looks. I thought I'd blown it. I got home, looked in the mirror and noticed these two long strands of nylon stitching, sticking straight up to the sky like antennae. I must have looked a right cock. I'm surprised they kept a straight face at all - I got the job.

Finale. I attended court nine or so months later, had to have a police escort from the train station on arrival and departure, with two of my oldest (biggest) mates, Willy and his son Gareth for protection. Turns out; the main character was part of some gang (just when you think it can't get any worse – it does). If they'd wanted to teach me a lesson – they had some success.

AAAAAGGGGGHHHHH!

Hammer attack

Second week in my fifth unit, I thought I'd seen it all - silly me. First I knew, was noticing a fracas by one of the side entrances. Apparently, some chap had dragged a lad out and attacked him with a hammer. I ran outside to find this lad in the middle of the road, blood pumping in the air like a fountain in surges, a surreal scene I can tell you. What do you do? This lad wasn't saying or moving an awful lot. I pressed two of my fingers where the blood was oozing from and kept them in place. It seemed to stem the flow, but I was stuck then - I couldn't move. I yelled at someone to ring an ambulance immediately, another to get me tissues or anybloodything to help apply pressure to the wound. Young lads were creating chaos all around me threatening this and that. A girl who knew him took over from me, whilst I stopped traffic and people from getting in the way (humans really are a pain in the arse sometimes). An ambulance arrived and more police than I'd ever seen in one place. After giving statements, I had a few drinks and woke up to ITV and BBC reporters knocking on my door at half seven in the morning – unbelievable.

Biker attack

It was Saturday night with a hundred or so in, watching a really talented funky rock band. Earlier in the evening, I had observed a few jackets marked with a different biker chapter than my usual crew. At about 10pm, I got this feeling something was up. I did the rounds a couple of times, but couldn't put my finger on it and moved towards the front doors again for another look around. It was then I noticed three vehicles pull up opposite, in the train station approach: a jag, a range rover and a transit as far as I can remember.

Like in some action movie, every door on every vehicle opened at once. Out piled all these denim and leather clad chaps, tattoos abound, brandishing hammers of all sizes (what is it about bloody hammers?), including one of the sledge variety; big bats, and one scary chap dragging a chain behind him.

AAAAAGGGGGHHHHH!

If I'd have had time to shit myself . . . I probably would have!

I didn't have door staff on, and as a backdrop to that; my daughter was in the pub kitchen with my girlfriend of the time, preparing food for her twelfth birthday party, to be held in the pub the next day (we were shut on a Sunday, a bit like London city pubs that are completely surrounded by office blocks). I pulled the lock bars across the front doors. With that, all hell broke loose. The band was halfway through a number at the time, when all this glass started to fly everywhere. My only train of thought was to stop them entering. I ended up leaning against the front doors to stop them caving in and managed to secure the mortise lock somehow, as the windows of these very doors started splintering all over me. I felt now would be a good time to ring a taxi. Like on the titanic, the band was still playing, but I guessed it wouldn't be very long until one of my double doors caved in. If they got in - we were all buggered. I remembered Lynn and my daughter innocently baking cakes in the pub kitchen. Within seconds I was shouting at Lynn, "Get her upstairs now". Lynn started to ask why and I blurted out in no uncertain manner, "do as your fucking told and do it now!" I realised at that point I was in panic mode. I took a deep breath and made back for the bar to find out if anyone was still alive. What I encountered then was surreal to say the least.

Opening the door, I was greeted by absolute silence and no movement by **ANYBODY**. The five piece band were all stood like statues, along with the hundred odd customers. You could have heard a pin drop. I could hear the hum of one of the valve amps from the band. There was all this glass on the carpet and windows, sort of missing. I saw and heard a car pass, unusually quite loud. We all just stood quiet and still for what seemed like ages - no one was dead as far as I could see, the doors intact. What seemed like an age was probably only seconds, but a **STRANGE** experience nevertheless. I'd like to say this was all character building stuff, but it probably took years off me. Regaining the ability to speak, I muttered something like . . . "I would suggest all the biker gang, whom are clearly and obviously **NOT WELCOME** – leave by the side door ASAP (which they did). And come on you lot (pointing at the band); I'm not paying you to stand around. And you lot (pointing at the crowd), start buying some beer for Christ's sake." I said all this with obedient silence in the room. There was a slight hiatus. Then, everybody all at once started talking, as if they'd been on pause and the band started. I asked my staff if they were ok and reached for the dust pan and brush.

> # I exaggerated on the phone to the glaziers – I said it was thirteen windows that had been smashed . . .
> # It was only twelve!

I had rang the police whist in the kitchen (wiping my ass at the same time), expecting the door to open and some big biker start attacking me. I rang the glazier afterwards, and the bloody glazier arrived before the police. What's that all about?

Personally. If I experienced a biker gang going off again, I certainly wouldn't say that on the phone to the police. I'd just say there was a fight going on, they might wait until mob handed before arriving. Would I be lying?

Michael. Turns out; there is political correctness within the hells angel fraternity. If a rival gang want to visit another chapters designated meeting place, they have to request permission from that chapter in advance or else. The last thing my daughter said to me that night after all the commotion had died down, and the glazier was putting boards up was – "I'm still going to have my party tomorrow aren't I dad?"

AAAAAGGGGGHHHHH!

Upshot. I took me three hours to get all that glass up. When the parents dropped their kids off the next day, a few remarked on the windows and had I had any trouble? I of-course replied we were just having the windows replaced as part of on-going maintenance. If you say something with conviction and don't blink too much, people can believe you. They did until the Tuesday, when the front page of the local rag had the headlines, 'Hells angels attack on pub, leaves a dozen windows smashed' or something to that effect. Those parents all thought of me as a bare faced liar from then on.

Lesson. If you have gangs of bikers frequenting your hostelry, they do so because **YOU** allow them to. It is not **THEIR** place, it is **YOURS**. Again, I was totally green on all this crap. Luckily, no one was injured, bar a few cuts glass collecting (pardon the pun). The biggest loss; several historic etched glass windows, plus the damage to my central nervous system. The local chapter did send a rather large bunch of flowers, but it'll never replace those beautiful windows.

Cabaret night

I banned this guy for bad behaviour. He was a tough old school builder bloke – **BIG DAVE**. He ripped his shirt off in the pub and took me on. I somehow managed to get him out, but he was strong as an ox and very proud. That was that. One of my door guys - Tony, invited my partner and me to a cabaret night at a local social club. We didn't get out much, mostly due to the fact, that going out might mean bumping into one of the two hundred and eighty customers I'd banned by then. Sod it, bored stiff, life's for living. I took my daughter too, and we arrived, sat down at this huge table and got sociable with new found friends. There were two free seats on this table. Just as the cabaret was about to start, this fella and his missus arrived just in time. You've guessed it, it was **BIG DAVE** - the builder I'd banned six months previous. In all the places in the entire world, he gets directed over to our table and sits down almost right beside me. I looked at him, he looked at me. Bloody great, thank you very much, you couldn't make it up. I wanted the earth to open up, and so did my partner. To be fair, I don't think the irony was lost on **BIG DAVE** either. Crueller still, we both ended up at the bar, stood right next to each other. I looked at him and he looked at me. We both smiled at the same time and I asked him how he was. He asked the same back and a good time was had by all. That night I invited Dave to come back in the pub and he accepted. Dave was one of a very few people I ever allowed back in amongst the thousand plus I banned for life - including my own brother.

To be fully in control and make wise decisions means you can never drink whilst on duty! – (Mick Brown 2015)

33 STAFF AT IT

Lots for me, Sod you story

I went to pick a mate of mine up from a venue just out of town from his Xmas do; I was completely sober, everyone else ten parts to the wind. Failing to obtain a coffee at the bar, a fella approached straight afterwards, ordering a couple of pints and four shorts. It tallied up to about £25. The customer paid the barman the exact money. As the customer turned his back after paying, the barman rang a no sale in the till. How do I know he rang a no sale in the till? It came up on the display as a no sale. There was no free bar and he was not the owner. He had a quick look around and pocketed the money there and then – **WHAT A BASTARD!** I couldn't see any cameras in the bar area and no one else was looking - nice work if you can get it. He didn't blink - I'd love to look at their stock results.

Warning. Once an individual crosses that line, steals from **YOUR** till and gets away with it - it'll be like a **DISEASE** every time they work a session. Does it happen? It really does.

What effect does this have on your business? If somebody is stealing cash; generally speaking, they will **NOT** have rang in, convenient (for them) items at the till. It gets expensive.

How much? Add what the stock **STOLEN** cost you in the first place and the money lost from the sales to the twenty five in cash – suddenly it's cut your wrists territory. In layman's terms; £25 in cash will lose you at least sixty quid plus the wages you're paying the **SCROAT** for the honour of . . .

Pocketing the cash as part of their personal yacht appeal!

Prevention

Can you stop fraud or theft? Probably not entirely - more a never-ending damage limitation battle I'm afraid.

How can you prevent it? Regular stock takes (weekly, if need be) and managing the audit trail of every bartender on a daily basis. If you have no track of voids, no-sales, handover of tills and stock loss; there's more chance of witnessing the Martians landing, than proving someone's on the take. The correct choice of staff in the first place certainly helps, but a till/stock system where you can check anything at any time, is probably the biggest weapon against fraudulent activity by staff. CCTV coupled with eyes wide open will complete your armoury. Humans will not usually steal in front of you. They'll wait till you're too busy in the kitchen, the cellar, or preferably out of the building. You'd have to be really lucky to catch someone red handed. I reiterate – **VERY LUCKY!**

You cannot just accuse staff of nicking . . . You have to have concrete proof!

Advice. Concrete evidence, might mean a guilty person walking there and then, but the last thing you want before possessing concrete proof - is make the suspect aware you **THINK** they're at it. As soon as you do that, **THEY** might shut down. Even if guilty; accusing without - they might stay.

AAAAAGGGGGHHHHH!

If you accuse, you'll more than likely have to suspend them on full pay - until such time as you can call a disciplinary meeting adhering to any rights the employee may be entitled to by law.

Warning. Just make sure you don't accuse an innocent person or else this **WILL** come back to bite - and rightly so.

Stealing money and stashing the cash

Historically, a favourite place for staff on the take to stash a note, might be under the drawer in the casing of the till, but the most dangerous money grabbing bastards won't leave a note in the drawer - they'll save it up within the till itself.

Random cash checks. Finding a till up by anything larger than a fiver, could be indication an individual is saving (your) money, before opportunely removing a convenient note towards that personal yacht appeal. From personal experience, 9 times out of a 10; finding excess cash in a till, signifies a staff member on the take. If your tills are spot on, but you're losing stock and can't find a reason – there could be the answer in a nutshell.

Random cash checks are a weapon.

Example. Discovering an extra sixteen quid in a till; I wouldn't necessarily bring this to the attention of the server. I might leave it like that; check any other tills in use, finishing with a safe check in your office to see if **YOU** have made a cock up in the first place. If sixteen quid down in the safe, that might explain that, but if you're not - alarm bells might ring.

What might you do? If an individual has solely used that till, I might let it run. By that, I mean let them finish their shift and remove the till at that point. If it's still sixteen quid up, I could prove nothing, but that might be clever on their part. If it was near enough correct, they'd have had it away. Real time recording of CCTV would be rather useful at that point.

Tip. If you suspect a bartender, it's pointless carrying out a cash check on their till twenty minutes into a session - choose your moment wisely. Remember: unless you carry out cash checks as a norm', you may alert that person they may now be under suspicion. Honestly, what a pile of shit it really is.

Health warning

From personal experience. It can be frustrating; suspecting
or convinced someone is being naughty and unable to prove it.
I've been there many times. You'll lose sleep over it. It can take
over your whole life. It sort of consumes one, leaving **YOU**
feeling desperately inadequate. Control your emotions at that
point. Remember: its only business. It may be a few quid
you're losing, but be patient. It's the hardest thing to carry on
business as usual, whilst inside feeling like a volcano is going to
erupt, but an opportunity will arise to bring matters to a head.
Act like a pig in a china shop and it might never.

Eyewash story

I inherited a barman upon takeover of a unit. This guy was a
really nice chap, salt of the earth and all that. I was consistently
down on one particular lager, by about three or four gallons
every couple of months. I was brand new to the trade, not yet
up to speed, what with learning all the other five hundred
bloody jobs I'd now discovered. After about a year, this loss
turned into eight or nine gallons every two months. Christ, I
thought I was going to get the sack! Every time someone
bought me a drink, I'd ring it in to make up the loss on that
product. I had a Welsh stock taker named Graham, who helped
me enormously. He must have recognised I wasn't a complete
tosser. We only sold an 11 gallon keg a week. Firstly, he
suggested we get rid of it altogether: this might not solve the
problem, but it was a start. I was always about six or seven
gallons up on each of my other lagers. I naively suggested this
would at least hide the problem, but was forgetting the lager
surplus helped hide stock loss in other areas.

Secondly, Graham pointed me towards my staff; what was the story there? I hadn't even given it a thought – what a cock. A couple of nights later I was in bed staring at the ceiling, sweating, and thinking about all this crap, when the penny started to drop. The only person I knew who actually drank this lager was my barman, whose nickname was **EYEWASH**. What was that all about? I made it my mission to find out.

Answer. This guy always worked the daytime shift weekdays. A couple of months previous, there was a right old jolly going on as he was finishing his shift. He usually disappeared quite abruptly, but the regulars and I had made a bit of a fuss about him staying for a couple - just this once. The most amazing thing happened. After about two pints he said he had to go. He got up and nearly fell over against the bar. It was one of those surreal moments when you can't work out what just occurred. Honestly, I must have been as thick as shit. Two months later, laid in my bed, sweating over this loss, I suddenly sat upright and new exactly what was going on. That day, he'd obviously been drinking all day long behind my flaming bar. No wonder he used to bugger off sharpish, he didn't want us knowing he was three parts to the wind already. Two more pints and he could barely walk or talk, let alone stay any longer.

Concrete proof. I arranged for one of my colleagues to visit while we went out for the day. I'd found out what eyewash referred to; it was the action this guy made, when he would quick as lightning consume a half of lager in about two seconds flat. He'd sort of raise his arm above his head and almost hide the half glass behind his arm. If he'd missed his mouth it would have caught him in the eye. I'd heard him called eyewash from the moment I'd moved in. What a donkey (and that's just me). On ringing my spy in the bar, he said he hadn't seen anything.

I went through the eyewash action again over the phone and he rang back half an hour later. He said he'd witnessed this guy do three eyewashes in 30 minutes flat. He said the guy was brilliant; he'd probably been doing it the whole time, but was so clever he hadn't clocked it. And there you go - **EYEWASH**. The next day my man left by mutual agreement – immediately. I stand by my judgement that this was a nice guy, but he had a problem. Unfortunately, it became my problem.

Story of Dim

I had another salt of the earth guy, held in high affection by the whole team. Let's call him Dim. He was always boasting about his tills being penny perfect. A dispute occurred over change given by Dim, requiring an immediate cash check. I grabbed my paper roll calculator, took a reading off the till and removed the till drawer. When I bent down to peer into the darkened drawer, I noticed a red ten pound note in the base. I left it there lurking in the dark and didn't blink. It took me all of about three minutes to count the till on the back of the bar, whilst keeping an eagle eye on the till area to see if Dim went near it to retrieve the evidence – I had assigned that till for his use only. The till was a further twenty six quid up.

AAAAAGGGGGHHHHH!

The customer dispute was only over four quid. I handed the customer back their four pounds, apologised profusely and told them their next drink was on the house. Giving the customer back four pounds left the till twenty two pounds up, plus a tenner still left in the till base. I went to the office; cash checked the safe, including two extra till drawers floated up ready for the evening, it was all penny perfect - I let it run.

Turns out his claim of penny perfect tills was a load of old bollocks then!

Sitting in my castle (office) pondering over all this crap gave me time to reflect on recent affairs. Dim had started to look slightly dishevelled, turning up to work unshaven, having previously been always well turned out. Instinctively, the moment I clocked the note in the drawer, I knew there was a spanner in the works; Dim had developed a problem. I always tried to look after my **FAMILY**, but if they've crossed that line of actually stealing from **YOU**? I let Dim finish his session. True to form, he hung about downing a couple of pints before leaving (one in and one paid in cash – with a ten pound note). The note **HAD** disappeared from the base of the till, and the till was (you've guessed it) almost **PENNY PERFECT**. So that's £32 stolen from my till, except it isn't just thirty two quid is it? Its £32, plus what the stock cost, plus the retail value. So I'm paying this scumbag to rip my company off and laugh in my face in the process – bring back public hanging I say.

Lesson. I was always way up on my lagers and hadn't noticed I wasn't quite as much up as normal. By chance, I'd interrupted his personal savings scheme. There were no extra no-sales or voids. He was serving a lager and a short, only ringing in the short. How do I know this? Before he left I went round and collected glasses noticing three or four couples with a lager and a wine for example. I did a timed hard copy print out for the last hour of Dim's shift. There hadn't been any lager sold for those rounds. Unfortunately for me, the CCTV wasn't real time; it recorded a frame every ten seconds (bloody useless). It didn't catch our Dim relieving the tenner from the base, or removing the extra from the till itself. Bloody hell.

Upshot. I suppose if I hadn't noticed the tenner in the base, I might have thought I was going slightly mad, but it not being there at the end of the shift clinched it for me. Dim was a long standing employee so I had to be careful, but – he had to go. The next morning when he came in, I took him to one side and told him I knew he was at it. I told him about the tenner and bluffed the CCTV, merely pointing at the camera above the bar and awaiting a reaction. He put his hands up just like that, told me his problems and burst out crying. There was no apology, just a blame game. It wasn't him it was the drugs.

AAAAAGGGGGHHHHH!

I then made another mistake. I told him he was still welcome in the pub as I feared for his mental state, but all he did was slag me off to customers and staff alike. Sometimes being able to lip read more or less, comes in really handy too. I banned him with gusto after that. If you've got concrete evidence . . .

Sack and ban in one foul swoop!

Long story cut short

Wherever there exists a candy store with pots of cash flying around, there will always be some smart Alec who thinks it's ok to skim off the top. Vet your staff, make sure your CCTV is real time recordable, install a till system linked to stock, operate random till checks and be alert. Irregular losses on stock should stick out like a sore thumb. The ability to spot problems early on can save you pots of cash and heartache.

The bonus. If you're obtaining regular 100% stocks and not losing any cash, it will signify you have mostly eradicated waste and thieving. It will also indicate you've trained your people to a fair degree. These are profit building milestones.

34 THE KITCHEN

Honest

I cannot simply bullshit my way through this chapter making out I know what I'm talking about, when truthfully I'm the least cooking friendly human you will ever meet. What I can do however; is share lessons learnt, (cures and consequences) mixed with a few ideas around the kitchen operation itself. I will hint towards the kind of people you should be looking to work your kitchen, and add, not subtract value to the customer journey. Here's one thing I do know for sure . . .

A badly run kitchen will fight against any battles you win front of house!

It's a place that should only be inhabited by humans who are organised and love cooking; possess the art of timing and a desire to be there – just not me. When I entered the trade in 1996 I would have struggled to make myself beans on toast. In 2000 when my cook left, the other going sick; I was forced into the role, pumping out 2K a week of £2.99 steak & chips and breakfasts at £1.99, at the same time preserving brilliant sales on liquor already achieved. It went on for months. Sex was a distant memory around then. I just wanted to run away.

Life in a pub/hotel/restaurant kitchen is not for the faint hearted!

I would personally rather have hot pins poked under my finger nails than be subjected to work a busy lunchtime session in a kitchen ever again.

It's hard to run any unit, let alone being based in the kitchen, but there are exceptions to the rule. I know a very talented chef who successfully runs an extremely busy unit, still managing to be very hands on front of house. This guy is highly motivated, conscientious and respected by staff and customers alike. High personal standards of food hygiene, coupled with years of experience, has set him in good stead to cope with some ridiculous EU rulings that beset us all - well done Shane! These individuals are as rare as rocking horse shit and should be coveted, but he and units all over this land offering even a limited menu, will suffer from the same eternal problem . . .

Finding RELIABLE kitchen staff with high standards and a strong work ethic!

In many areas, just finding a cook of any kind is nigh on impossible. Why do governments make **ALL** kids believe they can and **SHOULD** go to university? Whatever happened to working your way up from the bottom and learning a trade? We have to find kids with flair, talent and a true vocation - whilst still at school; offer them a real future instead of bullshit rainbow chasing. All I ever see is signs outside pubs – chef wanted. We need tens of thousands of these people.

Pertinent questions when setting up a food offer

- If you only employ one cook, what happens when they go on holiday or go sick for three weeks?
- Does the kitchen have to shut?
- Are you able and experienced enough to cover?
- What is your plan B?

What's the point of building up food trade only to have it decimated the moment your cook isn't there for one day?

Food offer

Decide what you want your food offer to do. 2k a week offering a simple menu, might still make a small profit, but the overwhelming advantage might be the gain on the wet side. A customer only ordering a club sandwich will invariably consume a pint, a softie, or a coffee to bump the bill.

Advice. The menu should be an easy fit within with the overall picture you paint. Whatever your food offer – profit it must. It must pay all the X's connected with the delivery of that food.

Advice. Even the most basic food offer is better than none at all. There aren't many wet only units being built these days - if any. How much more profitable could a wets only unit be by adding food at the very start, or at a re-launch? Yes it takes passion and commitment, but every single successful unit I visit, incorporates a strong, targeted food offer – full stop.

What's it like working in a pub kitchen?

Working the kitchen was painful for me and everyone within earshot. Yes I could cook one or two meals at the same time, but after that I was bloody useless. A customer enjoying a trouble free, enjoyable meal won't happen by accident; there are scores of affiliated jobs in a smooth running kitchen. If you're not cooking, you'll be prepping and filling out a whole host of kitchen protocol paperwork: all the rest of the time you'll be cleaning. At times it can be unbearably busy; orders spewing out of a printer in the kitchen to join the dozen already waiting - I seriously wanted to smash the bloody thing to smithereens on occasion. The pressure ramps up and you really have to step up to the plate. As if to pour salt on the wounds – it can get really hot. Hard graft – no question.

The right people

You can have the newest kitchen with all the right kit, the latest technology in place to deliver orders, and plenty of customers wanting to take advantage of your scrumptious looking menu, but it will all be reduced to a shower of shit, if you have made some really bad choices in whom you choose to drive this engine. Same damned equation as employing the wrong candidate to work the bar; it will cost you thousands of pounds in lost revenue and act like a cancer from within.

So much time and resources are wasted employing square ended individuals . . . attempting to fit in curvy round holes!

Employing the right people in your kitchen, will be the one decision you make, that will mostly determine whether **YOU** have **ANY** quality of life - other than work. Mark my words; a food offer with crap staff, is comparable to walking across a football pitch, only to discover a thousand self-exploding land mines have been planted all around – one going off every 5 minutes as a rule. I loved working the bar. **YOU'VE** got to find individuals who love - and are suited to working the kitchen.

Advice. Hold weekly meetings to discuss progress and failings. Regularly ask staff if they're ok. I don't mean lick their feet or let them take the mick, but liaise with them on a regular basis. The moment you start taking them for granted is the moment it all falls apart. People like to be respected and thanked if they've done a good job. They will like working for someone who cares about them, with genuine interest in improving the efficiency of the job in-hand. By looking after them, they might well look after you - it's **THEIR FUTURE TOO**.

Tips and advice

If you're the guvnor; generally, all you'll be interested in is the overall efficiency of your kitchen. Is it pumping out the meals fast enough? Are they presented in the correct manner? Are they served on hot plates? Why am I running out of certain items? Who ordered a hundred boxes of chips instead of ten? Where will we keep them? Why aren't there any knives and forks wrapped? Did you say the cook hasn't turned up yet?

AAAAAGGGGGHHHHH!

Customer love. Front of house staff are the key in the door to an efficient kitchen. Working backwards, if a bartender doesn't invest time, energy and attention in the customer staring them in the face, how will they eke the most profit and reputation for your business? Failing to add value to every single sale, will mean they are not worth the money you are paying them. Instil this quality in all bartenders and watch profits rise.

Following on. Crucial, will be the correct taking of the order and passing that information successfully to the kitchen.

Sounds simple doesn't it? It isn't. Cock ups happen all the time!

First rule of comedy. Without appearing patronising; before sending an order, ask your servers to repeat the order in its entirety - **BEFORE** taking the money and despatching that information to the kitchen. If you have the facility; print a receipt and ask the customer to check it over whilst still at the point of service. Delivered constructively; this will add value to the customer, at the same time as double and treble checking the order. The kitchen will thank you for that and so will your food stocks benefit; mistakes are costly and mostly avoidable.

Order queries. There is nothing worse, than a customer coming back to the bar to query an order and having to wait again; whilst **YOU** serve three other customers before getting back to them – regardless of how much they've spent.

Wait? – I'd want to lay a red carpet out!

Staff need to be alert and switched on, able to act on their own initiative and quickly deal with a query from a customer already served. Once again it relies on employing the right person, instead of a - couldn't give a shit, profit exterminator.

Printer-roll. If the bar printer runs out of paper mid-print; have you facility to re-print the order for the customer? Make sure printers have alarms or markings indicating the end of a roll. What if the kitchen printer runs out with a dozen orders **NOT** printed **NO** spares in house? Bloody mayhem I should imagine. If a glitch happens and you cook the same meal twice over - solve the glitch, so it never happens again. Fully communicate that information to the **WHOLE** team. Removing obstacles like this will add **VALUE** to the journey both sides.

Food stocks. A good result on a food stock is I would say, far harder to achieve than a wet stock. Probability of mistakes in the process of cooking food and storage of that food, means food stocks tend to be rather unforgiving, with little chance of surplus to cover loss. In translation; the fewer cock-ups you can make in the ordering, cooking, delivery and storage of those ingredients, the better the outcome for your business. I don't belittle this subject, but simply haven't the luxury of another 200 pages to invest here. In a nutshell – the reliability, honesty, skill, man management and overall efficiency of the person you charge to run your kitchen - will determine how food stocks result. And all you wanted was to pull a few pints?

Food service times. If you advertise food till ten at night; make sure someone can still order a mixed grill at ten to ten, unless otherwise stated. Attempting to order food in the clearly stated hours and being treated to "I'd just better check with chef to see if that's ok," will do nothing but wind a prized customer right up. They might have fought hard to reach you within time, only to be left dangling on a bloody string. That kind of retort ruins the customer journey in one foul stroke. State cooking hours and welcome that order – with gusto.

Be fair to staff. If you advertise food till ten at night, but come 9.30pm the kitchen has eight orders hanging depressingly from some string, like a sentence of slavery to the staff within - instruct the bar not to take any more orders. You won't lose return custom by apologising; it will be the manner in which you communicate the apology. Next time they'll order earlier, **INCREASING** trade and probably encourage friends to do the same. Contrary to popular belief – you can't please all the people all the time - but you can be **NICE** about it.

How long is the wait? Don't ever lie about waiting times. Try putting five minutes on top of any estimate during a busy session. If the meal comes out five minutes earlier, it'll make the business look pretty efficient. On the flipside; if it took a little longer, you've already covered your back in advance.

Remember your aim. A happy customer journey, will almost guarantee a return visit at some time or another. After leaving; if they think fondly of their stay and the service they were **TREATED** to - you will have succeeded. If you say it'll only be ten minutes and they've waited forty, I expect they'll be asking for a refund and part of your anatomy on a chopping board - you'll certainly **NEVER** see them again. Worse than that, they'll tell everyone they know – word of mouth works both ways.

Prep and shutdown. Staff need time to prep a kitchen for use. By the same token, kitchen areas must be left spotlessly clean for the next day. This really isn't just a five minute job at the end of a shift - far from it. When an environmental health officer (the food police) knocks your door at eight the following morning, their clip board aimed true; you'll be wishing you hadn't left two sinks full of dirty dishes and the floor still greasy because you couldn't be bothered to mop down with boiling hot water. A truly conscientious team member, cleaning all the nooks and crannies, leaving no stone unturned - is also prepping for the next day and covering **YOUR** back. I'll remind you once again – it isn't a five minute job. A spring clean once a month wouldn't go amiss either – not once a year.

Warning. Employing someone to leave your kitchen spotless is pointless - if you sink half a dozen lagers that night and raid the pub fridge before you retire upstairs. Leaving crumbs and debris to be found by staff, EHO or ABM - is really **NOT** the cleverest of moves. Pre-buy some pizzas and don't fall asleep!

5 Star scores. Every fridge/freezer temperature sheet and all relevant paperwork should be authentically up to date. Hairnets, gloves, you name it, whatever it takes; do the courses, do your homework – get it done. It can get a bit messy whilst cooking takes place, but there's a stark difference between messy and un-clean. Don't underestimate the importance of a 5 star score these days. It is recognised by the public. It will be one of the first things they spy before choosing to darken your doorstep – another profit assassin.

Big warning. Anything other than being completely thorough and professional when it comes to the handling and storage of food, coupled with fastidious cleaning habits; is tantamount to leaving yourself wide open for - a kick in the nether region.

Washing up. This job falls into the never-ending preparation category; the better the finish, the smoother the ride. I have been ready to serve a meal and reached for a dozen, before finding a suitably clean plate. Not only is it bloody infuriating, but what's the point? Someone who can wash up properly is worth their weight in gold and just as important as any other!

Knives and forks. If you usually go through thirty odd knives and forks in a dinner time session, make sure you've got at least double that wrapped and ready beforehand. Having to wrap as meals are served, is a pain in the ass and draws the server away from just that. Running around like a blue assed fly isn't enjoyable for anyone, especially if preventable.

Plan to win – not fail!

Dirty fryers. Stink! Not all customers will link that familiar burnt oil, well past it's sell by date smell, with a badly run kitchen, but a bit like *THAT* smell emanating from men's loos; it will consume the whole building and at the very least - limit your success. Oil is expensive, but cleaning fryers and adding new oil regularly is a no brainer (and I'm being polite).

Locks on coolers. Keep all fridges and freezers locked; not only will it erase accidentally leaving the door open scenarios, but trust is a wonderful concept, until **YOU** end up losing a pile of money, or – your job. Do it as a rule and do it from the start; it'll cut the odds of accidents or plain theft. No lock – fit one.

Use by dates. Play it by the book. Out of date? – chuck. It's just not worth the risk to your 5 star score and the fines that follow, to take **ANY** risks whatsoever with use by dates. A manager may have the pressure of a bad dry stock result next time round, but that ain't nothing compared with the shit that would hit the fan - if you give a dozen people food poisoning!

Under pressure?

An independent or manager, only able to afford one cook/chef will face the everyday risk of that person ringing in sick. In that position - **YOU** may feel pressured to cook, finding cover for the bar; it happened to me on a regular basis. I survived; more importantly - so did my customers. You might feel pressured to have your food offer in place, from opening time till ten at night; a harsh sentence indeed – mostly for you.

Antidote. Without waving a magic wand, I'm afraid the only way out; is to raise the wet's income to a level that affords proper cover in the kitchen. Food takings will rise in tandem, more customers to fire at. Common sense though that may be, it's easier said than done. It takes stamina and determination, but - it can be done, it really can. I know . . . I did it.

Kitchen long story cut short

If you already have a rehearsed, organised and attractive front of house operation; a well-run kitchen, is like adding an extremely efficient chip to an already capable motor car. A room full of people eating is great, but more customers equal; more liquor, coffee, softies, machine income and pot's more **ATMOSPHERE**. A survivor of the kitchen, I openly beg cooks and chefs to provide written insight; not about cooking, but as to what it takes to work a busy kitchen. I would be only too willing to publish under the *howtoandwhatsitlike* banner (up to 50% of profit royalties paid). Let's educate - mail me.

Last but not least. I reiterate - from the washer-up to the head honcho; if you find the right staff – don't take them for granted, include the whole team in plans and meetings. If they do a good job, make sure you thank them – personally.

35 MAINTENANCE

Licensed premises are continually battered from the footfall of customers, staff and just lately - weather conditions that defy the odds. Bills to keep buildings safe and secure, can on occasion be the most damaging hits your pocket will meet.

New venture your responsibility for repairs?

Before signing on the dotted line, paying God know how much for the honour of receiving the keys to your new kingdom, do yourself a favour - get some roofing guy up on the lid. Is it in good nick? How much would it cost to make good?

Common sense. Being duly informed it will cost at least 5K to bring the roof up to scratch, the question I might be asking is; why am I being asked to pay full whack on the original ingoing price? At that point – true colours may be revealed.

Lesson. Think about maintenance – add **VALUE** for **YOU**.

> ## Being highly determined to succeed won't stop getting the shit kicked out of YOU by unexpected repairs!

Flooding story

I experienced a roof caving in through a build-up of water; a faulty **VALLEY** up on the roof. After several different tradesman visiting and a bodge it and scarper crew on the receiving end of some strong cash . . . you guessed it – it flooded through two storeys, taking the men's loo out in the process.

Consequences. Not only did it cost about 10K to put right, a week shut, loss of takings, goodwill and still having to pay staff; I'm pretty sure that caper put paid to my yearly bonus. After much effort beforehand, the business suffered and I became de-motivated for a while; luckily I'm supremely conscientious. Whatever your position you can't drag your staff down. Business as usual ASAP and extra motivation is called for to get things back on track. I felt this was all completely preventable.

Lesson. Mostly - bodging doesn't work.

Heating story

I've got a mate with a small pub, an old three story building. The boiler went down over a year ago. Five grand to fix, is five grand he just hasn't got. A log burner in the bar costs him a hundred quid a week to furnish. Heaters of all types upstairs send his electric bill through the roof – literally. I just can't bear to ask him whether he's actually got hot water in the unit.

AAAAAGGGGGHHHHH!

Beware. There are units all over this country in the exact same position. Customers don't like entering a cold place. The lounge might be warm enough, but the loos might be freezing. This accentuates a deterioration in the building itself and to the people living within it. There is only one way this scenario will end. This is the effect maintenance can have on your business; a harsh lesson, but one you should be conscious of.

I repeat. Before signing on the dotted line for a new venture, get the heating and plumbing checked out throughout the whole building. Add the cellar cooling, python and roof to that list and you might have a better idea whether you'll make it through the first Xmas – better to be wise before the fact.

Day to day maintenance

Example. If you've got sixty odd light fittings around the unit and two aren't working, but for one reason or another you don't fix them; the following week another four might stop working. You'll suddenly start wondering why one area seems quite dim. You might call an electrician out and get charged sixty quid for them just to assess and quote a repair fee. This doesn't get them fixed - it might just provide a quote.

AAAAAGGGGGHHHHH!

If you're a managed house. The electrician may have a hundred pound limit to work to, so no way will he fix all six for a hundred quid. Permission from your ABM will then be required. They might have just broken the area bank having to repair some idiot's roof that cost 10K (I'm not bitter).

Advice. Don't let problems build up. Obviously you will have to prioritise sometimes, but try and deal as dealt. Learn the ins and outs of your maintenance system to get work progressed. Ask other experienced house managers how to eke the fastest route to fix heaven. Don't wait six years like I did, only to stumble over answers, spending hours and hours on the phone chasing some donkey to turn up and fix this or that.

Michael. I lost loads of hair in those first six years!

An independent. Find people that aren't gonna rip you off. Half the repair herbert's I've encountered, seem to have the theme tune to *JAWS* permanently playing in the background. On the flip side of that; I encountered completely genuine people who did a superb job, with great advice to boot. Get these characters on board as soon as you possibly can. Check what they're doing and check once they're done. If you find reliable people, treat them nice – make them tea.

Toilets

I've extensively covered this subject already, but I joke not; if I owned a pub company I would bring a plumber in to teach all my managers how to sort urinals out in an emergency.

Machine maintenance

Example. If you buy a new glass washing machine, with recommendation of cleaning once a week and six monthly servicing; bloody well clean it once a week and service as requested. Don't be surprised, when after a few months of ignoring that advice and not teaching staff to clean it regularly; customers start drinking elsewhere - the glasses will stink.

Maintenance long story cut short

Ignore maintenance at your peril. It can affect turnover in a subtle manner, or with dramatic effect. Paintwork, guttering, plumbing, doorway's, ventilation, carpet's, gardens, car parks, electrics, alarms, machinery - just to mention a few. Purchase some clipboards, design rotas and get organised. If you call someone out to fix something, act like a voracious Rottweiler; be on the phone checking time of arrival and chasing if late. It's funny how service improves when they just know - you ain't putting up with jack shit. Much like customer service, it is a percentages game. If you cover 99% of maintenance 99% of the time - things should run reasonably to plan. Yes you're always going to get the odd nasty surprise, but mostly you can concentrate on taking money instead of drowning in repairs.

PS. Have out of hours/maintenance phone numbers to hand.

By the way! I wasn't joking about the glasses stinking – it happens more than you'd think was possible.

36 MANAGERS

What's it all about?

Do you need to be a special type of individual? Do you need to have flair and flamboyance, the personality of a talk show host? Do you need qualifications? What are the qualities of an ideal house manager in the licensed trade? Well actually . . .

You simply need to be the right person, with a passion for serving humans!

Example. You may have been the team captain at school, recognised and acknowledged by all. You may enjoy the largest social circle known to man and personal magnetism to die for, but none of that will count for tuppence, when and if you're lucky enough to secure a job for a managed house company.

Why? If you can't get your head around counting tills, the computer system that controls everything, understand, manage and execute all health, safety and hygiene rules and regulations, command respect from staff and develop training skills – you'll struggle. Not to mention cleaning the shithouse at a moment's notice when the cleaners don't show, shortly after beginning a whole day on the bar when two staff ring in sick.

Lonely too! Being the most popular cock in the world, won't count a jot when a company offers that first opportunity a hundred miles away from family and friends; the added complication of guests becoming a pain in the arse. They'll want to party party the night of their stay, which'll suddenly become a whole load less attractive, what with your new workload and an imminent visit from a stock taker or ABM.

Good news. That was the bad news.

Important qualities

Aspiration. It may sound strange, but you need to **WANT** to be there an awful lot; someone who gets a kick out of putting a smile on a customer's face, a desire to serve and please, no matter what personal crisis **YOU** may be living through.

Stamina. Not many jobs demand the amount of hours at the coalface - double shifts, day in day out on occasion. Flitting from the cellar, to the office, to the kitchen, is punishing; not only physically, but mentally. Even not on duty, maybe upstairs; you'll need to turn on at the flick of a call, or a shocking sound from below. Being alert at **ALL** times becomes a necessary evil, still able to deal differing scenarios with patience and good judgement. It takes a certain kind of stamina to smile through really odd or challenging moments.

Jack of all trades. Quite honestly, you don't have to be **SPECIAL** at anything. It does however; pay to be pretty damned **GOOD** at almost everything in the frame. In layman's terms: you don't necessarily have to have a university degree in sod all, but do need to have a grasp on what you're doing, the end effect and consequences of actions. No pressure then.

Physically able. Goes without saying.

An example to staff. Always pay for your own food and drink. Don't ring it in the till personally; ensure a member of staff takes the cash. Teach staff - **ALL** products must be **PAID** for. Breed and cultivate that custom across the board.

Streetwise/awareness. This can be a horrible shitty world we live in, where nasty little herbert's abound. Have your wits about you at **ALL** times - completely knackering.

Never lie or make things up. Either to your customers, staff and more especially - your boss.

Leadership and teambuilding. You can't build a team without a leader. Your crew need to know they can count on **YOU**. Encourage, train, and thank when deserved. If the shit hits the fan; before you leap - think about their wellbeing. Get behind them at busy times. It may be your night off, but if they're unexpectedly swamped at the bar - jump in and get some ice, collect some glasses, set a wash going, change that barrel, cut fruit for the bar. Very often, all they'll need is a twenty minute dive in and they'll be thankful. If sitting at the bar watching your crew struggle is your idea of fun, the trade won't miss you – **NEITHER WILL YOUR STAFF**.

Motivation. Not that busy? Get everyone busy; clean everything there is to clean – continually **TEACH**. Be the firework and provide the push. Motivation requires energy; tired humans = bad motivation; sleep is a fundamental requirement. Are **YOU** getting enough sleep?

Ability to listen. Actually listening to what people say, takes a lot of patience and valuable time, but can be a superb way of gathering intelligence and clues of how to improve trade. Staff especially, need to know you're completely accessible for help and guidance. Customers will chew your ear off all day long given half a chance. Sometimes that will be very funny, other times it'll drive you insane – apparently . . . patience is a virtue.

Tow the company line. This Company will be providing **YOU** with employment - be thankful for that. The least you can do; is promote their ethos and the brand you represent. You don't **HAVE** to work for them, but **THEY** will have gambled somewhat on you - pay them back. If you're not happy with the salary you're on, no amount of moaning to all and sundry will change it. Boosting turnover, will afford you ammunition in that respect. The only way to boost your income is to prove it.

Being told what to do. Everyday life as a house manager, feels a lot like being self-employed and running your own show, but with a stark difference. You'll have a dark lord (that's your area business manager or ABM) hovering in the background, watching every move you make, either in the form of their human self (appearing at the oddest of times without warning), or from afar via a laptop or mobile phone. Most of these people will be extremely clued up and experienced. They will have heard every excuse under the sun and suffer fools very badly. Most will have some sense of humour, but this will stop; the moment **YOU** start talking a pile of shite, or are not taking care of business. Sometimes you've got to bite the bullet, accept a bollocking like a grown up and hit the wall later. This always spurred me on to prove a point - raising turnover and beating targets is always good retort. To be fair to an ABM; if you're not performing, they'll be under the cosh from their very own dark lord. Of course it's in their interests for **YOU** to flourish. Having been appointed will usually indicate - **THEM** having observed qualities in you they have warmed to. As well as reigning you in on occasion, they will be your guide and mentor, a valuable tool in **YOUR** box.

Honesty. Is it really worth losing your job and living quarters for fiddling a tenner here and there? Don't even think about it. Being straight as a dye will let you sleep at night.

Perseverance. If you have a problem affecting the smooth running of your unit - don't stop until solved. Problems don't vanish - they escalate, damage profit and **YOUR** quality of life.

Learn everything you can. You have to have an in-built desire to **WANT** to learn every damned thing there is to know, about every single aspect of the trade. Never think you know it all - there's always a little gem waiting.

Self-control. The moment you lose control of your brain, is when you put your job and future at risk. Thinking before you leap takes self-control. Steaming in like a bull in a china shop will only end in tears, a one way ticket. Keeping calm in chaos can provide options - I don't just mean dealing with trouble. As previously mentioned; an irate customer sparking off over an hour wait for a meal, might well be unforgivable on **YOUR** part. The ability to **LEARN** and **IMPROVE** your delivery, will only transpire through thinking on your feet and self-control.

Professionalism. In everything you say and everything you do. This can only rub off on staff and reputation.

Learn to say no. I remember having to state that more times than anything else. Mick, can I have a fag break? Can I bring my three dogs in? Can I eat my takeaway in here seeing as you stopped food at ten? Play fighting in the bar, resting a pint on the side of the pool table, asking for a drink five minutes after time. You don't have to be nasty; in fact, quite the opposite, but still – no. This leads me nicely on to the next point.

Treat all staff and customers the same. Just said no to one of your regulars for another drink, when a family member asks the same question? The answer has got to be no. I've witnessed a huge brawl caused by just this scenario.

Creativity and attention to detail. You can get big things right, but still end up looking like a cowboy outfit. Taking care of the small stuff in a fashionable manner, is akin to adding finishing touches to a cake. Mess with displays, wipe those tables constantly, set the scene and create that atmosphere.

Gaining respect. Generally, you only gain respect by example. If customers and staff see you pulling your finger out in a host of ways, that'll make a big impression. If they see you getting ratted all the time - they'll think you're a prick.

Confidence. If you considered yourself reasonably confident before entering the trade, initially this might take a knock. You might still have the face of confidence, but inside your stomach churning, simply not possessing enough knowledge. So many subjects to master will leave your head spinning at times. It took me years to gain some quality of self-assurance.

Faith. Don't be afraid of the unknown. When I started, I had doubts. Then again; when my partner and I split up and I took on the books and kitchen (previously her job), I had doubts. Have some faith in yourself, you can do it – I did.

Bollocking staff. If you have to tear a strip off someone, don't do it in public. How many staff have walked after a public reprimand? Do it behind closed doors and use that self-control. How much time and money have you invested in training that person up? Take a step back and think what needs to happen.

Realism. Don't expect the biggest unit straight away. This might mean not enough budget to staff properly. This will mean **YOU** having to work long hours to cover. The only way to afford more staff, is to raise the turnover. Raising the standard of customer love can do that, no question.

For you. The scale of this job can take your breath away. There are so many different aspects to learn and manage all at once, with so many moving parts. You need to possess a hunger to achieve success and an outline plan that can be tailored and modified as you go along. The buck will stop with you, so don't get in to the habit of delegating blame. The more you learn about stocks and current tricks of the trade, the greater your control and profitability. You can have an extremely rewarding career as a manager, both inwardly and financially, it's all doable. I was so green for the longest time, but then I was reluctant in the first place.

First impressions story

First impressions are crucial when trying to land a job as a house manager. The job my partner and I had applied for was with one of most respected companies. We were sent to a pub in Swindon (a unit I ended up running) for an arranged meeting with the existing manager Keith; he would explain what life as pub managers might be like. We had worked out all the pertinent questions and arrived an hour early. We sat at the bar and I was drinking smooth bitter at the time. The bartender pointed out the only smooth bitter on offer. I settled for that – it was gorgeous. After about an hour, we introduced ourselves to Keith. He seemed nice and then got called off to take care of something. I took my chance to visit the loo and ran in to a problem - my legs wouldn't move. I suddenly had the horrible realisation . . . I was completely pissed.

AAAAAGGGGGHHHHH!

The only thing I could think of was; we cannot let him see me like that, a total disaster - I was so embarrassed. Somehow I made it to the door, with my partner asking me what the hell was going on. All I could muster was 'we've got to go.' I had visions of this Keith, being rung up by someone from human resources at head office, asking what he thought of the couple they had sent down. I could just imagine him saying in his broad scotch accent, 'och aye, they were ok like, but the bloke got so drunk he had to leave before I had a chance to chat - I thought I was gonna' have to ring an ambulance!'

AAAAAGGGGGHHHHH!

I've never drank smooth bitter since that day. We hadn't eaten before coming out and were both very nervous. I hadn't been nervous for as long as I could remember. There you go.

Manager's long story cut short

Whist theirs no magic formula for the ideal candidate to manage a pub; like any job, it's a game of percentages. If, after reading my interpretation of qualities desirable for suitability, you decide it's not for you - I'll have saved you from your worst nightmare. I'll also have saved the general public. Retail in general is littered with people who couldn't give a crap about the customer – you won't have to look far for an example. If however you tick a lot of the boxes mentioned, it could be your true vocation – **TRULY BRILLIANT**. Ask yourself . . .

How bad do you really want it?

An equal playing field. I know managers that have no previous qualifications to speak of, aren't the life and soul of the party, but have a certain charm in dealing with staff and customers alike. I know managers that really are the sharpest tool in any company box; switched on to a really high degree. Is the second any better than the first? - Of course not.

Like any apprenticeship. You won't know a lot to begin. You'll learn a darned sight quicker if you **WANT** to be there.

At interview. The best thing you can do is - be yourself. The licensed trade thrives on characters; the rest can be developed if suitable. You've just got to hope and pray the interview panel recognise something in **YOU**, that gives **THEM** confidence to proceed. All the successful managers I know have something about them that stands out like a beacon.

Above all. This business is not about you, it's all about the customer. You need to possess a passion for serving humans that translates to the customer feeling the value – a treat.

It's the biggest kick . . . Can you do that?

37 ASSISTANTS

Freedom

There are two types of assistants. One, you will train up to leave at some point to pursue their own career. The other will be quite happy to stay, in and around the family and social circle they already own. How many attributes a manager must possess, will not always apply to the second type. They might not have the hunger for success you retain, but bestowing pots of training in someone that isn't going to leave you at the end of the day - can be an asset. They might be considered to run that unit when you eventually chip, or might be happy just as. On one occasion, I pushed someone down the road; too far as it goes and lost them completely - silly Michael. The better the quality of assistant, the more down time you will enjoy away from the coal face - to recharge those batteries.

Wrong choice of assistant will definitely make one person's life a misery – yours!

Consequences. Be aware of issues arising from appointing the wrong candidate - let me be the public asshole.

- In the long term you might expect them to cover your holiday relief, a definite advantage. If not a requirement; don't even mention - it might scare them off.

- Not straight away of course, but if you can't have a day off leaving your subordinate in charge – **WHATS THE POINT?**

- If your choice of assistant suddenly becomes a little Hitler overnight - that won't work either. He got beaten the crap out of, and that's how you'll feel when two of your best staff quit out the blue. It happened to me – a bad mistake.

Promotion story. I appointed an idiot, who thought promotion meant constantly leaning on the bar socialising, while queues of customers waved notes at the bar. Come Halloween, I seriously thought my regular staff might burn this character at the stake - with me as tinder. Don't just promote without re-interviewing. It might sound anal, but literally spell out the change in job description and expectations.

Long story cut short

What you really require an assistant to deliver - is continuation of what **YOU** normally provide. When handing over the next session to your buddy, it should be smooth and harmonious, not bumpy and volcanic - a safe and secure pair of hands to pass the baton until you return. It's a big ask; depending entirely on the quality of training you lavish and enthusiasm displayed, by what is in effect - your protégé. A loyal, trustworthy assistant is a fantastic tool and sheer necessity; you simply cannot be there all of the time. Through consistently high turnover, the last unit afforded me the luxury of two assistants, one of these able to cover my holidays. Melanie was a superb right hand for me, possessing a great work ethic and willing to listen, learn and say no, even to formidable foe – thank you Melanie. Manager or independent, these people become family; this can prove difficult when having to reprimand, but like a naughty child; it's a learning process and reprimand you must. Remember: this game is all about putting the customer #1, persuading them to return time after time – even in your absence.

Will the person you are considering add or detract from that goal?

38 HOLIDAY RELIEF COVER

Every licensee needs a break. Like it or not - you emphatically must take time away from the lunatic asylum. Time to replenish smiling ability and reflect on how the business is performing can be hugely beneficial – downtime **ESSENTIAL**. Being a relief manager is not easy by any stretch, but before reliefs slag me off - this is not written from a relief stand point. It is advice for **YOU** . . . the one employing them.

What are the fundamentals a relief should fulfil?

If you're a licensee in the business of building trade 24/7, care passionately about the future and are totally committed; the reality is – **NO-ONE** is going to look after your business the way **YOU** do. Accepting that fact early on, will allow you to concentrate instead, at limiting the damage in your absence.

The overriding ingredient of relief cover should be – continuity!

How do I achieve this? The week before a vacation, hold a staff meeting. Delegate responsibility as a challenge to them; it's their jobs and future too - how well can they do? Ask them for co-operation that no one rocks the boat while you're away.
Brief incoming. Make it simple, like ABC. Supply daily schedules. Plan a break like a military manoeuvre – it works.
In reality. There's only so much information humans can take in before it all goes to mush, but leave enough time to brief the incoming. If I was a relief manager, I'd want instruction to make my life bearable and be a success in the resident's eyes.

Warning. Leaving twenty minutes with cases packed, is akin to just throwing the keys at an incoming relief and deserting!

Anger management story

I had a relief, that within twenty minutes of me being back in the building, completely removed my ability to utter even a simple sentence. I was so angry, I could feel my eyes bulging like some psycho-killer; the damage that guy inflicted to previous hard won gains in teamwork and service standards - a bitter pill to swallow. It seemed like this individual had been hitting my business with a sledgehammer, from the moment I'd left, till the day I returned – the stock was shit too.

AAAAAGGGGGHHHHH!

Warning. A licensee returning from holiday to find all the furniture has been moved to positions . . . **YOU** tried two years ago (and didn't work); bottle displays altered that took the longest time to perfect, and the only cook you have has put their notice in – might be a tad upsetting. It happened to me.

Warning. Flip that. When the relief first drops their cases in the accommodation and you've left it looking like you've had burglars – that won't be a good start. If **YOU** don't give a shit about them, they sure as hell won't look after you.

Long story cut short

Again, it's a game of percentages; the better prepared, the better the outcome. Of course there will be things that go wrong, but how they're dealt with will probably be mostly down to **YOU** - have a great holiday.

P.S. Leave tea, quality coffee, fresh milk, bread, bacon and eggs for the relief, sometimes bribery has its uses.

39 INDEPENDENT OPERATORS

Firstly, if you're a prospective, or current independent and have skipped the managers chapter - go straight back and read it intently. Without big company backing, you'll require **ALL** the attributes mentioned just for starters.

Word of warning. Money invested in any business, might well be your own. Committing yourself is one thing, but the pressure that goes with it - might not have crossed your mind. The ability to very quickly lose direction and self-confidence might be devastating. How many times has an individual poured their whole redundancy into securing a tenancy agreement, only to find they can't meet the first quarters VAT bill? That might mean loading up a credit card, or cashing in a pension plan just to carry on - it won't stop there.

AAAAAGGGGGHHHHH!

Do your homework

I wouldn't dream of undertaking complicated brain surgery on one of my pals, unless I was trained to do so - even though a couple of them warrant it at times. Why then, would you think you were capable of running a pub, with no formal experience and training of any kind?

At the very least. Go work in a pub or licensed premises. Find out what it's like to do an eight hour shift behind the jump. Could you get on with people? Would you enjoy it? Do you have the right mentality? Be a sponge; gather as many skills as humanly possible in a short space of time – better those odds.

Ideally. Having gained some experience and deciding this really is the career desired - go work for a managed house estate. You'll be well trained, gaining skills and regimentation you might otherwise lack. You might well find; working in that field suits **YOU** down to the ground, providing a new career path - **THAT** Company gaining in the process.

Later. The benefits of being trained properly for any job would set you in good stead - should you then decide on wanting to branch out on your own.

Failing that. You might think all of the above is a load of old bollocks. You may decide to gamble your personal crown jewels on *THE DOGS MUCK* down the road from where you live, and off you'll jolly well go. Good luck with that.

The gamble. To be fair, there are business owners all over this country that have done just that . . . and been very successful. Being in the right place at the right time, with a deal in your favour; coupled initially with a supreme effort, half descent employees (even by accident) and off you'll sail. Lots of others will lose it all – within a very short period.

Plan. Before starting any venture, make a detailed business plan, including realistic estimations of costings – not a pie in the sky wish list. Meticulous planning may seem a boring chore, but success is in the detail. If you end up with multiple units – very shortly you'll have developed a blueprint that works every time. That plan will start and evolve from the first unit. You at least, have to know every single bill that'll hit the doormat, on top of minimum staffing requirements. Can you pay **ALL** of these bills? What is the minimum income you can work from? **YOU** can't live on fresh air, what are you going to pay yourself? Make a list of what Strengths, Weaknesses, Opportunities and Threats are relevant (SWOT analysis).

How does an independent succeed?

To fully understand the extra drive and commitment required to flourish as a small business, you **MUST** compare your task to that of a professional managed house.

Example. A professionally managed house will have a proven working system in place for every facet of that unit. They will be linked to a small army of well trained and briefed teams at head office, designed to facilitate all requirements and problems on a daily basis; you'll have - **NONE OF THAT**. A manager always has that **DARK LORD** hovering in the background, silently breathing red hot fire behind the coattails of the manager. That manager in turn, will spread their own fire across the team they lead; continually chasing targets, adhering to every health and hygiene box they may have to tick. A stock taker will appear, often randomly unannounced, asking pertinent questions about the odd missing bottle of lager, the vodka being ten shots amiss and the whereabouts of several steaks. An auditor will appear a couple of times a year, accounting for every single penny taken in the last seven months, and why is the two thousand pound float two quid down? Perish the thought they arrive **TOGETHER** on a cold winter morning (like the grim reaper and his brother making a dark shadow in your doorway).

My point. A professional manager will be the sergeant instigating controls, training and motivation. A managed estate provides framework making that possible; rewarding the whipping boy or girl with accommodation, wages and bonuses for high performance. In return they'll want their pound of flesh and who can blame them? My question . . .

Who's going to be chasing your ass?

Showtime. As an independent; yes you'll be the boss and that's fine and dandy, but from where I'm sitting – **YOU** need to be at least twice as motivated as any manager would ever need to be. Imagine me shouting at you right now . . .

> # Do not enter this trade if you do not possess the drive, stamina and determination to learn fast and achieve.

I make no apologies for pointing out the bad stuff – you need to know. I want you to succeed, but **YOU** need to know . . .

> # If you're a lazy bastard – DON'T even bother thinking about it!

Long story cut short

Billy public is crying out for a higher standard of customer love and personal hygiene. The licensed trade is crying out for hard working characters - to **MAKE IT HAPPEN**. Raising the level of customer service to a whole different level, will separate **YOU** from any competition I can think of. Huge opportunity.

> # I firmly believe this is where the growth will be in the licensed trade!

Yes you can run a unit in your own style, but you must emulate the professional traits of a well-oiled managed house and beat them by a country mile. Set your own targets, make a detailed plan of action and drive it home. Make careful choice of employees and implement the sharpest tools in tills and stock control you can afford. Learn how they work inside out and stay off the sauce. You will be solely responsible for success or failure. It can be done - I wish you well xxx

40 COMPANIES AND ABM's
(Reference managers)

Managed house estates

Quite honestly, being offered a position with any size company will have been a huge wall to climb by any standards. Whether the estate has ten or two thousand units, they will expect only one thing – profit. **YOU** will be expected to contribute towards that profit, and **THEY** will have seen something in you that made them think that possible - **WELL DONE** to achieve that.

Michael. Almost all my working life I'd been self-employed. I hated people telling me what to do, but I have to say – I mostly relished the whole experience and challenge. At times I found it totally frustrating thinking I knew best. Sometimes I did, but sometimes I really didn't. Working within a company ethos can be restricting, but also exhilarating. Big companies have big bills to pay, so you really will have to pull your finger out; hopefully this book has given you the heads up on what that life might be like, a few ideas thrown in for good measure.

Opportunity. When considering a career in the trade, don't walk around with blinkers on; don't think you **HAVE** to run your own joint. Starting out, I knew I didn't have the knowledge or finance to stand a cat in hell's chance of successfully running my own place - I discounted it before the first post. Companies are crying out for serious minded talent to run units on their behalf. You'll be paid for the privilege, well trained in the process and given somewhere to live; an apprenticeship by any standard. I'm not suggesting it would suit everyone, but it worked for me – it might work for you too.

Your boss

I had the pleasure of being mentored by some excellent human beings. The encouragement invaluable; their support and experience fundamental, occasional reprimands part and parcel after veering on to the hard shoulder – thank you Mark.

However. I did have one so called ABM that made me hallucinate violent scenarios on more than one occasion. This poor excuse for a boss, just out of nappies and obviously never having served behind a bar in their life; may have possessed a degree or six in business studies, but had absolutely no man management skills or common sense . . . in any bodily vain. If you do run in to an idiot like this - don't worry, what goes around comes around. Sorry folks . . . bit of therapy there.

Advice. You don't have to like your boss, but it helps an awful lot. Like them or not - essential you develop a healthy working relationship. Companies and the ABM's they employ will want **YOU** to succeed. Listen to their advice and don't be afraid of asking awkward or embarrassing questions. Above all, never ever lie, that'd go down like a bag of shit.

Thought for ABM's

Managers who take a unit to its fullest capacity are the *Holy Grail* for a company. The ability to grow at that point becomes negligible bar inflation, therefore blotting out the possibility of bonuses. It begs the question - shouldn't there be a generous yearly gratuity for management achieving this climb? In effect; turnover insurance, providing momentum for a management team to stay in place - ensuring continuity. Taking any unit to cash saturation point will have been hard; even **TOUGHER** remaining at that level. Please reward – it's a **NO BRAINER**.

LAST ORDERS PLEASE

I would **NEVER** have finished this book without an inbuilt desire to do so. Furthermore, without total commitment and determination, it still wouldn't be anywhere near completion. To succeed in running a pub or any licensed premises, requires **ALL** those qualities and a shitload more. Paying a case full of money for a tenancy or lease, or merely **THINKING** working as a manager seems a good crack, won't automatically guarantee success - far from it. I do not apologise for repeating the same mantra throughout. The licensed trade is a repeat business. Learning is **ALL ABOUT** repeating and practice until mastered. A large part of **YOUR** job will be educating your team on the **CORRECT** procedures and **WHY!** Getting all the big things right is very bloody clever, but not paying attention to the little things, can reduce the customer journey to a shower of **SHIT!**

Improving beyond measure, the delivery of your products is the **GAME CHANGER.** I continually visit units and am constantly treated to **AWFUL** service. In the UK, the government is introducing the living wage, and I'm all for that. **BUT** – this is an ideal **OPPORTUNITY!** If you have no choice but to pay your cherubs more cash – I'd be asking a lot more for it. In taking on the task of improving all round service beyond recognition, it will pay for any enforced pay rise ten times over. Paying some moron to stand behind **YOUR** bar, texting on their bloody phone, lent on the bar staring in to space wishing closing time nearer; eating **YOUR** crisps, continually touching their bloody nose, ears, hair, and keeping customers waiting at the bar without apology – **BEGGARS BELIEF!**

YOU need to inject into your team the **VALUE** of tuning into the customer and smiling while they do it. Just like **YOU** unlocking the doors in the morning, and expecting busloads of customers to arrive without putting in massive effort to make that happen: plonking Jack or Jill behind your bar, spending forty minutes pointing them in the right direction, expecting superior love to be showered on your audience – is **NAÏVE** . . .

I have other expressions!

The big wigs need to smell some serious coffee, and **TOGETHER** formulate a plan for a new standard of customer love – to enable long term growth in the licensed trade.

For **YOU** the independent or manager: enforcing the 4 points of the **PREMIUM SERVICE EQUATION** launches an improved platform to travel. You'll know by now how **FURIOUS** I am about current service standards. I would enquire . . .

What service standards?

This book is **ALL** my **OWN** personal view, pulling from my experience in the trade and watching thereafter. If it saves you time, makes you an extra few quid, or even points you in the right direction – I'll consider that a success.

If you have a different view, or speciality you could educate and benefit a targeted audience from your experience; I have developed *howtoandwhatsitlike.com Publishing*. Mail me at howtoandwhatsitlike@gmail.com for a chat.

I'm off to sit in a darkened room with a bottle of brandy and lots of ice. My love to you all Xxx - Mick Brown.
P.s – It is **DOABLE!**

Acknowledgements

Personal

When the shit is really flying, it always comes back to the upbringing my mum and dad **TREATED** me to. My brother Clive and I are indebted. They give us the strength to carry on when sometimes running away seems the easy option.

After moving in to my fourth pub, my eldest daughter Kelly came to stay for the weekend. As she descended the fire case from the upstairs accommodation with my stepdaughter Elle, she peered through the window of the door. I was dragging this bloke by the neck past that window at that very moment. I thank god Kelly has turned out the wonderful human being she really is and hasn't been tainted by my actions. My grandson Charlie too – brave Charlie. I love you both.

To my youngest children Ella and Oliver, I'm so sorry this flipping book has taken so much of my time in the past four years. Daddy thanks you for that accommodation - I love you.

To my friends, Kit, Jamie and Diane. I've banged on about this **IDEA** for bloody years. I've bored you shitless on numerous occasions. You've always told me the **TRUTH**. I love you.

To my neighbour Tom; same as that, always there, and always true. We've put the world to rights. Love you.

Big love to dear Willy and Pauline in Swindon for just always being there and fundraising for beautiful Charlie.

To my friend Ciaran at Prescott, for caring and showing it.

Special thanks go to my two door guys in Exeter - Brian Soanes and Ian Morris, who gave me a life and will always be the real dog's bollocks by any stretch of the imagination.

The business end

I'd like to thank all my ABM's; Andrew Buchanan for taking a chance on Tracie and I initially, and Peter Dutfield for getting me the hell out of there. Gerry for choosing me to front a refurbishment and Jenny Potter for letting me escape. Mark Sutherland for giving me enough rope to perform, but strong enough to lasso me in on occasion – thank you Mark.

The really important people here were Dereck and Andrea who trained us at the Swan at Ash Vale near Aldershot. You got us through and believed in us, even when the pressure of leaving Elle in full time child care became **TOO MUCH!** Tracie and I will never be able to thank you both enough.

Thanks to all my assistants – Kaz, George and Debbie in Swindon. Darren, Steve, Kirsty and Melanie in Exeter.

This book

To Jennie Gray, Emma Donaldson Wood, Kelly Brown, Tom Price, Andy Bowkett, Nick Cassidy, Ian Whitmore, Vicky and Gazza (cellar extraordinaire) for constructive feedback.

A whole load of thanks to Cathy Dey, who's proofreading skills pointed us in the correct direction of travel - **BRILLIANT**.

Special thanks to Diane Roberts who has been my continual friend and bounce. I could not have completed this without your help and developing the *howtoandwhatsitlike* brand. I will continue to be a pain in the ass.

Special thanx go to Stuart Crawshaw for his **EXPERT** graphic assistance and of course Carole for the tea.

My thanks for helping me navigate the publishing game goes to Miles and Rachel at Choir Press in Gloucester – **SUPERB!**

A special thank you to **AMAZON** for providing me the platform to launch this project – **PERFECT!**

Printed in April 2021
by Rotomail Italia S.p.A., Vignate (MI) - Italy